THE PASTRY CHEF

THE PASTRY CHEF

by

Bert J. Phillips

BONANZA BOOKS · NEW YORK

This edition published by BONANZA BOOKS
a division of Crown Publishers, Inc.
by arrangement with A. S. Barnes and Co., Inc.
a b c d e f g h
Printed in the United States of America

Contents

Introduction

The Pastry Chef was written to fill specific needs—to give professional chefs a source of excellent international recipes, and to enable the housewife to produce the same specialties with ease at home. Last, but not least, it should be a guide for apprentices who want to make baking their occupation.

A glance at the Index will indicate the broad scope of the subject, which here is meant to touch on each department in the realm of sweets. Here then is the basic guide for all pastry shops and additional material for the hotel chef. And here also is the guide for the discriminating hostess who desires to give her family and guests only the best.

To enable the reader to follow the formulas easily, the commercial measurements used by the professional are listed at the left side of the page, while the right side is used to list the quantities and measurements in home recipes. If there is only one list in the formula, it can be used without difficulty by all readers.

What is greatly needed on the American bakery scene is a new striving for excellence and individualism. *The Pastry Chef* should be helpful in supplying new ideas in this search for excellence. Europe is noted for its many fine eating places, the majority of which are famous for one or more specialties developed in their own kitchens. The formulas in this book have been collected from many of those as well as other countries, and a number I have myself developed through experiments. Many recipes included have been closely guarded by members of the pastry profession until now. In my teaching years I often received requests from students for formulas. This book is a partial answer to them. Most of the formulas in this book are rich with fine ingredients. Don't hesitate to use them—let the customer or family be the judge. Their reaction will be immediate and gratifying.

Sugar art work has been dealt with in some detail, as I feel that foods should appeal to the eye as well as the palate. Most artistic creations are made by hand. However, a set of simple tools is essential in the performance of certain jobs. The beginner is advised to get his own set of tubes, modelling woods or carving chisels. Tools are much like pens, and once broken in by one hand will not work well for anyone else.

I have put great emphasis on the book's illustrations. They will help explain methods and procedures where words are not sufficient.

I would like to express my gratitude to all those who helped in completing this book—especially to my wife, Janet, who so patiently helped to put my thoughts into words.

I hope my readers get as much pleasure and use from these formulas as I have. It seems fitting to close these remarks with a quotation that has always guided me through many countries of the world : "If You Are Not Proud Of It—Don't Serve It."

BERT J. PHILLIPS

THE PASTRY CHEF

I

CANDIES AND CHOCOLATES

The Preparation of Chocolate - Candies, Chocolate - Jelly Fruit Bonbons - Chocolate Truffle Bonbons - Cream Chocolate with Liqueur - Fondant Cream Pralines - Marzipan Confections - Glazed Fruits - Marzipan Confects - Bonbonnières of Candy - Liqueur Pralines.

THE PREPARATION OF CHOCOLATE

Chocolate is composed of cocoa, sugar, and cocoa butter. Cocoa butter is lighter than cocoa and will therefore lay on top of molten chocolate at high temperatures. Because of this separation, chocolate which has just been melted can not be used without further preparation. If this preparation is not carried out, the result will be a gray, streaky, and possibly sticky product with no shine.

In order to obtain chocolate-glazed sweets with a dry, shiny finish, the molten chocolate must be cooled. For this purpose, place the container in cold water and stir constantly until the chocolate feels neither cold nor warm to the touch. The correct temperature cannot be determined with a thermometer—it is strictly a matter of experience. Do not use ice or ice water for the cooling process, as this will make your chocolate stick to the bottom of your pan. There is also the danger of getting lumpy chocolate. Should you notice that the chocolate is beginning to harden on the bottom, put the container into hot water for a few seconds, stirring constantly. The greatest care must be taken to prevent even a drop of water from being mixed into the chocolate, as the chocolate would become thick and clotted, and unfit for glazing purposes.

It is advisable to sample the chocolate before beginning to glaze. Put a few drops on waxed paper and let stand a few minutes. If the chocolate hardens with a shine, the preparation is completed. If silvery streaks are visible on top, it indicates that the cocoa butter and cocoa have not blended. The chocolate then requires further cooling and stirring.

Before beginning to glaze the candies, place the container on a warm baking sheet to prevent the chocolate from cooling or hardening too quickly. If the chocolate becomes too thick while you are in the process of glazing, it indicates that its temperature has dropped too low. Place the container in hot water for a few seconds, stir well, and continue glazing.

It is advisable to use only first-quality chocolate. Cheap chocolate has a very low percentage of cocoa butter, and when melted will be sticky, will not pour smoothly, and will have no shine. Milk chocolate is usually very dry. This type, as well as other types of chocolate, can only be thinned-down with melted cocoa butter. Another thinning medium, such as salad oil is recommended only for use on chocolate-iced cakes, cake rolls, pastries, et cetera. Thinning with oil is especially helpful in the winter when the outside temperature aids in keeping the chocolate dry and hard. Chocolate thinned with oil will retain a certain amount of flexibility which is helpful on cakes to be cut in the store or hotel.

All professional people who use a large amount of chocolate in their daily work are advised to work with a time-saving automatic chocolate warmer. These units have built in thermostats which keep the chocolate at the desired temperature, and constitute a wise investment. Chocolate warmers with dry heat should be given preference over those with water heaters.

CANDIES AND CHOCOLATES

A. Mocha Bonbons*

* Left is a commercial formula, and right is a home formula. This is the procedure followed for every recipe presented in two formulas.

1½ ozs. pulverized coffee	1 tbsp. pulverized coffee
2 lbs. hazelnut nougat	8 ozs. hazelnut nougat
11 ozs. semi-sweet chocolate	3 squares semi-sweet chocolate

Method

Mix the coffee and nougat together thoroughly. Stir in melted, cooled chocolate. Let harden in a cool place. Roll out candy in a sheet about ¼" thick. Cut shapes with cooky cutter. Decorate with leaf gold or silver dragées.

B. Sea Waves

8 ozs. butter	4 tbsp. butter
8 ozs. shortening	4 tbsp. shortening
2 lbs. semi-sweet chocolate	8 squares semi-sweet chocolate
vanilla	vanilla

Method

Cream together butter, shortening, and vanilla. Melt and cool chocolate, add slowly to first mixture. Using a small star tube, squeeze candy from pastry bag onto waxed paper. Glaze with chocolate.

C. Mandoletti

1½ ozs. egg whites	2 egg whites
1 lb. water	½ cup water
2½ ozs. gelatine	1½ tbsp. gelatine
9 lbs. sugar	5 cups sugar
1 lb. filberts, chopped	1 cup filberts, chopped
4 lbs. glucose	1¼ cups glucose
6½ ozs. sugar	¼ cup sugar

Method

Soak gelatine overnight in the egg whites. Beat stiff with the smaller portion of sugar. Combine sugar, water, glucose and boil to 264° F. Pour last solution slowly into egg whites, mixing at low speed constantly. Add filberts. Stir well over low heat until mixture will crack (Test: put a small piece in cold water. If it breaks clean without stickiness, remove candy from fire). Pour onto marble slab, let cool, and cut to desired sizes.

D. Walnut Bonbons

10 ozs. hazelnut nougat (See Index.)	5 ozs. hazelnut nougat
5 ozs. semi-sweet chocolate	2½ squares semi-sweet chocolate
walnut halves	walnut halves

Method

Melt chocolate and mix it slowly with the nougat. Fill mixture into a pastry bag with large star tube. Form stars on waxed paper and put walnut halves on top. Cool in refrigerator.

E. Coffee Bonbons

2 lbs. sugar	1 cup sugar
1 quart whipping cream	scant ½ cup honey
5 ozs. glucose	1 cup whipping cream
coffee to taste	coffee to taste

Method

Cook all ingredients, stirring constantly, to the medium-crack stage. It is most important to be sure there is no crystallization of sugar on the walls of the pan. (See Index the "Boiling of Sugar.") With regard to the coffee, the best professional results have been obtained with one-quarter pint of strong coffee reinforced with three teaspoons of instant coffee. Roll candy on oiled marble slab and cut into squares.

A. Chocolate Rum Bonbons

1¼ lbs. butter	½ cup butter (generous)
2 lbs. fondant	½ cup fondant (generous)
2 lbs. semi-sweet chocolate	8 squares semi-sweet chocolate
vanilla and rum flavoring	vanilla and rum flavoring

Method

Cream butter, add melted chocolate and fondant. Add flavorings to taste. This formula is of a paste-like consistency, and can be used for modelling different figures such as animals, fruits, flowers, et cetera. For bonbons, simply roll sticks of 1″ in diameter, cut into small pieces and form little balls, squares, or other shapes.

B. Cherry Bites

Soak the desired amount of canned, stoned cherries in brandy over night. Drain and let dry. Dip each cherry into hot, vanilla-flavored fondant. When they have cooled, ice with melted chocolate and decorate with glazed cherry pieces.

C. Mint Patties

1 lb. 3 ozs. fondant	¾ cup fondant
2½ ozs. crème de menthe	1¼ ozs. crème de menthe
2 drops mint extract	1 drop mint extract

Method

Warm fondant in a double boiler. Add flavoring. Pour into rubber or powder molds. (See Index, "Fondant Cream Pralines.") After the patties have hardened, remove them from the molds and dip in melted chocolate.

D. Peanut Mounds

1 lb. toasted peanuts (or other nuts)	1¼ cups peanuts (or other nuts)
8 ozs. melted chocolate	4 squares melted chocolate
rum flavoring	rum flavoring

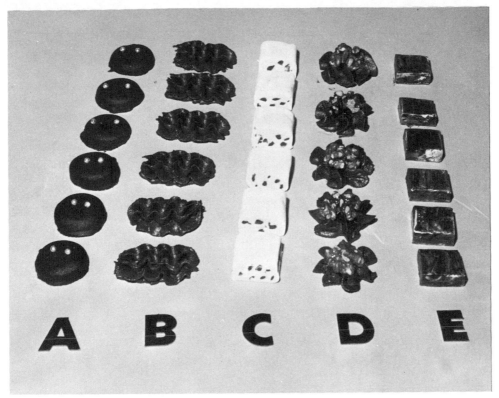

Grouping of bonbons: A. Mocha B. Sea wave C. *Mandoletti* D. Walnut E. Coffee.

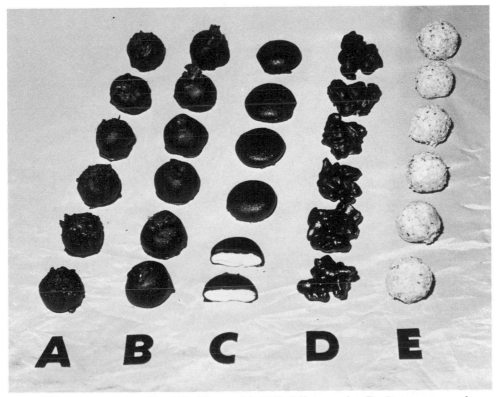

A. Chocolate rum bonbons B. Cherry bites C. Mint patties D. Peanut mounds
E. *Cocosettes*.

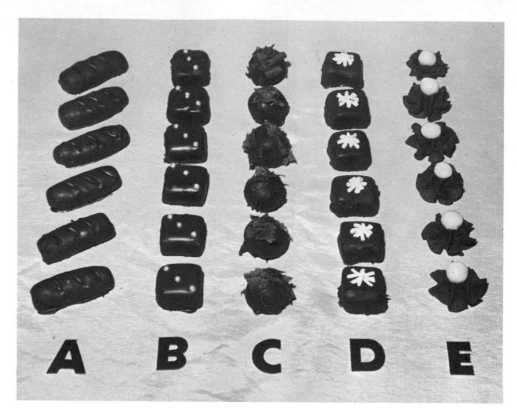

Grouping of truffles : A. Tea B. Butter C. Mocha D. Egg E. Creamy milk.

Cream chocolates with liqueur

Method

Mix all ingredients well. With a teaspoon form small mounds on waxed paper and allow them to harden.

E. Cocosettes

Warm fondant in a double boiler and flavor with rum. Add enough finely shredded cocoanut to give the fondant the consistency of a thick dough. Form balls. Roll in pink-colored shredded cocoanut.

JELLY FRUIT BONBONS

This type of bonbon is often neglected in favor of candies using other materials, and yet, properly manufactured and flavored, it will compare very favorably with other sweet delicacies.

We know of different types of jellies, such as the natural jelly, which hardens through its pectin content and is found in most fruits. Manufactured, artificial jellies are not recommended for jelly bonbons as they spoil very easily. The best jelly, not only for this type of bonbon, but also many other products of the baking and cooking industry, is agar-agar. It is an ocean plant found in the Far East. It is sold in bundles and looks very much like dry, transparent grass.

Basic Jelly

3 ozs. agar-agar	1 oz agar-agar
6 lbs. sugar	4½ cups sugar
4 lbs. glucose	1¾ cups honey or syrup

Note: This formula can be altered to suit individual tastes without complications. However, it is advisable to try a small portion of the above formula first, before making any changes.

Method

Because agar-agar takes a long time to soften, it is recommended to soak it in water for twenty-four hours before using. Use just as much water as you plan to use the next day to boil the six pounds of sugar. After twenty-four hours put the agar-agar-water solution on the stove and cook over medium heat until all of the agar-agar strings have dissolved. Add sugar and glucose. Dissolve the sugar over low heat to make sure that there are no crystals in the water or on the walls of the pan, as this would cause total crystallization of the mixture.

When the mixture has become clear, cook over high heat until the proper stage has been reached. This cannot be determined with a thermometer. Use the following test: Dip a wooden spatula occasionally into the syrup and hold it vertically over the pan. At first you will notice that the excess jelly runs into the pan in large drops. However, as soon as the proper stage has been reached, the jelly on your spatula will slide off in large, solid pieces. Remove the pan from the heat and place it in cold water or ice to prevent after-burning. Cool the jelly completely. You now have a natural jelly. Divide the jelly into different utensils for individual flavoring and coloring. This formula will give you approximately twelve pounds of jelly bonbons.

Following are six of the most popular flavor and color combinations:
(1) Two ounces raspberry jam, or extract to taste, plus red coloring
(2) Two ounces lemon pulp, or extract to taste, plus yellow coloring
(3) Two ounces orange pulp, or extract to taste, plus yellow and red coloring
(4) Mint extract to taste, plus green coloring
(5) Two ounces cherry jam, or extract to taste, plus light red coloring
(6) Two ounces pineapple jelly, or extract to taste, plus yellow and green coloring

The jams or jellies used for flavoring must not be too liquid, or the bonbons will become too soft. To imitate the fine fruit acids, a few drops of lemon juice should be added to all combinations.

Method

Pour the flavored, colored jelly into a baking sheet which has been lined with waxed paper. Refrigerate the jelly for several hours. Using a sharp knife, dipped occasionally into hot water, cut the jelly into squares. Roll the cubes in plain or colored granulated sugar. In the event that different fancy forms are desired, the jelly must be poured into powder trays. (*See Index*, "Fondant Cream Pralines.")

Truffle chocolate is a chocolate filling consisting of whipping cream, chocolate, and flavoring. To assure lasting freshness, the whipping cream must be boiled. As soon as the boiling point is reached, add the chopped chocolate and remove the mixture from fire. Stir well until smooth. Add flavoring. If desired, add butter to the mixture before stirring to increase the delicate flavor and improve the consistency of the final product. Cool completely before using the mixture. Following are several of the most popular recipes for truffles.

A. Tea Truffle

1½ pints whipping cream	1 cup whipping cream
1 lb. 3 ozs. milk chocolate	9 squares milk chocolate
10 ozs. bitter chocolate	3 squares bitter chocolate
2½ ozs. strong tea	2½ tbsp. strong tea

Method

Proceed as described under "Chocolate Truffle Bonbons." When the mixture has cooled, roll it out and cut into cubes. Ice with chocolate. Decorate as desired.

B. Butter Truffle

8 ozs. butter	½ cup butter
½ pint whipping cream	½ cup whipping cream
1 lb. 3 ozs. milk chocolate	9 squares milk chocolate
3½ ozs. nougat (*See Index*)	1¾ ozs. nougat (*See Index.*)

Method

Boil cream and butter. Proceed as directed under "Chocolate Truffle Bonbons."

C. Mocha Truffle

1 quart whipping cream	1 cup whipping cream
1 lb. 8 ozs. sweet chocolate	6 squares sweet chocolate
3 ozs. instant coffee	1 tbsp. instant coffee

Method

Proceed as directed under "Chocolate Truffle Bonbons." Allow mixture to cool. Cream well and form balls. Roll in chocolate decorettes.

D. Egg Truffle

10 ozs. whipping cream	¼ cup whipping cream
5 ozs. sugar	3 tbsp. sugar
2 egg yolks	½ egg yolk
1 lb. 6 ozs. milk chocolate	5½ squares milk chocolate
7½ ozs. cocoa butter	2 ozs. cocoa butter

Method

Boil cream, sugar, and egg yolks. Proceed as directed under "Chocolate Truffle Bonbons."

E. Creamy Milk Truffle

½ pint whipping cream	½ cup whipping cream
1 lb. chocolate	8 squares chocolate
8 ozs. nougat (*See Index.*)	4 ozs. nougat (*See Index.*)
1½ ozs. powdered milk	scant ¼ cup powdered milk
1½ ozs. fondant	1½ tbsp. fondant

Method

Boil the cream, add chocolate and nougat to melt. Let cool. Stir powdered milk into warmed fondant. Combine the two mixes and beat well. Using a pastry bag with star tube, drop small mounds onto waxed paper.

CREAM CHOCOLATES WITH LIQUEUR

Because of its soft, creamy center, this type of chocolate is considered one of the most delicious. In modern candy manufacturing, chemicals are added to the sugar which help soften the centers after the chocolate coating has been applied. These chemicals are often harmful to the flavors and may also cause crystallization of the cream. The chemical most often used in this process is citric acid.

Method

For this purpose we use small waxed paper or aluminum foil cups up to 1″ in diameter and ¾″ high. Have your melted chocolate cooled as described at the beginning of this chapter. Hold the paper cup in your left hand and fill it to the top with chocolate, using a small teaspoon. As soon as the cup is filled, turn it upside down onto a wire screen. This allows the liquid chocolate to run out, leaving only a film of chocolate on the cup's wall. As soon as all the cups have hardened cut them loose from the screen, smooth the edges and set them aside in a cool place.

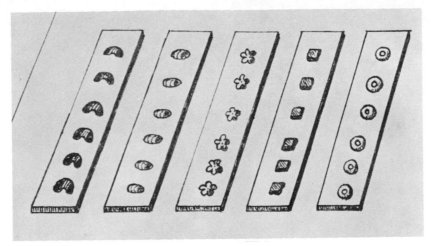

Form the desired shapes of pralines from plaster of paris. Allow them to dry thoroughly. Glue the plaster-of-paris pralines onto a strip of wood.

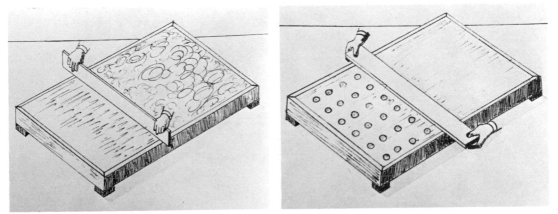

Sift completely dried wheat or rice starch into the powder trays. Smooth the surface with a wooden slat.

Form powder impressions with plaster-of-paris molds.

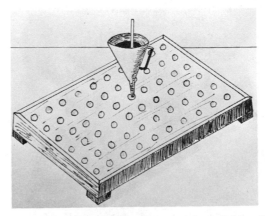

Pour the prepared fondant, using a funnel, into the molds. Cover entire surface with powder. Allow pralines to harden for approximately twenty minutes.

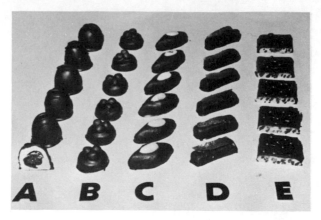

A. Kirsch chocolates B. Filbert treats C. Almond chocolates D. Orange bites E. Butter krokants.

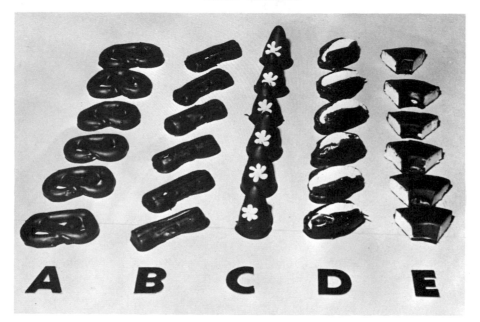

A. Marzipan pretzels B. Marzipan sticks C. Daisy Pyramids D. Date pralines E. Pineapple delights

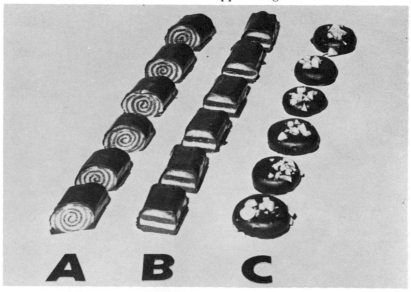

A. Roulades B. Nougat cubes C. Chartreuse bonbons

We are now ready to prepare the cream centers. Put fondant into a saucepan and heat until luke warm, stirring constantly. Remove from heat. You will notice that the fondant is still quite stiff. Add the desired flavoring and soften with either liqueur or sugar syrup. *(See Index.)* Mixture should be of heavy, cream-like consistency. The filling must be thoroughly cooled to prevent the chocolate cups from melting. When the fondant is cool, pour it into the prepared cups, leaving 1/16″ free at the top for the cover. Allow the filled cups to stand for about thirty minutes or until a thin skin has formed on top. Put cooled chocolate into a paper tube and fill cups to top. The final product will be a delicacy greatly appreciated by your friends or customers.

Following are nine of the most popular cream fillings :

(1) Fondant plus lemon rind and gin.
(2) Fondant plus fine, toasted almonds and rum.
(3) Fondant plus half a cherry and brandy or kirsch.
(4) Fondant plus coffee and rum.
(5) Fondant plus crème de menthe.
(6) Fondant plus strawberry jam and egg nog.
(7) Fondant plus apricot jam and apricot brandy.
(8) Fondant plus cocoa and curacao.
(9) Fondant plus fine cocoanut and rum.

As mentioned above, if no liqueur is desired, thin the fondant with a sugar syrup. Add a few drops of lemon juice to the fondant in all fruit-cream combinations. Decorate each variety in a distinctive way, to facilitate identifying each type.

FONDANT CREAM PRALINES

The manufacturing of fine fondant cream pralines requires a special treatment unlike that of other chocolates or candies, with the exception or liquid liqueur bonbons. In order to obtain soft and creamy pralines, cream of tartar must be added to the sugar. The pralines should be coated with chocolate as soon as they have hardened. If they are left unglazed for several days, the pralines will become almost liquid, and too soft to handle. The softening process is a chemical reaction of the cream of tartar, which absorbs the humidity in the air and thus dissolves the sugar crystal formation. The cream of tartar destroys the sugar crystals within twenty-four hours.

The following formula will give the finest product possible :

4 lbs. granulated or cube sugar	2⅓ cups granulated or cube sugar
3 grams (1/10 of one ounce) cream of tartar	1 pinch cream of tartar
1½ pints water	¾ cup water

Method

Mix all ingredients together and boil rapidly to 242° F., observing all rules and regulations concerning the "Boiling of Sugar." *(See Index.)* Pour sugar onto a marble slab and stir with a wooden spatula in a circular motion until the sugar has hardened. Then knead it well by hand to get it as fine and as soft as butter. Store away under cover.

Take a small portion of the above mixture, place it in a sauce pan, add flavors and coloring. Heat, stirring constantly, until the mixture is very hot. This is important, as sugar which is not hot enough will not harden properly. As a test, from time to time put your little finger into the mixture. When you cannot stand the heat anymore, remove sugar from fire.

The fondant is now ready to be poured into the molds. The molds may be made of rubber or pressed into powder trays. The rubber forms are more expensive, but there is no better way of doing it. The fondant is poured into the molds and removed after twenty minutes. The illustrations which follow demonstrate the powder-mold method, the alternative to the rubber molds.

After the pralines have been properly prepared, as demonstrated in the foregoing illustrations, place them on a wire screen to remove all excess powder from candies. It is of the utmost importance to clean the pralines thoroughly to prevent possible fermentation. As previously mentioned they should be chocolate-coated immediately. In a day or two the cream of tartar will have dissolved the sugar crystals and a fine tasting, creamy-smooth product will delight guests and customers alike.

MARZIPAN CONFECTIONS

A. Kirsch Chocolates

12 ozs. marzipan (*See Index.*)	6 ozs. marzipan
2½ ozs. sugar	¼ cup sugar
5 ozs. cherries, chopped	½ cup cherries, chopped
kirsch liqueur	kirsch liqueur

Method

Soak cherries in kirsch for several hours. Drain well. Mix them lightly with the rest of ingredients. Roll sheet about ½″ thick, and cut squares or form little balls. Ice with chocolate.

B. Filberts Treats

6 ozs. filberts	1½ cups filberts
6 ozs. sugar	scant ½ cup sugar
10 ozs. marzipan, rum flavored (*See Index.*)	5 ozs. marzipan, rum flavored

Method

Grind filberts finely. Mix with rest of ingredients to form smooth dough. Roll dough and cut round with a cooky cutter. Arrange filberts on top of each round and dip them in milk chocolate.

C. Almond Chocolates

10 ozs. marzipan (*See Index.*)	5 ozs. marzipan
3 ozs. almonds, chopped, toasted	½ cup almonds, chopped, toasted
vanilla	vanilla

Method

Knead all ingredients together to make a dough. Roll and cut almond shaped pieces. Ice with chocolate and decorate with toasted, blanched almonds.

D. Orange Bites

10 ozs. marzipan (*See Index.*)	5 ozs. marzipan
10 ozs. powdered sugar	1 cup powdered sugar
orange extract or liqueur	orange extract or liqueur

Method

Knead ingredients to a dough of rolling consistency. Cut oblong pieces. Ice with semi-sweet chocolate.

E. Butter Krokant

10 ozs. sugar	¾ cup sugar
7½ ozs. butter	scant ½ cup butter
5 ozs. cocoa butter (*See Index.*)	2½ ozs. cocoa butter
1½ ozs. marzipan (*See Index.*)	¾ oz. marzipan
3 ozs. almonds	⅓ cup almonds
1½ ozs. whipping cream	1½ tbsp. whipping cream
½ orange rind, grated	¼ orange rind, grated

Method

Place sugar in saucepan and melt over medium heat, stirring constantly until all crystals have dissolved. Add the rest of ingredients. Mix well. Spread evenly onto waxed paper. When firm, cut in squares and dip in chocolate.

A. Marzipan Pretzels

Method

Flavor the desired amount of marzipan with melted, bitter chocolate. Form pretzels. Dip in either sweet or semi-sweet chocolate.

B. Marzipan Sticks

1 lb. marzipan (*See Index.*)	½ lb. marzipan
3 ozs. filberts, ground and toasted	½ cup filberts, ground and toasted
egg whites	egg whites
rum flavoring	rum flavoring

Method

Soften the marzipan and filbert mixture with enough egg whites to beat well. Add flavoring. Place dough in pastry bag with small star tube. Form sticks. Ice with milk chocolate.

C. Daisy Pyramids

1 lb. marzipan (*See Index.*)	½ lb. marzipan
4 ozs. pistachios	½ cup pistachios
1 oz. gin	½ oz. gin

The Basket woven with pale colored marzipan onto a basket board. The handles
are made of the same material. The fruits have othello centers, covered with
marzipan and polished with gum arabic.

Bonbonniere made from chocolate (50% sweet chocolate plus 50% cocoa butter).
The ornaments are from royal chocolate icing and the picture is a cocoa painting.
The box is filled with fondant pralines

Covered marzipan bonbonnière.

Bonbonnière made entirely from sugar plastic and filled with marzipan fruits.

Mint stand made from colored sugar plastic. The bird and the carnations are freely modelled from the same material. The stand holds mint patties.

Method

Mix all ingredients well. Form little pyramids. Dip bottom in sweet chocolate. Daisy is made of royal icing.

D. Date Pralines

Method

Split open dates lengthwise. Remove stone and replace with green-colored, rum-flavored marzipan. Dip bottom half in semi-sweet chocolate.

E. Pineapple Delights

Method

Set pineapple rings on a wire screen to allow the excess syrup to drain off. Roll out a very thin sheet of marzipan, and, with a cooky cutter the same size as a pineapple ring, cut two rounds of marzipan for each ring. Place each pineapple ring on a round of marzipan and cover with the second round. Cut each pineapple ring into ten or twelve pieces and ice with semi-sweet chocolate. Decorate as desired.

A. Roulades

Method

Color one mass of marzipan with light green coloring and a second, equal mass with melted chocolate. Roll each mass of marzipan to a layer 1/16″ thick. Join the two layers with sugar syrup, and roll them as a jelly roll. Ice with sweet chocolate, cut small pieces, and decorate as desired.

B. Nougat Cubes

Method

Roll two sheets of nougat-flavored marzipan *(see Index)* and two sheets of lemon-flavored marzipan. Join the layers with sugar syrup, alternating colors. Ice with melted chocolate. Create a wavy design on top with a decorating comb. Cut into cubes.

C. Chartreuse Bonbons

12 ozs. marzipan (*See Index*.)	6 ozs. marzipan
3 ozs. chartreuse liqueur	1½ ozs. chartreuse liqueur
3 ozs. powdered sugar	¼ cup powdered sugar

Method

Knead ingredients together thoroughly and roll to ¼″ thick. Cut with a small cooky cutter. Ice with melted chocolate and decorate with green pistachios.

GLAZED FRUITS

All fruits which have been preserved in sugar syrup may be glazed. Fresh fruits can not be glazed. Before using, the fruit must be drained thoroughly so that its surface is dry.

The glaze consists of sugar to which eight percent glucose has been added. Add water and cook to 242° F. Put the fruit into the solution and bring back to a boil. Remove from heat. Take a spatula and begin to mix the syrup against one side of the container's wall. As soon as the syrup has reached a light, milky color, remove the fruit from the liquid and place it onto a wire screen. Allow the fruit to dry thoroughly in a warm, dry place. When glazed, differently colored fruits are an attractive asset to all chocolate selections.

Candied Orange Peel

Cut orange peel into narrow strips. Place in a container and cover with water. Float waxed paper on top of the water and let stand three days. Drain, cover with water and add sugar to equal the weight of the orange peel. Boil until the syrup has thickened. Drain off the excess syrup and roll the pieces of orange peel in granulated sugar.

If chocolate coated orange peel is desired, remove the peel from the thick syrup and place it between two layers of clean towels. When the excess syrup has been absorbed by the towel, dip the orange peel in melted chocolate.

Contrary to other marzipan items, the sugar content must be kept very low to avoid over-sweetness of the confects (1lb. almond paste to 8 ozs. of powdered sugar).

The marzipan must be perfectly smooth and may be colored or flavored with different kinds of liqueurs. The small individual pieces are decorated with candied fruits, nuts, filberts, almonds, candied orange, lemon peel, or cherries.

The confects should be left to dry for a few hours and then glazed with caramel sugar as follows :

Place desired amount of sugar plus twenty to twenty-five per cent glucose in a stainless steel utensil. Add enough water to get a thick solution. Boil swiftly to 280° F., strictly observing all the rules governing the "Boiling of Sugar." (*See Index.*) Dip the objects into the hot sugar and set on a slightly greased pan. Use only cocoa butter or glycerin for greasing. The confects should be set into small paper cups and stored or displayed in a cool, dry place.

BONBONNIÈRES OF CANDY

Chocolate or candy boxes come in a variety of different shapes, materials and colors. Above all, the attractive appearance and display of chocolates is important.

In the manufacture of edible candy boxes, two excellent materials are available—sugar plastic and chocolate plastic. The sugar plastic has been given special attention in Chapter XI.

Chocolate plastic

1 lb. semi-sweet chocolate	8 squares semi-sweet chocolate
5½ ozs. glucose	scant 3 ozs. glucose
1 tbsp. gelatine solution	½ tbsp. gelatine solution

Method

Melt chocolate, (36° F. to 38° F.) stir in glucose, and add approximately one tablespoon of dissolved gelatine, or any other kind of acid-free jelly. Allow the mixture to harden slightly, then knead to a smooth paste. If the chocolate does not become smooth after a few minutes of kneading, allow the mixture to cool on a marble slab. Do not mix the chocolate by machine. Over-beating of plastic will cause the cocoa butter to separate from the cocoa and the plastic will not bind together. When storing, keep chocolate plastic wrapped in aluminum foil.

Before making the boxes, the designs are to be cut from cardboard. When rolling chocolate plastic, use powdered sugar for under dusting. The thickness of the chocolate depends upon the size of box desired. After the chocolate has been rolled out, brush off all excess sugar on both sides. Rub the top gently with palm of hand. This will produce a deep lustre. Then place card board pattern on top and cut with sharp knife. The individual pieces may be assembled immediately. Use cocoa butter or melted chocolate to glue the pieces together. Chocolate plastic will harden in a few hours when left in a cool, dry place.

Bonbonnières which are made strictly for display purposes may be preserved for greater durability with a special chemical chocolate polisher.

Chocolate plastic has a modelling consistency similar to clay and may be used for making flowers or other decorative items.

LIQUEUR PRALINES

Pralines with liquid liqueur fillings are a special delicacy. Although expensive, they are certainly the finest chocolates of all.

In modern times we use special metal forms which are filled with melted, firstgrade, semi-sweet chocolate and turned upside down to allow the excess chocolate to run out. Shortly before the remaining chocolate walls begin to harden, the excess chocolate must be cut off smoothly. The hollow spaces are then filled up to three-quarters with liqueur such as rum, arrak, chartreuse, kirsch, cherry brandy, or curacao. Chopped fruits such as cherries, pineapples, et cetera, may be added if so desired. The greatest care must be taken that not a drop of liquid spills onto the edges. This would prevent the bottoms from sticking properly and result in a partial or total loss of the filling. The forms are closed off by spreading chocolate onto cellophane strips and placing them over the openings. In order to secure tight-fitting bottoms, slightly press on back of cellophane with roller or side of a knife. The pralines will fall easily from the molds, when left to harden for a few minutes in a cool place. The pralines are usually wrapped individually in aluminum foil.

This method is very simple and even the most inexperienced will be able to produce good pralines. However, the metal forms will require a considerable investment if large quantities are sold regularly.

Liqueur Pralines with Crust

This method was invented by a French confectioner in 1821. Sugar and liqueur are boiled to a certain degree and poured into powder molds as described under "Fondant Cream Pralines." (*See Index.*)

The principle is based on the fact that sugar will crystallize under certain conditions, which are given at the moment of contact with the powder. As soon as the liquid has been poured into the molds, cover it up with powder completely. The solution will crystallize all around, leaving a liquid center. It will take a little experimenting to get the crust very thin and yet strong enough to hold the liquid center it encloses.

How to Make Pralines with Crust

Dissolve one and one-half pounds of sugar in one-half pint of water over low heat, stirring constantly. Strictly observe all rules governing the "Boiling of Sugar." (*See Index.*) Boil solution briskly to 227° F. Put one-quarter of a pint liqueur into a stainless steel saucepan, add boiled sugar quickly. Cover and let stand for a few minutes. Pour liquid into prepared powder trays, cover with powder and let stand in a warm place for three hours. The crystallization process will advance faster from the bottom. This makes it necessary to turn the pralines over after three hours. After approximately eight hours the crystallization process should be completed. The pralines must be freed of all excess powder in order to prevent fermentation. As soon as the pralines have cooled, dip them in sweet or semi-sweet chocolate.

Note. The boiling degree is approximate. If the crust becomes too hard or too thick, decrease temperature by two degrees. If the crust breaks easily, increase temperature by two degrees.

II

FRENCH PASTRIES

Othello Desserts - French Pastry Slices - Éclair Products - Roulades - Short Bread and Cake
Combinations

The term "French Pastries" is commonly used in America for all small, individually decorated cakes or dessert pieces. Most French pastries have basic centers such as cake or shortbread, and are usually distinct from one another in appearance. For example, a layer of sponge cake may be cut into four or five sections, joined together with creams of different flavors, cut into a variety of shapes, iced in several colors, and decorated. The same base thus yields a selection of pastries. However, the pastry chef should include five or six basic centers in the daily selection offered to the public.

The decoration and final touch applied to French pastries gives the pastry chef or housewife a unique opportunity to display his or her artistic ability. There are no specific rules as to how this is done. I present here a few ideas about the basic appearance of a selection. As a general rule, the following could be kept in mind —too much is just as bad as too little. In other words, an over-loaded pastry looks just as unappetizing as a square of plain cake. Bear in mind at all times that the final destination of each culinary effort is the guest's stomach. No one likes a pastry that looks like a piece of wood or like a paint box.

Speaking of colors, a good many professionals as well as housewives have spoiled the guest's appetites simply by over-coloring. Use your food colors as carefully as you would your salt shaker.

When coloring a variety of French pastries, the icings should be kept very pale, and a certain color coordination should be maintained in each assortment.

For example, you may have the following colors on one plate starting from the left.
 (1) white, cream, pale yellow, yellow, orange
 (2) white, pale green, green, light blue, mauve, violet
 (3) white, pale pink, pink, brilliant rose

Food colors should be liquids, and placed in bottles with drip corks on top. Powdered or paste colors should not be used in their original form as the quantity is hard to control. Instead they should be dissolved in water and used as described above. Clear glass bottles are recommended as they show the colors at a glance.

Decorating mediums are chocolate, butter cream, marshmallow, marzipan, glazed fruits, dragées, shredded cocoanut, all kinds of nuts and royal icings.

French pastries should not be made in large quantities for use a few days in advance. Refrigeration is usually harmful to the delicate icings and decorations.

BASIC FORMULAS FOR FRENCH PASTRIES

Basic temperatures given in this book are approximations. Most professionals do not depend on the temperature indicators only, as they usually differ from one another.

Othellos

18 egg whites	9 egg whites
14 egg yolks	7 egg yolks
6 ozs. sugar	scant $\frac{1}{2}$ cup sugar
6 ozs. cornstarch	$\frac{3}{8}$ cup cornstarch
4 ozs. flour	scant $\frac{1}{2}$ cup flour
vanilla	vanilla

Method

Beat whites to stiffness, adding sugar a spoonful at a time. Mix yolks and vanilla together with a hand beater. Fold yolk mixture into whites carefully. Sift the flour and starch, and blend into the egg mixture. Using a pastry bag with a large, round tube, squeeze dough onto a paper-lined baking sheet. Different shapes can be made as shown in the illustration above. Before baking, dust some powdered sugar over the othellos. This will give a smooth top. Bake with little bottom heat.

Note. There should be no steam inside the oven, as this will make the othellos tough. Bake at 300° F.

A SELECTION OF OTHELLO DESSERTS

A. Mozart Balls

Take round othellos, make a shallow hollow in the bottom of each, and join pairs together with rum-flavored butter cream. Roll a thin sheet of marzipan and cut into squares 3" x 3". Brush the squares with sugar syrup. Wrap a square of marzipan thoroughly around each othello to make it look like a ball of marzipan. Melt granulated sugar without liquid, dip the balls into the caramel, and set them on a greased baking pan. When cool, dip them into melted semi-sweet chocolate and set on a screen. Shortly before the chocolate hardens, roll the balls over the screen a few times. This will give the desired fuzzy appearance.

B. Cocoanut Balls

Take round othellos and hollow as above. Join with cocoa-flavored butter cream. Roll into marzipan squares. Coat the balls with butter cream and then roll in toasted, shredded cocoanut. Dust with powdered sugar.

C. Mocha Crescents

Crescent shaped othellos are used. Hollow out and join the pairs with mocha butter cream. Brush hot jam on top and ice with mocha fondant. Decorate.

A. Almond Hearts

Heart-shaped othellos are hollowed and joined with almond butter cream. Brush with hot jam, ice with pink fondant. Decorate.

B. Raspberry Balls

Join round, hollowed othellos with raspberry-flavored custard cream. Pierce the balls with a fork and dip them upside down into hot raspberry jam. Roll the sides in chopped, toasted almonds.

C. Cherry Desserts

Hollow out oblong-shaped othellos and join them with a mixture of butter cream and chopped cherries. Brush with hot apricot jam. Ice with white fondant. Decorate.

A. Chestnuts

Round, hollow othellos are joined with nougat butter cream. Roll in marzipan as described under "Mozart Balls." Stick with almond slivers and ice with green fondant.

B. Orange Drops

Join pear-shaped, hollowed othellos with orange-flavored custard cream. Cover with marzipan. Ice with orange-colored fondant. Decorate.

Indian Puffs

Hollow out round othellos. Place single othellos upside down in paper cups and set aside. Brush hot apricot jam on the other halves and dip in chocolate fondant. Let dry. Join the tops to the bottoms with vanilla-flavored whipped cream pressed through a large star tube from a pastry bag.

FRENCH PASTRY SLICES

A. Dobosh Desserts

8 ozs. sugar	½ cup sugar (generous)
6¾ ozs. cake flour	¾ cup cake flour
3 ozs. butter, melted	⅓ cup butter, melted
12 egg whites	6 egg yolks
12 egg yolks	6 egg whites
vanilla	vanilla
½ lemon rind, grated	½ lemon rind grated

Method

Beat together egg yolks, flavoring, and one-half of the sugar until fluffy. Beat whites to stiffness, adding remaining amount of sugar slowly. Combine the two mixes. Blend in flour and melted butter. Spread mixture on greased, floured baking sheets. Bake at 325° F.

When cold, cut the sheets into equal strips about 4" wide. Join five or six strips together with chocolate-nougat butter cream. Keep top layer separate. Melt sugar to the caramel stage. (*See Index.*) Spread over top layer. Cut top layer into strips about 1" wide, using a greased knife. Place small strips on top of the other layers and cut pieces right through.

Note. Do not try to glaze top layer placed on cake. The final product would be too hard to

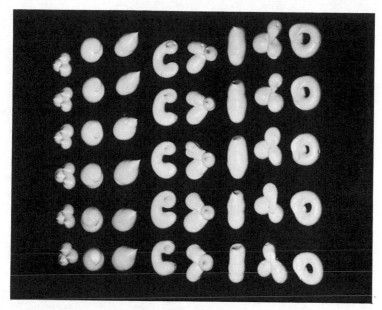

Othellos, variously shaped.

Mozart balls B. Coconut balls C. Mocha crescents.

A B C

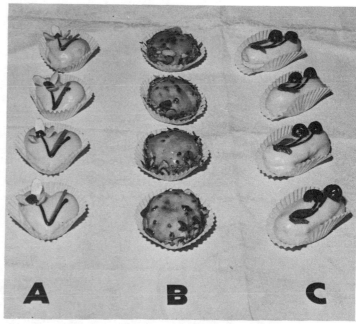

A B C

A. Almond hearts B. Raspberry balls C. Cherry desserts.

A. Chestnuts B. Orange drops

Indian puffs topped with chocolate.

A. Dobosh dessert B. Dobosh pyramids C. Dobosh cubes.

cut. Mocha butter cream, or chocolate butter cream may be used for the whole cake, instead of glazing the top layer with caramel.

B. Dobosh Pyramids

Join strips together as described above. Cool in refrigerator. Set the strips on the extreme edge of the table, long side parallel to the edge. Using a knife dipped in hot water, cut the cake, holding the knife at an angle between the back edge of the top and the front edge of the bottom layer. Join the two sections together like a pyramid and set on a base strip. Cover the pyramid lightly with butter cream and ice with sweet chocolate. Use a hot knife to cut pieces 1″ wide.

C. Dobosh Cubes

Proceed as directed under dobosh desserts. Cut into cubes and ice with sweet chocolate. Decorate.

A. Sacher Slices

Cut a sheet of sacher cake into three layers. (*See Index.*) Join layers with hot raspberry jam. Glaze with hot jam and ice with chocolate icing. Cut pieces 1″ wide.

B. Mocha Squares

Cut a sheet of walnut cake in half. (*See Index.*) Join with hot apricot jam and cut into squares 1½″ x 1½″. Spread all over with butter cream, either mocha or rum flavored, and roll in toasted nuts. Decorate with butter cream.

C. Mocha Walnut Slices

Bake a sheet of shortbread. Cut a walnut cake in half, fill with apricot jam, and set on the shortbread which has also been spread with jam. Glaze with mocha fondant, cut, and decorate.

A. Rainbow Slices

Line a half-round tin or mold with sponge cake. Moisten cake with rum-flavored syrup.

Build up differently colored and flavored layers of butter cream. Close bottom with a thin strip of cake. Refrigerate. Turn upside down onto a wire screen. Coat with semi-sweet chocolate and decorate.

B. Punch Slices

Cut a sheet of chocolate cake in half. Take a layer of white cake, soak it well in rum-flavored syrup and place between chocolate layers. Join layers with jam. Glaze with pink fondant. Decorate with butter cream and glazed cherries.

C. Arcadia Slices

Line the bottom and sides of a rectangular loaf tin with chocolate cake. Fill one half with parisienne cream and the remaining half with mocha cream. Close with a strip of cake. Coat with chocolate, and decorate.

A. Fruit Slices

Line a loaf tin with pound cake or almond sponge. Whip together butter cream, grated lemon rind, and a little lemon juice. Add chopped, glazed fruits, mix, and fill cake-lined tin. Close tin with a strip of cake. Invert on wire screen, spread with apricot jam, and glaze with lemon fondant.

B. Chestnut Slices

Join white and chocolate cake together as shown in the illustration. Add a layer of chestnut fudge. Top with whipped cream and decorate with chestnuts.

Note. Chestnut fudge consists of boiled, mashed chestnuts mixed with the equivalent weight of sugar. Decorative chestnuts are made of fudge and glazed with semi-sweet chocolate.

C. Diplomat Slices

Put a layer of sponge cake between two layers of puff pastry. Join layers with vanilla butter cream. Before putting on top layer, soak the cake with rum-flavored sugar syrup. Ice with butter cream and decorate.

A. Tropical Treats

Join a sheet of macaroon cake and a sheet of chocolate cake with lemon-flavored custard cream. Spread top with hot apricot jam. Cover top with sliced pineapple, papaya, and oranges. Glaze with hot apricot jam or transparent jelly. Cool and cut.

B. Marzipan Slices

Sprinkle white wine on a strip of cherry cake. Glaze with hot jam. Cover top and sides with a thin layer of pale green marzipan. Decorate.

C. Cocoanut Slices

Roll a sheet of shortbread dough $\frac{1}{4}''$ thick. Bake at 350° F. until half done. Cover with $\frac{1}{2}''$ layer of cocoanut dough as used in cocoanut macaroons. (*See Index.*) Glaze with egg whites. Bake at 350° F.

A. Marshmallow Flammé

Set a strip of pound cake on a sheet of baked puff pastry, using custard cream to join the layers. Top with marshmallow cream. *(See Index.)* Put into a hot oven with overhead heat until light brown.

B. Elite Dessert

Form a small cake roulade of your choice. (*See Index.*) Cover with vanilla-flavored whipped cream. Decorate and cut.

C. Checkerboard Slices

Cut five pieces of chocolate cake about 1" square by the length of the cake, and four similar pieces of sponge cake or pound cake. Join strips with butter cream as shown in illustration and glaze with hot jam. Cover top and the sides with a thin layer of marzipan. Decorate and cut.

A. Gypsy Slices

12 whole eggs	6 whole eggs
8 egg yolks	4 egg yolks
10 ozs. sugar	$\frac{3}{4}$ cup sugar
8 ozs. cake flour	1 cup cake flour
vanilla	vanilla
1 lemon peel, grated	$\frac{1}{2}$ lemon peel, grated
sugar *couleur* (*See Index.*)	sugar *couleur* (*See Index.*)

Method

Proceed as directed under "Sponge Cakes." (*See Index.*) Spread on greased and floured baking sheet. Dough should be about $\frac{1}{4}''$ thick. Bake at 350° F. Cut strips and join with nougat butter cream. Ice with milk chocolate.

B. Cardinal Slices

Part 1

9 egg whites	4 egg whites
3 ozs. sugar	$\frac{1}{4}$ cup sugar
13 ozs. sugar plus water	1 cup sugar plus water

Part 2

8 egg yolks	4 egg yolks
5 whole eggs	3 whole eggs
$6\frac{1}{2}$ ozs. sugar	$\frac{1}{2}$ cup sugar
5 ozs. cake flour	$\frac{1}{2}$ cup cake flour

Method

Part 1 — Beat whites until stiff, using the smaller amount of sugar. Dissolve remaining sugar in water and boil swiftly to 242° F. Add to whites and continue beating until cooled.

Part 2 — Mix all ingredients, except flour, first warm and then cold as directed under sponge cake. Make three long strips with the egg-white mixture on a sheet of paper in a baking pan. Leave enough room between the strips for two strips of the sponge mixture. On the next pan reverse the strips, having three of sponge and two of egg whites. Continue making alternate groups of strips until all the dough is used. Bake at 325° F. When cold, turn upside down, wet, and remove paper. Join two groups of strips with hot apricot jam, sprinkle with powdered sugar, and cut.

ÉCLAIR PRODUCTS

The basic éclair dough is unlike any other dough. A clear understanding of its formation and baking will contribute noticeably to the excellence of the final product.

Strong flour must be used because of its high binding quality. This will produce the necessary

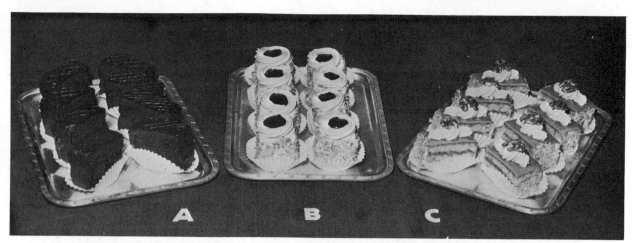

A. Sacher slices B. Mocha squares C. Mocha walnut slices.

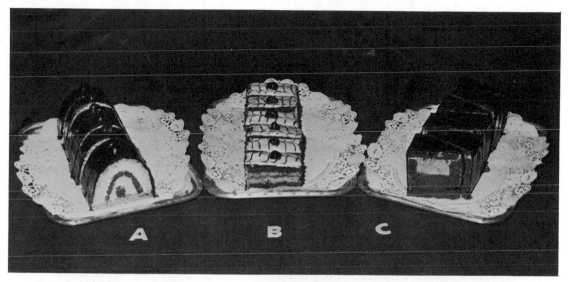

A. Rainbow slices B. Punch slices C. Arcadia slices.

A. Fruit slices B. Chestnut slices C. Diplomat slices.

A. Tropical treats B. Marzipan slices C. Coconut slices.

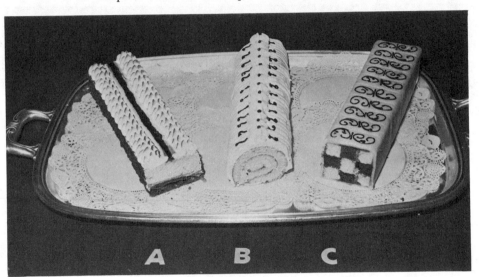

A. Marshmallow *flammè* B. Elite dessert C. Checkerboard slices

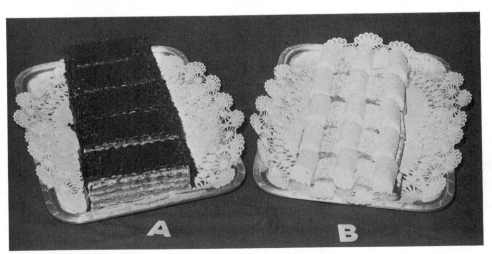

A. Gypsy slices B. Cardinal slices.

solid outside shell. In the high baking temperature the moisture will evaporate quickly. This will cause the mounds to rise, leaving a hollow center. If the oven is set at the proper temperature the outside walls will harden and prevent the pieces from collapsing. Care must be taken to leave the damper at least partly open. If there is no damper on the unit, the oven door should be kept open just far enough to allow the excess steam to escape.

Éclair dough may be cooked in a copper pot if necessary, but under no circumstances should the mixing be done in the copper utensil. This would immediately oxidize the eggs, which not only discolors them but also makes the product dangerous to consume.

Some professionals add sugar and ammonium to the dough, but this practice is not recommended. The amount of eggs used varies with the size of the eggs and the length of time the dough is cooked. The longer the dough is cooked, the more the moisture will evaporate. This moisture may have to be replaced with more eggs. The texture of the dough before baking should be creamy and soft.

Basic Formula for Éclair Dough

2 quarts milk	1 pint milk
14 ozs. butter	½ cup butter
1½ tsp. salt	dash salt
1 lb. 4 ozs. strong flour	1 cup strong flour (bread
20 eggs (approx. 2 lbs.	flour)
3 ozs.)	5 eggs

Method

Bring to a boil the milk, butter, and salt. Add flour. Cook until mixture will loosen from pot wall. Stir well during entire cooking time. Put into mixer and blend in the eggs one at a time. Force through a round tube onto greased baking pans. Bake at 375° F. to 400° F.

Éclairs

Form lady-finger-shaped figures on a greased pan, using a round tube. Bake as above. Cool and fill with rum-flavored custard cream. Ice with chocolate fondant. For mocha éclairs, flavor custard cream with coffee and ice with mocha fondant. Whipped cream may be added to custard, if desired.

Cream Puffs

Force dough through a star or plain tube to make small mounds on a greased baking pan. Dab lightly with egg wash. Bake as directed. Cool, cut in half and fill with vanilla-flavored whipped cream, or a mixture of whipped cream and custard cream. Replace tops and sprinkle with powdered sugar or ice with fondant.

Carolines

Using a small round tube, make mounds the size of a dime on a greased pan. Bake as directed. Cool, then poke a small hole in the bottoms. Put custard or whipped cream filling in a paper tube and fill holes completely. Glaze with chocolate fondant. An interesting selection can be made by varying the fillings and icings. Carolines are served as *petits fours*.

Caroline Hors d'Oeuvres

Small carolines may be filled with curried chicken, cheese fillings, meat, or egg, fillings to suit the individuals' tastes and provide a wide selection.

Croquembouche

Fill small carolines with custard cream, flavored to taste. Glaze by dipping into light brown caramel sugar. Set on a greased pan and allow to cool. Form a pyramid as shown in illustration. Decoration is made of krokant. (*See Index.*)

Éclair Ornaments

Use basic éclair dough formula. Fill paper bag and cut very small opening. Form flowers or ornaments as shown in illustration onto lightly greased and floured pan. Bake at 280° F. Care must be taken that there is no steam formation during baking. Ornaments bake very quickly.

ROULADES

Under the classification of roulades we find all the types of cakes which are rolled in the fashion of a jelly roll. A variety of formulas will provide a suitable one for each purpose. Most jelly rolls cannot be rolled after they have cooled. However, roulades which will be spread with either butter cream or whipping cream must be cold. Special formulas are provided for these roulades.

All roulades are rolled the same way. Turn the baked sheet of cake upside down onto paper or canvas which is slightly larger than the cake sheet. Remove baked-on pan-liner swiftly. Spread with filling. Lift up top ends of paper or canvas and pull towards yourself. Cake will form a roll. Make sure roulade is rolled tightly, and wrap with same paper or canvas to prevent uncoiling. Refrigerate before cutting.

Walnut Roulade

9 egg yolks	9 egg yolks
6 egg whites	6 egg whites
4 ozs. sugar	1 cup sugar
3½ ozs. walnuts, ground	¾ cup walnuts, ground
1 oz. flour	1 tbsp. flour
¾ oz. butter, melted	⅛ cup butter, melted

Method

Beat together the whites and one-half of the sugar until stiff. Beat together yolks and remaining half of sugar. Fold the two mixtures together slowly. Add flour and nuts. Add melted butter last. Spread mixture ½″ thick on a paper-lined baking sheet. Bake with overhead heat at 350° F. to 375° F. Cool completely. Spread with nut-rum butter cream. Roll and decorate.

Strawberry Roulade

10 egg yolks	10 egg yolks
8 egg whites	8 egg whites
8 ozs. cake flour	2 cups cake flour
5½ ozs. sugar	¾ cup sugar
vanilla	vanilla
1 lemon rind, grated	1 lemon rind, grated

Method

Proceed as directed under "Walnut Roulades." When cold, spread with pink-colored butter cream and sliced strawberries. Roll, then decorate with whipping cream and fresh strawberries.

Jelly Sponge Roulade

20 eggs	5 eggs
13 ozs. sugar	½ cup sugar
14½ ozs. cake flour	¾ cup cake flour
vanilla	vanilla
1 lemon rind, grated	¼ lemon rind, grated

Method

Proceed as directed under "Sponge Cake." (*See Index*.) Bake at 350° F. After baking remove from heat immediately. Turn upside down onto a sheet of paper or canvas. Remove baked-on paper and spread with raspberry jam or apricot jam. Roll and sprinkle with powdered sugar.

Dream Chocolate Roll

25 eggs	6 eggs
1½ lbs. sugar	¾ cup sugar
32 egg whites	4 egg whites
¾ oz. salt	dash salt
½ oz. cream of tartar	pinch cream of tartar
4 ozs. cocoa	4½ tbsp. cocoa
1 lb. 4 ozs. cake flour	1 cup cake flour
12 ozs. powdered sugar	½ cup powdered sugar
8 ozs. salad oil	¼ cup salad oil
vanilla	vanilla

Method

Sift together flour, powdered sugar, cocoa, tartar, and salt; stir in oil and vanilla. Add whole eggs gradually, mixing well after each addition. Beat together whites and sugar until stiff; fold into first mixture. Spread on a paper-lined baking sheet. Bake at 350° F. Cool completely, spread with whipped cream and roll. Decorate with chipped chocolate.

Madeira Roulade

1½ quarts eggs	1½ cups eggs
1 lb. 13 ozs. sugar	1 cup sugar
1 lb. 13 ozs. cake flour	1¾ cups cake flour
vanilla	vanilla
1 lemon rind, grated	¼ lemon rind, grated

Method

Proceed as described under sponge cake. Cool completely. Spread with rum-nougat-flavored

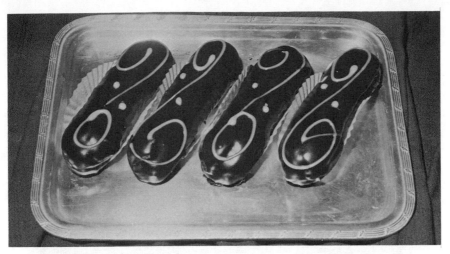

Decorated eclairs, chocolate covered.

Powdered cream puffs

Caroline *petits fours*

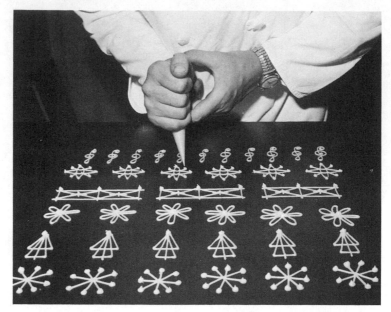

Styling éclair ornaments

Croquembouche

Walnut roulades

Strawberry roulades

Jelly sponge roulades

Dream chocolate roll

Madeira roulades

Marzipan roulades

Grouping of tarts : A. Strawberry B. Pineapple C. Mexican D. Almond E. Mocha
F. Fruit.

butter cream and roll. Spread cream over surface of roll and cover with toasted almonds. Cut slices 1½″ thick, place on sides in paper cups, decorate with butter cream and cherries.

Marzipan Roulade

Roll a thin layer of marzipan approximately 20″ x 12″. Cover with a layer of rum-flavored butter cream. Place a thin layer of cake on top. (Cake ends may be used.) Over the cake spread another thin layer of cream. Roll, coat with chocolate, and decorate.

Petits Fours

Petits fours as well as French pastries in general can be made in a large variety of shapes and flavors with different icings, colors, and decorations. Almost any of the many French pastries described in this section could be used as petits fours, providing they were made small enough to fit into the classification of *petit*. This brings us right to the source of many failures involving professionals and amateurs alike. *Petits fours* must be small, in fact so small that they can be consumed in one bite. To serve a *petit four* the size of a clubhouse sandwich is both unappetizing and ignorant.

The illustrated selection of petits fours was cut with various small cooky cutters from a frenchipan sheet cake *(see Index)* sprinkled with kirsch liqueur and glazed with pale colored fondant. The decoration consists of royal chocolate icing, candied cherries and fruit peel.

Note : If sponge cakes are used they must be coated with hot apricot jam before icing.

SHORTBREAD AND CAKE COMBINATIONS

Basic Tart

Line small tart forms with shortbread or sweet dough. Put a dot of apricot jam on the bottom of each tart. Fill the tarts up to three-quarters with almond sponge, Vienna sponge, or chocolate sponge, et cetera. *(See Index, "Cakes Part One.")* Bake at 350° F.

A. Strawberry Tarts

Brush sugar syrup on top of basic tarts. On each make a circle of pink butter cream. Put a spoonful of strawberry jam or fresh fruit in each center. Decorate with chopped nuts.

B. Pineapple Tarts

Follow same procedure as above, using pineapple jam. Use yellow butter cream. Decorate with nuts.

C. Mexican Tarts

After sprinkling with sugar syrup, make a circle on the tarts with chocolate, butter cream. Trim with thinly chipped chocolate. Sprinkle with powdered sugar.

D. Almond Tarts

Make a small hole in the cake part of basic tarts. Fill with almond butter cream and top with a half cherry. Roll out a thin sheet of marzipan. Cut rounds the same size as tart tops with a cooky cutter. With a sharp knife, cut a cross in the center of each marzipan round, and place on top of tart so the cherry shows slightly.

E. Mocha Tarts

Brush basic tarts with sugar syrup. Decorate with mocha butter cream.

F. Fruit Tarts

Place fresh or preserved fruits on top of prepared basic tarts. Glaze with hot apricot jam or tragant glaze. *(See Index.)*

Almond Soufflé

2 lbs. almonds, ground	1¾ cup almonds, ground
4 ozs. rum	1 oz. rum
3 lbs. sugar	1¾ cups sugar
12 egg yolks	4 egg yolks
12 whole eggs	4 whole eggs
12 ozs. butter, melted	⅜ cup butter, melted
6 ozs. pastry flour	⅜ cup pastry flour
8 ozs. almond paste	2 ozs. almond paste
vanilla	vanilla
1 orange peel, grated	¼ orange peel, grated

31

Method

Cream together almond paste, egg yolks, whole eggs, and flavoring. Add melted butter. Blend in sifted flour and finely ground almonds. Line small tart forms with puff paste. Put a dot of apricot jam in the bottom of each tart. Using a large round tube, squeeze the souffle mixture from the pastry bag into the forms. Bake at 350° F. Sprinkle with powdered sugar after baking, or decorate with butter cream if so desired.

Prince of Wales

20 whole eggs	5 whole eggs
20 egg yolks	5 egg yolks
1 lb. 8 ozs. sugar	scant 1 cup sugar
1 lb. 4 ozs. cake flour	1⅛ cups cake flour
1 lb. 8 ozs. almond paste	6 ozs. almond paste
12 ozs. butter, melted	¾ cup butter, melted
vanilla	vanilla
1 lemon rind, grated	¼ lemon rind, grated
1 orange rind, grated	¼ orange rind, grated

Method

Proeed with mixing as described under "Almond Sponge Cake" *(see Index)*. Squeeze mixture into paper cupcake forms. Bake at 350° F. After they have cooled, remove the paper, cut horizontally and join with jam. Decorate with butter cream and toasted nuts.

Florentines 1

3 lbs. sugar	1¾ cups sugar
1 lb. 5 ozs. butter	½ cup butter (generous)
1½ pints whipping cream	¾ cup whipping cream
1½ lbs. honey	½ cup honey
1¼ lbs. blanched, chopped almonds	1¼ cups blanched, chopped almonds
1¼ lbs. filberts, sliced	1¼ cups filberts, sliced
7 ozs. mixed fruits	½ cup mixed fruits

Method

Boil sugar, whipping cream, and honey to 265° F. Add rest of ingredients. Let cool to a manageable temperature. Form rolls and cool completely in refrigerator. Cut rolls. Form little balls and set on a greased baking sheet. Bake at 300° F. Remove from pan while still hot and place on rack to cool. Join pairs with chocolate butter cream.

Florentines 2

1 quart whipping cream	1 cup whipping cream
1 lb. 3 ozs. mixed fruit	1 cup mixed fruit
1 lb. 3 ozs. almonds, blanched, chopped	1¼ cups almonds, blanched, chopped
1 lb. powdered sugar	¾ cup powdered sugar

Method

Add all ingredients to hot whipping cream. Cook over low heat until thickened, stirring constantly. Drop hot mixture from a spoon onto a greased baking sheet. Bake at 300° F. Glaze with hot sugar syrup or tragant glaze *(see index)*. Remove from pan while still hot and soft. Cool on a wire screen or waxed paper. Ice bottoms with sweet chocolate.

Canadian Cheese

1 lb. 4 ozs. egg whites	½ cup egg whites
3 lbs. 1 oz. sugar	1¾ cups sugar
dash salt	dash salt

Mix all ingredients together. Place in a double boiler and beat until the mixture is hot. Remove from heat and continue beating until cool and stiff. On a paper-lined baking sheet form spirals approximately two inches in diameter, using a pastry bag with small tube. Sprinkle with icing sugar. Bake at 160° F. to 180° F. Remove from oven and let dry thoroughly in warm place. Disks must come loose easily from paper. Join pairs with mocha or chestnut-flavored butter cream.

Canolli Rolls

1¼ lbs. almonds, grated	1¼ cups almonds, grated
1¾ lbs. sugar	1 cup sugar
7½ ozs. butter, melted	scant ¼ cup butter, melted
3½ ozs. flour	¼ cup flour (generous)
1¼ lbs. egg whites, unbeaten	1¼ cups egg whites, unbeaten
½ pint whipping cream	¼ cup whipping cream
vanilla	vanilla

Method

Mix together the almonds, sugar, and vanilla. Add flour, butter, whites, and whipping cream. Grease and flour the baking pans. Cut a 4″ x 2″

Prince of Wales teacakes topped with cherries

Florentines

Canolli rolls

Grape tarts

Filbert boats

Orange tarts

rectangular hole in a piece of cardboard. Place it on the pan and, using a spatula, fill the rectangle with the above mixture. Lift cardboard and repeat process until all the mixture is used. Bake at 300° F. until very light brown. Have ready a cylindrical stick about one foot long and no more than ½″ in diameter. While they are still hot and pliable, roll the *canolli* sheets over the stick and set rolls aside. If the sheets get too cold to roll, put them back inside the oven for a few minutes. When rolls are cold, fill them with maraschino-flavored butter cream and dip the ends into chopped nuts. Whipped cream may be used instead of butter cream.

Filbert Boats

15 ozs. ground, toasted filberts	1¼ cups ground, toasted filberts
15 ozs. cake crumbs	1 cup cake crumbs
7½ ozs. powdered sugar	¼ cup powdered sugar
1 oz. orange rind, grated	1 tsp. orange rind, grated

Method

Line oval-shaped tart forms with Linzer shortbread dough. *(See Index.)* Bake at 350° F. Prepare above formula as follows : Add a little milk to nuts and crumbs, mix, and put through a meat grinder. Stir in orange rind, sugar, and if necessary more milk to get a thick, creamy texture. Fill the baked tarts, spread with apricot jam, and ice with vanilla-flavored fondant. Decorate with toasted filberts.

Grape Tarts

Partly fill baked tart shells with vanilla custard cream. Close tarts with round pieces of cake. Brush with apricot jam. Pile grapes on top and glaze with hot jam or jelly.

Orange Tarts

Soften marzipan with orange juice. Squeeze from a pastry bag with a large, round tube into baked tart shells. Peel oranges and cut circular slices. Place slices on top of tarts and glaze with hot apricot jam. Decorate outer edges with shredded nuts.

Cherry Tarts

6½ ozs. marzipan	6½ ozs. marzipan
6½ ozs. sugar	scant 1 cup sugar
juice of 1 lemon	juice of 1 lemon
4 egg whites	4 egg whites
2 ozs. flour	½ cup flour
2 ozs. water	¼ cup water
cherries, canned or fresh	cherries, canned or fresh

Method

Soften marzipan with water, sugar, and lemon juice. Cream thoroughly and add flour. Beat whites until stiff and fold into first mixture. Line tart forms with dough, then place cake or wafer crumbs in bottom of each shell. Half-fill each tart with cherries. Top with above mixture and dust with powdered sugar. Bake at 350° F. to 375° F.

Strawberry Tarts with Cottage Cheese

1 lb. cottage cheese	1 cup cottage cheese, generous
4½ ozs. sugar	⅜ cup sugar
3 ozs. butter	¼ cup butter
4 egg yolks	2 egg yolks
salt	salt
vanilla	vanilla
¼ oz. gelatine	⅛ oz. gelatine
1 pint whipping cream	1 cup whipping cream

Method

Put a thin coat of semi-sweet chocolate on the inside of baked tart shells. Melt the butter, add cheese, salt, yolks, vanilla, and mix well. Dissolve gelatine in a little cold water and add to first mixture. Whip the cream, blend in strawberries to taste, and fold lightly into the cheese mixture. Fill tart shells. Decorate with whipped cream.

Apple Tarts

6 ozs. butter	⅜ cup butter
7¼ oz. sugar	½ cup sugar
12 ozs. cake flour	1½ cups cake flour
⅓ oz. baking powder	1 tsp. baking powder
5 ozs. milk	¼ cup milk, generous
salt	salt
1 lemon rind, grated	½ lemon rind, grated
rum to flavor	rum to flavor
3 ozs. raisins	⅓ cup raisins
sliced apples	sliced apples

Method

Cream together butter and sugar. Slowly add yolks and milk. Sift together the flour and baking powder. Blend into first mixture. Add raisins. Line tart forms with dough, and fill to half with above mixture. Dip ¼″ thick apple slices into hot butter, and place on top of tarts. Bake at 350° F. Decorate with marzipan.

Mince Tarts

Roll a thin sheet of puff paste. Cut rounds with a cooky cutter and press into tart forms. The dough should be a little higher than the edges of the forms. Fill shells with mince meat. Brush outer edges with egg wash. Cut rounds of puff paste to cover tarts. Brush with egg wash. Let tarts rest a few hours in a cool place. Before baking, prick holes in tops of tarts. Bake at 375° F.

Rice Tarts

10 ozs. rice, washed	½ cup rice, washed
2 lbs. 2 ozs. milk	(generous)
10 ozs. sugar	2 cups milk
salt	¾ cup sugar
vanilla	salt
1 lemon rind, grated	vanilla
10 ozs. raisins	½ lemon rind, grated
12 egg whites	1 cup raisins
12 egg yolks	6 egg whites
2½ ozs. cornstarch	6 egg yolks
	⅛ cup cornstarch

Method

Cook rice and milk until soft. Mix in sugar, yolks, salt, flavoring, and raisins. Beat whites until stiff, and add starch to whites. Fold whites into rice mixture. Line tart forms with thinly rolled yeast dough. Put a dot of raspberry jam on the bottom of each tart and fill with rice mixture. Bake at 375° F. Sprinkle with powdered sugar.

Lemon Tarts

10 ozs. white wine	⅝ cup white wine
juice of 6 lemons	juice of 3 lemons
8 ozs. sugar	½ cup sugar
9 egg yolks	4 egg yolks
¼ oz. gelatine	½ tsp. gelatine
14 ozs. whipping cream, whipped	1 cup whipping cream, whipped

Method

Bring all ingredients except cream to a boil in a double boiler. Stir well and remove from heat. Let cool. Fold in whipped cream. Put into small, baked tart shells. Decorate with butter cream or whipped cream.

Macadamia Tarts

10 ozs. butter	⅝ cup butter
15 ozs. sugar	1 cup sugar
9 eggs	4-5 eggs
6 egg yolks	3 egg yolks
10 ozs. marzipan	5 ozs. marzipan
vanilla	vanilla
dash cinnamon	dash cinnamon
10 ozs. cake crumbs	1½ cups cake crumbs
12 ozs. milk	¾ cup milk
5 ozs. macadamia nuts, ground	½ cup macadamia nuts, ground
5 ozs. bitter chocolate	2½ squares bitter chocolate

Method

Soften marzipan with eggs and yolks. Add sugar, butter, and flavoring. Cream well. Soak crumbs and nuts in milk, add melted chocolate to crumb mixture. Blend well into first mixture. Grease and flour tart forms. Fill with mixture and bake at 375° F. Cool. Glaze with hot apricot jam and dip into macadamia nuts. Sprinkle with icing sugar. Decorate with cherries.

Cocoanut Tarts

2½ lbs. dessicated cocoanut	4 cups dessicated cocoanut
7½ lbs. granulated sugar	4¼ cups granulated sugar
1¼ lbs. potatoes, mashed	5 ozs. potatoes, mashed
1¾ lbs. egg whites	scant 1 cup egg whites
5 ozs. glucose	2 tbsp. glucose
2 lemon rinds, grated	½ lemon rind, grated

Method

Heat together whites, sugar, potatoes, glucose, lemon rind, and cocoanut, using a double boiler. Bring mixture close to a boil, stirring constantly. Remove from heat. Allow to cool. If necessary, soften the mixture with additional whites to make it manageable. Using a pastry bag with a medium

Apple tarts

Lemon tarts decorated with nuts and chocolate

Coconut tarts

Maraschino tarts

A selection of French pastries, including éclairs, sponge cake slices, cream horns, and Napoleons.

round tube, squeeze mounds 1½″ in diameter on greased, floured pans. Bake at 400° F. Use shortbread cookies for each base. Make a spiral of chocolate butter cream on each cooky and set baked cocoanut mounds on top. Dip in chocolate to upper edge. Cocoanut tarts will be hard at first, but will soften within a few hours under refrigeration.

Maraschino Tarts

Roll shortbread dough *(see Index)* and cut into 2″ rounds. Set on greased pans. Brush with egg wash. Sprinkle one-half of the cookies with sliced almonds. Place a half of a cherry in each center. Leave the other half of the cookies plain. Bake at 350° F. On the plain cookies make a spiral of maraschino-flavored butter cream. Cover with the almond-sprinkled cookies. Dip in chocolate to upper edge.

III

COOKIES AND FANCY TEA SWEETS

Basic Shortbread and Cooky Dough - Macaroons - Cookies

BASIC SHORTBREAD AND COOKY DOUGHS

The following formulas should provide a variety of differently flavored cookies, slices, and tarts. Some of the formulas are richer than others, some more and some less expensive. They may be used according to the individual's needs or the public's demands. The so-called "One-Two-Three" dough is the most popular. This mixture consists of one part sugar, two parts butter, and three parts flour. All ingredients are mixed together swiftly without too much kneading. The dough should be kept in a cool place.

Shortbread Dough 1

1 lb. pastry flour	4 cups pastry flour
8 ozs. butter	1 cup butter
8 ozs. powdered sugar	$1\frac{1}{2}$ cups powdered sugar (generous)
2 eggs	2 eggs
1 lemon rind, grated	1 lemon rind, grated

Shortbread Dough 2

15 ozs. pastry flour	$3\frac{3}{4}$ cups pastry flour
12 ozs. butter	$1\frac{1}{2}$ cups butter
4 ozs. powdered sugar	$\frac{3}{4}$ cup powdered sugar (generous)
8 egg yolks	8 egg yolks
1 lemon rind, grated	1 lemon rind, grated

Shortbread Dough 3

1 lb. 4 ozs. pastry flour	5 cups pastry flour
13 ozs. butter	$1\frac{1}{2}$ cups butter (generous)
$6\frac{1}{2}$ ozs. powdered sugar	$1\frac{1}{4}$ cups powdered sugar
4 egg yolks	4 egg yolks
1 lemon rind, grated	1 lemon rind, grated
vanilla	vanilla

Shortbread Dough 4

1 lb. pastry flour	4 cups pastry flour
8 ozs. powdered sugar	$1\frac{1}{2}$ cups powdered sugar (generous)
4 ozs. butter	$\frac{1}{2}$ cup butter
$\frac{1}{6}$ oz. ammonium	$\frac{1}{4}$ tsp. ammonium
1 lemon rind, grated	1 lemon rind, grated
little milk	little milk
vanilla	vanilla

Chocolate Shortbread

1 lb. 4 ozs. pastry flour	5 cups pastry flour
13 ozs. butter	$1\frac{1}{2}$ cups butter
12 ozs. powdered sugar	$2\frac{1}{2}$ cups powdered sugar
2 ozs. cocoa	$\frac{1}{2}$ cup cocoa (generous)
vanilla	vanilla
$\frac{1}{6}$ oz. ammonium	$\frac{1}{4}$ tsp. ammonium

Filbert Shortbread

1 lb. 4 ozs. pastry flour	5 cups pastry flour
10 ozs. butter	$1\frac{1}{4}$ cups butter
8 ozs. powdered sugar	$1\frac{1}{2}$ cups powdered sugar (generous)
7 ozs. filberts, toasted, ground	$3\frac{1}{4}$ cups filberts, toasted, ground
2 eggs	2 eggs
vanilla	vanilla

Almond Shortbread

1 lb. 5 ozs. pastry flour	$5\frac{1}{4}$ cups pastry flour
15 ozs. powdered sugar	3 cups powdered sugar
13 ozs. butter	$1\frac{1}{2}$ cups butter (generous)
5 ozs. almonds, blanched, ground	$2\frac{1}{4}$ cups almonds, blanched, ground
2 ozs. candied orange peel	$\frac{1}{4}$ cup candied orange peel
3 egg yolks	3 egg yolks
$\frac{1}{6}$ oz. baking powder	$\frac{1}{4}$ tsp. baking powder
1 lemon rind, grated	1 lemon rind, grated
$\frac{1}{2}$ tsp. cinnamon	$\frac{1}{2}$ tsp. cinnamon

Walnut Shortbread

1 lb. pastry flour	4 cups pastry flour
13 ozs. butter	$1\frac{1}{2}$ cups butter
6 ozs. powdered sugar	scant $1\frac{1}{2}$ cups powdered sugar
5 ozs. walnuts, ground	$2\frac{1}{4}$ cups walnuts, ground
$\frac{1}{6}$ oz. baking powder	$\frac{1}{4}$ tsp. baking powder
1 lemon rind, grated	1 lemon rind, grated
dash nutmeg	dash nutmeg

Linzer Shortbread 1

8 ozs. pastry flour	2 cups pastry flour
8 ozs. crumbs	$2\frac{2}{3}$ cups crumbs
8 ozs. powdered sugar	$1\frac{1}{2}$ cups powdered sugar (generous)
5 ozs. butter	$\frac{5}{8}$ cups butter
$\frac{1}{4}$ tsp. ammonium	$\frac{1}{4}$ tsp. ammonium
1 egg	1 egg
$\frac{1}{2}$ cup milk	$\frac{1}{2}$ cup milk
dash cinnamon	dash cinnamon
dash nutmeg	dash nutmeg
1 lemon rind, grated	1 lemon rind, grated

Linzer Shortbread 2

8 ozs. pastry flour	2 cups pastry flour
6 ozs. crumbs	$2\frac{2}{3}$ cups crumbs
8 ozs. powdered sugar	$1\frac{1}{2}$ cups powdered sugar (generous)
$3\frac{1}{2}$ ozs. almonds, ground	$1\frac{3}{4}$ cup almonds, ground
$\frac{1}{3}$ oz. cinnamon	4 tsp. cinnamon
dash cloves	dash cloves
1 lemon rind, grated	1 lemon rind, grated
2 eggs	2 eggs
7 ozs. butter	scant 1 cup butter
$\frac{1}{6}$ oz. ammonium	$\frac{1}{4}$ tsp. ammonium

MACAROONS

The basic ingredient of macaroons may be almonds, cocoanut, walnuts, or filberts. Sugar and egg whites must be in a certain proportion to the nuts to assure softness, shine, lift and crack. They may be produced cold or hot. The egg whites act as the binding medium, and at the same time, will keep the macaroons moist and soft. Macaroons made with egg yolks will not only dry out quickly but also lack the distinctive flavor obtained with egg whites as the binder. Instead of pure almonds or the equivalent amount of almond paste, kernel paste may be used to economize wherever necessary. Macaroons are to be squeezed through a pastry bag with a medium-sized, round tube. The mixture must have a soft and creamy texture, obtained by adding more or less egg whites. This very fact leaves the door wide open as to how soft is soft or how hard is hard. Generally speaking the mounds should have a smooth, firm consistency. If the top appears rough, it indicates that the mixture is too hard. Hard mixtures will not crack properly, bake small and taste gluey. Mixtures which are too soft will bake hollow, dry out and lose all flavor. The easiest way to find out whether or not the right texture is reached is by putting a few test samples in the oven before making up the whole formula. Macaroons will stay soft for weeks when kept in covered tins stored in the refrigerator.

White Almond Macaroons

$1\frac{1}{2}$ lbs. almonds, blanched, ground	3 cups almonds, blanched, ground
1 lb. 11 ozs. granulated sugar	$1\frac{1}{2}$ cups granulated sugar (generous)
3 ozs. powdered sugar	$\frac{1}{4}$ cup powdered sugar (generous)
1 lemon rind, grated	1 lemon rind, grated
egg whites	egg whites

Brown Almond Macaroons

14 ozs. almonds, ground	$1\frac{3}{4}$ cups almonds, ground
$1\frac{1}{2}$ lbs. granulated sugar	$1\frac{1}{2}$ cups granulated sugar
$1\frac{1}{2}$ ozs. powdered sugar	$\frac{1}{8}$ cup powdered sugar
1 lemon rind, grated	$\frac{1}{2}$ lemon rind, grated

Method

In both formulas use finely ground nuts. Blend dry ingredients together well. Add egg whites one at a time, mixing after each addition, until the mixture becomes creamy but remains fairly firm. Using a pastry bag with round tube, squeeze mounds the size of a fifty-cent piece on paper, approximately $\frac{3}{4}''$ apart. Dampen cloth, fold evenly and tap macaroons carefully on top. This will give smooth surfaces. Added moisture will help macaroons to crack. Sprinkle with very little granulated sugar (1 tsp. covers a 12 x 16 inch baking sheet). Bake at 325° F. to 350° F. To remove from paper, turn upside down, dampen paper thoroughly, turn right side up again and let stand for a few minutes. Macaroons will come off easily.

Marzipan Macaroons

3 lbs. almond paste	$\frac{3}{4}$ lb. almond paste
3 lbs. granulated sugar	$1\frac{1}{2}$ cups granulated sugar
approx. 1 pint egg whites	approx. $\frac{1}{2}$ cup egg whites
2 lemon rinds, grated	$\frac{1}{2}$ lemon rind, grated

Method

Soften almond paste gradually with egg whites. Otherwise proceed as directed.

Filbert Macaroons

2 lbs. filberts, ground	4 cups filberts, ground
3 lbs. granulated sugar	3 cups granulated sugar
approx. $1\frac{1}{2}$ pints egg whites	approx. $1\frac{1}{2}$ cups egg whites
2 lemon rinds grated	1 lemon rind, grated
vanilla	vanilla
dash nutmeg	dash nutmeg

A tray of macaroons before baking

Smoothing macaroon surfaces

Removing baked macaroons from baking paper

Cherry macaroons, Walnut drops, Macaroons duchesse *(left to right)*.

Macaroon crescents

Method

Use brown, finely ground filberts. Proceed as directed.

Walnut Macaroons

1½ lbs. granulated sugar	1½ cups granulated sugar
1 lb. walnuts, ground	scant 2 cups walnuts, ground
1 lemon rind, grated	½ lemon rind, grated
¼ tsp. cinnamon	⅛ tsp. cinnamon
approx. ½ pint egg whites	approx. ½ cup egg whites

Method

Proceed as directed.

Chocolate Macaroons

2 lbs. granulated sugar	2 cups granulated sugar
1 lb. almonds, ground	2 cups almonds, ground
2½ ozs. cocoa	5½ tbsp. cocoa
approx. 12 egg whites	approx. 6 egg whites
vanilla	vanilla
2 orange rinds, grated	1 orange rind, grated

Method

Proceed as directed. Before dressing macaroons onto paper, place mixture in double boiler and heat through.

Cocoanut Macaroons 1

12 egg whites	6 egg whites
1 lb. 12 ozs. granulated sugar	1¾ cups granulated sugar
1 lb. 12 ozs. cocoanut, shredded	4 cups cocoanut, shredded
4 tbsp. vinegar	2 tbsp. vinegar
1 lemon rind, grated	½ lemon rind, grated

Method

Beat egg whites until stiff, adding sugar slowly. Add vinegar and blend in cocoanut. Using spoon or pastry bag, dress small mounds on greased, floured pans. Bake at 325° F.

Cocoanut Macaroons 2

24 egg whites	6 egg whites
3 lbs. 6 ozs. granulated sugar	1⅝ cups granulated sugar
1 lb. pastry flour	1 cup pastry flour
1 lb. 7 ozs. cocoanut, shredded	1½ cups cocoanut, shredded
2 orange rinds, grated	½ orange rind, grated

Method

Beat egg whites, adding the sugar slowly, until stiff. Blend in cocoanut and rind. Place in double boiler and cook for a few minutes, stirring constantly. Add flour. Let mixture cool slightly. Dress onto greased floured pans. Bake at 325° F.

Cocoanut Macaroon 3

2 lbs. 8 ozs. cocoanut, shredded	scant 3 cups cocoanut, shredded
7 lbs. 8 ozs. granulated sugar	3¾ cups granulated sugar
1 lb. 8 ozs. cooked potatoes	1 cup cooked potatoes
1½ pints egg whites	¾ cup egg whites
5 ozs. glucose	2½ tbsp. glucose
2 lemon rinds, grated	½ lemon rind, grated

Method

Put egg whites, sugar, potatoes (mashed), and glucose into double boiler. Heat well, stirring constantly. Add cocoanut, rinds and bring to a boil. Stir mixture constantly. Remove from heat and let cool until just warm. If mixture is still stiff, add more egg whites. Dress onto greased, floured pans. Bake at 350° F.

Note: Mixture can be prepared one day ahead, but must be warmed before making up. Bake a sample first. If tops do not crack properly, put a little water in the oven to create steam.

Yolk Macaroons

2 lbs. almond paste	8 ozs. almond paste
10 ozs. powdered sugar	¼ cup powdered sugar (generous)
12-14 egg yolks	3-5 egg yolks
vanilla	vanilla

Method

Mix all ingredients together and warm well in double boiler. Dress mixture onto pre-baked shortbread bottoms. Brown tops in fast heat. After baking, glaze with syrup or gum arabic.

A. Cherry Macaroons

Use almond macaroon formula, mixed to medium firmness. Form small balls. Press glazed cherry halves in center, round well, and roll ball into chopped almonds. Set on paper-lined baking sheet. Bake at 325° F. Glaze after baking with gum arabic.

Note: The same formula may be used to form differently shaped macaroons such as ovals, crescents, sticks, cubes, et cetera. They may be rolled in chopped pistachios or any other nuts.

B. Walnut Drops

8 ozs. granulated sugar	1 cup granulated sugar
8 ozs. walnuts, ground	2 cups walnuts, ground
approx. ⅛ pint egg whites	(generous)
vanilla	approx. ¼ cup egg whites
dash cinnamon	vanilla
1 lemon rind, grated	dash cinnamon
	1 lemon rind, grated

Method

Mix all ingredients together well. Place in double boiler and warm through. Mixture must be smooth and firm. Using a pastry bag with star tube, form drop-like objects on plain paper. Set paper with macaroons on wet wooden boards. Bake at 300° F. to 325° F. Glaze with syrup or gum arabic. Remove from paper while hot and join in pairs.

Note: Wet boards will prevent bottoms from baking, thus leaving soft centers when joined.

C. Macaroon Duchesse

1 lb. almond paste	4 ozs. almond paste
2 lbs. 14 ozs. granulated sugar	1⅜ cups granulated sugar
1 oz. glucose	¾ tsp. glucose
2 tbsp. rum	½ tbsp. rum
10 ozs. almonds, ground	⅝ cups almonds, ground
egg whites	egg whites
1 lemon rind, grated	¼ lemon rind, grated

Method

On table mix together sugar, glucose, almond paste, lemon rind, and rum. Mix in egg whites until dough has become smooth and soft. Squeeze mounds the size of a quarter onto greased, floured pans. Let dry over night. Bake at 285° F. to 300° F.

Note: Duchesse mixture should be softer than normal macaroons and are expected to bake medium flat. The dry skin on top will force mixture to bake out on bottom, leaving a smooth surface. Use bottom heat only when baking.

Chocolate Macaroon Duchesse

Add four ounces (one square) melted bitter chocolate to above formula. Proceed as directed. After baking join macaroons with the following mixture : Softened almond paste with apricot jam to make it creamy and smooth, and a few drops of rum.

Almond Macaroon Arches

12 egg whites	6 egg whites
1 lb. granulated sugar	1 cup granulated sugar
1 lb. 5 ozs. sliced almonds	2½ cups sliced almonds
11 ozs. granulated sugar	¾ cup granulated sugar
vanilla	vanilla
rice paper	rice paper

Method

Beat egg whites until stiff, adding the larger amount of sugar slowly. Mix together almonds and the remaining sugar. Blend into whites. Add flavoring and heat mixture in double boiler. Spread mixture onto long strips of rice paper, which are cut 4″ wide. Cut to desired sizes. Place strips over round-bottomed loaf tin (A foil covered rolling pin may be used). Let cool. Bake at 300° F.

Note: Filberts may be used instead of almonds. If mixture appears too liquid, add a little flour. If sugar is added too fast, whites will become extremely soft. If this happens, add a dash of cream of tartar. Continue beating and whites will stiffen again.

Macaroon Slices Parisienne

13 ozs. blanched, sliced almonds	1½ cups blanched, sliced almonds
1 lb. 7 ozs. granulated sugar	scant 1½ cups granulated sugar
3/16 pint egg whites	scant ¼ cup egg whites
3 ozs. flour	⅜ cup flour
1 tsp. cinnamon	½ tsp. cinnamon
1 lemon rind, grated	½ lemon rind, grated
shortbread dough	shortbread dough

Anis toast, Mocha bites, Jewels, Raisin trios, *Spritz* cookies *(left to right)*

Hussar delights, Almond lady fingers, Palm leaves, Vanilla crescents, Chocolate pretzels *(left to right)*.

Medallion, Almond cookies, Chocolate slices, Butter nuts, Scotch shortbread, Lady fingers *(left to right)*.

Shortbread, Royal butter snaps (chocolate, plain and cherry), Fancy cookies made of white and chocolate shortbread *(left to right)*.

Method

Roll strip of shortbread dough the full length of a pan 4″ wide. Bake at 350° F. until half done. Proceed with above mixture as directed under "Macaroon Arches," without bending them. Spread mixture onto dough strips. Sprinkle with sliced almonds. Bake at 300° F. When cold, cut pieces 1″ wide.

Macaroon Crescents

2 lbs. almonds, ground	2 cups almonds, ground
4 lbs. granulated sugar	2 cups granulated sugar
20 egg whites	5 egg whites
1 lemon rind, grated	$\frac{1}{4}$ lemon rind, grated

Method

Mix all ingredients together until smooth and soft. Place sliced almonds on baking sheet. Using a pastry bag with medium tube, dress sticks four inches long into almonds. Roll sticks to cover thoroughly with almonds, form crescents and set on greased, floured pans. Bake at 375° F. After baking, glaze with gum arabic.

Pineapple Macaroons

Use "Macaroon Crescents" formula. Put generous layer of sliced almonds on board or table. Squeeze a long strip of mixture onto almonds. Place drained pineapple cubes down center of strip. Squeeze second strip over it. Roll double strips in almonds and cut pieces 2″ in length. Set on paperlined pans. Bake at 375° F. Glaze with gum arabic.

COOKIES

Anisettes

$\frac{3}{4}$ pint egg yolks	1 cup egg yolks
$\frac{1}{2}$ pint water	$\frac{1}{2}$ cup water
1 lb. 3 ozs. sugar	$1\frac{3}{8}$ cups sugar
1 lb. 7 ozs. cake flour	$2\frac{3}{4}$ cups cake flour
2 ozs. anis seed	1 oz. anis seed
vanilla	vanilla

Method

Beat yolks, sugar, and water to frothy batter.

Blend in vanilla and sifted flour. Use pastry bag with medium, round tube. Dress small oblong cookies $1\frac{1}{2}$″ in length on greased, floured pans. Sprinkle with anis seed. Bake at 325° F.

Note: If stronger flavor is desired, add few drops of anis extract.

Anisette Toast

18 egg yolks	6 egg yolks
21 whole eggs	7 whole eggs
$2\frac{1}{4}$ lbs. sugar	2 cups sugar
3 lbs. 4 ozs. cake flour	$4\frac{1}{3}$ cups cake flour
$1\frac{1}{2}$ ozs. anis seed	$\frac{1}{2}$ oz. anis seed

Method

Beat eggs, yolks, and sugar in double boiler until hot. Continue beating by machine until mixture becomes a cool, creamy froth. Add flavors. Blend in sifted flour. Use pastry bag without tube. Dress thick strips on greased and floured pans, covering the full length of the baking sheet and allowing 4″ to 5″ between the strips for expansion. Bake at 350° F. to 375° F. until golden brown. Remove from pan while still hot. Cut pieces $\frac{1}{2}$″ wide. Set cookies on pans, cut side up and toast in hot oven. When brown, turn upside down and toast other side as well.

Anis Rings

1 lb. 2 ozs. sugar	$1\frac{1}{4}$ cups sugar (generous)
10 eggs	5 eggs
1 lb. 2 ozs. cake flour	$2\frac{1}{8}$ cups cake flour
$\frac{1}{3}$ oz. anis seed	3 tsp. anis seed
vanilla	vanilla

Method

Beat eggs and sugar in double boiler until hot. Continue beating by machine until creamy and cool. Add vanilla and blend in sifted flour. Use pastry bag with medium, round tube. Dress small rings on greased floured pans. Sprinkle anis seed on top. Allow to dry for two or three hours.

Note: In both formulas the drying time is approximate. Top must form solid skin before baking. If the humidity is high this process may take overnight.

Armadas

10 ozs. cake flour	2¼ cups cake flour
6½ ozs. butter	¾ cup butter (generous)
4 ozs. filberts, ground	½ cup filberts, ground
4 ozs. powdered sugar	¾ cup powdered sugar
1 egg	1 egg
1 lemon rind, grated	1 lemon rind, grated
vanilla	vanilla

Method

Knead all ingredients together to form smooth dough. Roll dough ⅛" thick. Cut with small, round cooky cutter. Set on paper-lined pans. Egg wash. Place one whole filbert in center. Bake at 325° F.

Almond Bread Cookies

5 ozs. almonds, ground	scant 2 cups almonds, ground
7 ozs. powdered sugar	scant 1½ cups powdered sugar
7 ozs. cake flour	1½ cups cake flour
8 egg yolks	8 egg yolks
dash cinnamon	dash cinnamon

Method

Knead all ingredients together to form smooth dough. Roll dough ⅛" thick. Cut with round cooky cutter. Set on paperlined pans. Egg wash. Place one-half almond in each cooky center. Bake at 325° F.

Punch Stars

6½ ozs. butter	¾ cup butter (generous)
4 ozs. powdered sugar	¾ cup powdered sugar
1 egg	1 egg
2½ ozs. almonds, ground	1 cup almonds, ground
8 ozs. pastry flour	1⅞ cups pastry flour
2 tbsp. rum	2 tbsp. rum
½ lemon rind, grated	½ lemon rind, grated

Method

Cream together butter, sugar, rum, and rind. Add egg. Blend in flour and almonds. Using a pastry bag with medium star tube, dress mounds onto paper-lined pans. Place a piece of cherry in center of each cooky. Bake at 300° F. to 325° F.

Moscovites

1 pint milk	1 cup milk
4 ozs. pastry flour	½ cup pastry flour
4 ozs. butter	¼ cup butter
13 ozs. blanched, chopped almonds	2½ cups blanched, chopped almonds
3½ ozs. citron peel	¼ cup citron peel (generous)
3½ ozs. candied orange peel	¼ cup candied orange peel (generous)
2 ozs. sugar	3 tbsp. sugar

Method

Put one-half of the milk in saucepan and bring to a boil. Add flour and continue boiling for one minute, stirring constantly. Boil second half of milk with butter and sugar. Combine milk mixtures and beat well. Mix in fruits. Set small mounds on greased, floured pans with a tablespoon. Bake at 350° F. to 375° F.

Dragon Tongues

6 ozs. almond paste	3 ozs. almond paste
12 ozs. butter	¾ cup butter
4 egg whites	2 egg whites
4 ozs. powdered sugar	⅜ cup powdered sugar
13½ ozs. pastry flour	1½ cups pastry flour
vanilla	vanilla
½ lemon rind, grated	¼ lemon rind, grated

Method

Cream almond paste and butter together. Beat whites and sugar until stiff. Blend whites into first mixture and fold in flour. Using a pastry bag with a small, round tube, dress mounds 1½" long on paper-lined pans. Bake at 300° F. to 325° F. When cold, dip ends in chocolate.

Mocha Bites

13 ozs. pastry flour	3¼ cups pastry flour
6½ ozs. butter	¾ cup butter (generous)
3½ ozs. powdered sugar	scant ¾ cup powdered sugar
2 eggs	2 eggs
1 oz. cocoa	4½ tbsp. cocoa
¾ oz. instant coffee, dry	⅓ cup instant coffee, dry
vanilla	vanilla

Method

Knead ingredients together to form smooth dough. Roll dough $\frac{1}{8}''$ thick and cut with round cooky cutter. Egg wash. Bake at 300° F. Join together in pairs with jam or nougat.

Jewels

6 ozs. filberts, ground	2 cups filberts, ground (generous)
5 ozs. powdered sugar	1 cup powdered sugar
1 egg	1 egg
1 egg yolk	1 egg yolk
7 ozs. butter	$\frac{3}{4}$ cup butter (generous)
8 ozs. pastry flour	2 cups pastry flour
$\frac{1}{8}$ oz. ammonium	$1\frac{1}{2}$ tsp. ammonium
$\frac{1}{3}$ oz. cinnamon	3 tsp. cinnamon

Method

Cream butter and powdered sugar. Add egg and yolk. Blend in ground filberts. Fold in flour and ammonium. Using bag with star tube, form small stars on paper-lined pan. Sprinkle with colored, granulated sugar. Bake at 300° F.

Raisin Trios

5 eggs	5 eggs
5 ozs. sugar	$\frac{5}{8}$ cup sugar
8 ozs. pastry flour	2 cups pastry flour
6 ozs. butter, melted	$\frac{3}{4}$ cup butter, melted
1 lemon rind, grated	1 lemon rind, grated
vanilla	vanilla

Method

Beat eggs, sugar, and flavoring in double boiler until hot. Remove from heat and beat until cold and frothy. Blend in flour, then add melted butter. Squeeze small mounds through a pastry tube onto greased pan. Put three raisins on each mound. Bake at 300° F. Join in pairs with jam, and glaze with rum fondant.

Hussar Delights

1 lb. 3 ozs. pastry flour	$2\frac{3}{4}$ cups pastry flour
8 ozs. powdered sugar	$1\frac{1}{2}$ cups powdered sugar
8 ozs. butter	1 cup butter
4 eggs	4 eggs
vanilla	vanilla
1 lemon rind, grated	1 lemon rind, grated

Method

Knead all ingredients together well. Form balls $1''$ in diameter and set on paper-lined pans. Press hole in center with wooden stick and fill with raspberry jam. Bake at 300° F.

Sand Goulatsches

8 ozs. powdered sugar	$1\frac{1}{2}$ cups powdered sugar (generous)
8 ozs. butter	1 cup butter
5 egg yolks	5 egg yolks
5 eggs	5 eggs
12 ozs. pastry flour	3 cups pastry flour
vanilla	vanilla
$\frac{1}{2}$ lemon rind, grated	$\frac{1}{2}$ lemon rind, grated

Method

Cream together sugar, butter, and flavoring. Add eggs and yolks slowly. Blend in sifted flour. Form small mounds on paper-lined pans. Bake at 300° F. to 325° F. Join in pairs with apricot jam. Dip half in melted chocolate.

Pistachio Beans

4 ozs. butter	$\frac{1}{2}$ cup butter
4 ozs. powdered sugar	$\frac{3}{4}$ cup powdered sugar (generous)
2 eggs	
2 egg yolks	2 egg yolks
6 ozs. pastry flour	$1\frac{1}{2}$ cups pastry flour
vanilla	vanilla

Method

Cream together butter, sugar, and vanilla. Add eggs and yolks slowly. Blend in sifted flour. Form small half-moon shaped cookies on paper-lined pan. Sprinkle with chopped pistachios. Bake at 325° F.

Chocolate Rochettes

4 egg whites	4 egg whites
8 ozs. powdered sugar	$1\frac{1}{2}$ cups powdered sugar (generous)
9 ozs. toasted, ground almonds	$2\frac{1}{8}$ cups toasted, ground almonds
4 ozs. semi-sweet chocolate	4 squares semi-sweet chocolate
2 ozs. pastry flour	$\frac{1}{2}$ cup pastry flour
2 tbsp. rum	2 tbsp. rum

Method

Beat egg whites, adding sugar slowly until stiff. Blend in sifted flour and almonds. Add melted chocolate and rum. Using a star tube, dress 2″ oblongs on paper-lined pans. Let dry. Bake at 300° F.

Africanos

8 ozs. pastry flour	2 cups pastry flour
4 ozs. butter	½ cup butter
4 ozs. powdered sugar	¾ cup powdered sugar
1 oz. cocoa	(generous)
1 egg	⅓ oz. cocoa
1 egg yolk	1 egg
1 lemon rind, grated	1 egg yolk
2 tbsp. rum	1 lemon rind, grated
	2 tbsp. rum

Method

Knead all ingredients to form smooth dough. Form little balls and set on paper. Bake at 300° F. Join in pairs with jam. Brush outside with jam and roll in chocolate decorettes or chocolate cake crumbs.

Spritz Cookies

10 ozs. butter	1¼ cups butter
3¼ ozs. powdered sugar	½ cup powdered sugar
1 oz. almonds	⅜ cup almonds
10 ozs. pastry flour	2½ cups pastry flour
vanilla	vanilla
½ lemon rind, grated	½ lemon rind, grated

Method

Cream together butter, sugar, and flavoring. Blend in almonds and flour. Using a star tube, dress different shapes, such as wreaths, crescents, figure eights, et cetera. Decorate with glazed fruits. Bake at 325° F. to 350° F.

Czardas Cookies

1 lb. cake crumbs	2¾ cups cake crumbs
1 lb. filberts, ground	3¾ cups filberts, ground
1 lb. powdered sugar	1½ cups powdered sugar
5 ozs. butter	(generous)
10 eggs	¼ cup butter (generous)
vanilla	5 eggs
pinch nutmeg	vanilla
	pinch nutmeg

Method

Mix all ingredients together well. Spread ⅛″ thick on greased, floured pans. Bake at 300° F.

Join two or three layers with chocolate fudge or jam. Ice top with chocolate. Cut cubes or slices.

Sand Cookies

4½ ozs. butter	½ cup butter
4½ ozs. powdered sugar	¾ cup powdered sugar
7 ozs. pastry flour	(generous)
8 egg yolks	1¼ cups pastry flour
1 egg	8 egg yolks
vanilla	1 egg
½ lemon rind, grated	vanilla
	½ lemon rind, grated

Method

Cream together butter, sugar, and flavoring. Add egg and yolks slowly. Blend in sifted flour. Form small mounds with round tube on paper-lined pans. Bake at 320° F. Join in pairs with jam. Dip bottom halves in chocolate.

Note : Color one half of dough mixture red if desired.

Rothschilds

5 egg yolks	5 egg yolks
5 egg whites	5 egg whites
4 ozs. powdered sugar	¾ cup powdered sugar
5 ozs. pastry flour	(generous)
almonds	1¼ cups pastry flour
vanilla	almonds
	vanilla

Method

Beat egg yolks with one-half of the sugar for several minutes. Beat egg whites, adding the remaining sugar slowly, until stiff. Combine egg mixtures and fold in sifted flour. Using a pastry bag with small, round tube, dress small lady fingers on greased, floured pans. Sprinkle with chopped almonds. Bake at 300° F. When cold, dip bottom half in chocolate.

Neros

8½ ozs. butter	1 cup butter (generous)
4½ ozs. powdered sugar	scant 1 cup powdered
1½ ozs. cocoa	sugar
6½ ozs. cake flour	6½ tbsp. cocoa
2 eggs	1½ cups cake flour
1 egg yolk	(generous)
2 tbsp. rum	2 eggs
vanilla	1 egg yolk
	2 tbsp. rum
	vanilla

Method

Proceed as described under "Sand Cookies." After baking, dip in semi-sweet chocolate.

Raisin Galettes

6½ ozs. butter	¾ cup butter (generous)
8½ ozs. powdered sugar	1¾ cups powdered sugar
10 ozs. pastry flour	2½ cups pastry flour
½ pint whipping cream	1 cup whipping cream
2 eggs	2 eggs
vanilla	vanilla

Method

Cream butter, sugar, vanilla, and eggs. Stir in whipped cream. Blend in sifted flour. Use bag with small, round tube. Dress small mounds at 1½" intervals on lightly greased and floured pans. Sprinkle with raisins. Bake at 350° F.

Note : Mixture is soft and will flatten during the baking process. Properly baked *galettes* will have white centers and brown rims.

Cake Balls

15 egg yolks	15 egg yolks
5 ozs. powdered sugar	1 cup powdered sugar
6½ ozs. cake flour	1½ cups cake flour
vanilla	(generous)
1 lemon rind, grated	vanilla
	1 lemon rind, grated

Method

Beat yolks, sugar, rinds, and vanilla until frothy. Blend in sifted flour. Use pastry bag with round tube. Dress small mounds on paper-lined pans. Dust with powdered sugar. Bake at 300° F. Join together in pairs with apricot jam. Dust freely with powdered sugar.

Palm Leaves

8 ozs. almonds, ground, toasted	3¾ cups almonds, ground, toasted
8 ozs. powdered sugar	1½ cups powdered sugar
8 ozs. butter	1 cup butter
8 ozs. pastry flour	2 cups pastry flour
2 eggs	2 eggs
1 tsp. cinnamon	1 tsp. cinnamon
½ tsp. nutmeg	½ tsp. nutmeg
½ lemon rind, grated	½ lemon rind, grated
vanilla	vanilla

Method

Knead all ingredients together to form smooth dough. Roll dough ⅛" thick. Cut leaf-shaped cookies. Set on paper-lined pans. Egg wash. Bake at 350° F. When cold, brush ends with sugar syrup and dip into green-colored cocoanut.

Bishop Bread

6½ ozs. sugar	¾ cup sugar (generous)
6½ ozs. pastry flour	1½ cups pastry flour
12 egg yolks	(generous)
8 egg whites	12 egg yolks
4½ ozs. butter	8 egg whites
5 ozs. filberts, chopped	½ cup butter (generous)
6½ ozs. raisins	2¼ cups filberts, chopped
6 ozs. mixed fruits	1½ cups raisins
½ lemon rind, grated	1½ cups mixed fruits
½ orange rind, grated	½ lemon rind, grated
vanilla	½ orange rind, grated
	vanilla

Method

Whip whites, adding one-half of the sugar slowly, until stiff. Beat yolks, vanilla, and the remaining sugar for a few minutes by hand. Combine the two mixes, stirring gently. Blend in sifted flour. Add melted butter. Fold in fruits carefully. Line loaf tin with paper and pour in mixture. Bake at 300° F. When cold, cut loaf lengthwise into four or six sections, depending upon size of loaf. Spread thinly with apricot jam and roll the individual sections in green-colored marzipan. Slice thin.

Cat Tongues

¾ pint whipping cream	1½ cups whipping cream
6 egg whites	6 egg whites
5 ozs. powdered sugar	1 cup powdered sugar
5 ozs. pastry flour	1¼ cups pastry flour
2½ ozs. cornstarch	¼ cup cornstarch
vanilla	vanilla

Method

Beat whites, adding sugar slowly until stiff. Whip cream and add to whites. Sift together the flour and starch. Blend into soft mixture. Use pastry bag with small round tube. Dress small lady-finger shapes onto greased, floured pans. Bake at 300° F. When cold, dip one end in sweet chocolate.

Vanilla Crescents

8½ ozs. pastry flour	2 cups pastry flour
3 ozs. almonds, ground, toasted	1½ cups almonds, ground. toasted
6½ ozs. butter	¾ cup butter (generous)
2½ ozs. powdered sugar	½ cup powdered sugar
vanilla	vanilla

Method

Knead all ingredients together to get smooth, firm dough. Form long rolls of finger thickness. Cut pieces 1″ long. Roll the individual pieces 3″ long. Form crescents and set on paper-lined pans. Bake at 325° F. Roll crescents in vanilla-flavored powdered sugar while still hot.

Note : If dough does not bind properly, add one or two eggs. Do not over-knead as this will cause the butter to separate.

Chocolate Pretzels

10 ozs. pastry flour	2½ cups pastry flour
5 ozs. powdered sugar	1 cup powdered sugar
8 ozs. butter	1 cup butter
2½ ozs. cocoa	⅔ cup cocoa
3 egg yolks	3 egg yolks
vanilla	vanilla

Method

Proceed as described above. Roll pieces slightly longer and form pretzels. Bake at 325° F. When cold, dip in semi-sweet chocolate.

Almond Mounds

8 ozs. almonds, toasted, sliced	3¾ cups almonds, toasted, sliced
semi-sweet chocolate	semi-sweet chocolate
vanilla	vanilla

Method

Place sliced almonds in mixing bowl. Add as much melted, cooled chocolate as necessary to bind the nuts. Use a teaspoon to form small mounds and set on paper-lined pans. Let dry in a cool place.

Note : Chocolate must be prepared as directed under the "Preparation of Chocolate." (*See Index.*)

Fruit Sticks

5 egg yolks	5 egg yolks
2½ ozs. powdered sugar	½ cup powdered sugar
2½ ozs. pastry flour	½ cup pastry flour (generous)
1½ ozs. raisins	scant ½ cup raisins
1½ ozs. mixed fruits	scant ½ cup mixed fruits
1½ ozs. walnuts, chopped	scant ½ cup walnuts, chopped
vanilla	vanilla

Method

Beat yolks, sugar, and vanilla until frothy. Blend in sifted flour. Fold in fruits gently. Use pastry bag without tube. Dress strips full width of opening and full length of pan. Keep strips 4″ apart. Bake at 300° F. Ice top with chocolate. Cut pieces ½″ wide.

Venetians

3 ozs. powdered sugar	½ cup powdered sugar (generous)
3 ozs. nuts, ground toasted	1½ cups nuts, ground, toasted
5 ozs. pastry flour	1¼ cups pastry flour
3 ozs. butter	⅜ cup butter
1½ ozs. mixed fruits	scant ½ cup mixed fruits
1½ ozs. candied orange peel	scant ½ cup candied orange peel
1½ ozs. almonds, chopped	½ cup almonds, chopped
4 egg yolks	4 egg yolks

Method

Knead all ingredients together to form smooth, firm dough. Form long rolls 1″ thick. Egg wash. Roll sticks in granulated sugar and cut pieces ¾″ thick. Set on paper-lined pans. Egg wash. Bake at 325° F.

Chocolate Slices

5 ozs. butter	½ cup butter (generous)
10 ozs. powdered sugar	2 cups powdered sugar
10 ozs. filberts, ground, toasted	4½ cups filberts, ground, toasted
6½ ozs. pastry flour	1½ cups pastry flour (generous)
1½ ozs. cocoa	7 tbsp. cocoa
4 eggs	4 eggs
1 tsp. cinnamon	1 tsp. cinnamon
vanilla	vanilla
½ lemon rind, grated	½ lemon rind, grated

Method

Knead all ingredients together to get smooth, soft dough. Spread mixture over baking sheet $\frac{1}{4}''$ thick. Bake at 350° F. When cold, join two or more layers together with raspberry jam. Ice top with chocolate icing. Cut pieces to desired sizes.

Meringue Kisses

20 egg whites	10 egg whites
1 lb. granulated sugar	1 cup granulated sugar
2 lbs. powdered sugar	1 cup powdered sugar
$\frac{1}{4}$ tsp. cream of tartar	$\frac{1}{8}$ tsp. cream of tartar
vanilla	vanilla

Method

Beat whites to medium stiffness. Add granulated sugar slowly. Continue beating to stiff froth. Add tartar. Blend in sifted powdered sugar and vanilla. Divide mixture into two or more parts for different coloring. Use pastry bag with large star tube. Dress mounds onto paper-lined pans. Bake at 200° F. Let dry completely by keeping goods overnight in turned-off oven. Pack in cellophane bags.

Patience Cookies

15 egg whites	7 egg whites
1 lb. 7 ozs. sugar	$1\frac{3}{8}$ cup sugar
11 ozs. powdered sugar	1 cup powdered sugar
1 lb. 1 oz. pastry flour	2 cups pastry flour
couleur	*couleur*
vanilla	vanilla

Method

Mix granulated sugar with a little water and boil to 244° F. (soft ball stage). Beat whites until stiff, adding the cooked sugar slowly. Continue beating until mixture cools. Stir in vanilla and enough *couleur (see Index)* to get a light brown color. Blend in powdered sugar and sifted flour. Using a pastry bag with small, round tube, dress different shapes such as figure eights, *v*'s, *s*'s, circles, or triangles onto greased, floured pans. Allow cookies to form skin on top. Bake at 200° F. to 225° F.

Medallions

10 ozs. flour	$2\frac{1}{2}$ cups flour
$6\frac{1}{2}$ ozs. butter	$\frac{3}{4}$ cup butter (generous)
3 ozs. powdered sugar	$\frac{1}{2}$ cup powdered sugar
1 egg yolk	(generous)
$\frac{1}{2}$ lemon rind, grated	1 egg yolk
vanilla	$\frac{1}{2}$ lemon rind, grated
	vanilla

Method

Knead all ingredients to form smooth dough. Roll dough to one-eighth of an inch thick and cut three-inch disks with cooky cutter. Set on paper-lined pans. Using another cutter $1\frac{1}{2}''$ in diameter, cut out the centers of half the cookies. Egg wash remaining rings and sprinkle with granulated sugar. Use center cuts for rolling more cookies. Bake at 325° F. When cold, spread strawberry jam on bottom and set rings on top.

Linzer Crescents

1 lb. powdered sugar	$\frac{3}{4}$ cup powdered sugar
2 lbs. butter	1 cup butter
3 lbs pastry flour	3 cups pastry flour
1 pint milk	$\frac{1}{2}$ cup milk
1 lemon rind, grated	$\frac{1}{2}$ lemon rind, grated
vanilla	vanilla

Method

Cream together butter, sugar, vanilla, and rind. Add milk. Quickly blend in sifted flour. Using a pastry bag with medium star tube, dress crescents on paper-lined pans. Bake at 300° F. When cold, dip ends in chocolate.

Note: To make chocolate dough, leave out four ounces ($\frac{1}{4}$ cup) flour and add same amount of cocoa.

Vienna Biscuits

8 ozs. flour	2 cups flour
5 ozs. butter	$\frac{5}{8}$ cup butter
5 ozs. powdered sugar	1 cup powdered sugar
2 eggs	2 eggs
1 tsp. baking powder	1 tsp. baking powder
vanilla	vanilla
1 lemon rind, grated	1 lemon rind, grated

Method

Knead all ingredients to form smooth dough. Roll out and cut in various shapes with cooky cutters. Egg wash and bake at 300° F.

Lady Tea Cookies

1 lb. 7 ozs. pastry flour	$2\frac{3}{4}$ cups pastry flour
1 lb. 2 ozs. butter	$1\frac{1}{8}$ cups butter
$8\frac{1}{2}$ ozs. powdered sugar	$\frac{3}{4}$ cup powdered sugar
6 egg yolks	6 egg yolks
1 lemon rind, grated	1 lemon rind, grated

Method

Cream butter, sugar, and rind, adding yolks slowly. Blend in sifted flour. Using a round tube, form small mounds on paper-lined pans. Bake at 300° F. Join in pairs with apricot jam and sprinkle with powdered sugar.

Nut Patties, Noisettes

1 lb. 12 ozs. butter	$1\frac{3}{4}$ cups butter
1 lb. powdered sugar	$1\frac{1}{2}$ cups powdered sugar (generous)
5 egg yolks	3 egg yolks
2 eggs	1 egg
2 lbs. pastry flour	4 cups pastry flour
8 ozs. filberts, ground	$1\frac{3}{4}$ cups filberts, ground
vanilla	vanilla

Method

Knead all ingredients to form smooth dough. Roll dough $\frac{1}{8}''$ thick and cut with various cooky cutters. Egg wash. Sprinkle all or part of each cooky with ground, sliced, or halved filberts. If desired, some designs may be made on cookies with jam before baking. Bake at 300° F.

Scotch Shortbread

6 lbs. bread flour	6 cups bread flour
$2\frac{1}{4}$ lbs. powdered sugar	$1\frac{3}{4}$ cups powdered sugar
$4\frac{1}{2}$ lbs. buter	$2\frac{1}{4}$ cups butter

Method

Cream butter with sifted powdered sugar. Blend in sifted flour. To make shortbread fingers, roll dough $\frac{1}{2}''$ thick. Cut pieces $2\frac{1}{2}''$ long by $\frac{3}{4}''$ wide. As shortbread dough molds easily, designs pressed into it will stay during baking. Dough pressed into fancy, carved wooden forms provide excellent shortbread cakes. Set cookies on paper and bake at 290° F. to 300° F. Finished product should be very light in color.

Note: If large amounts of shortbreads are made, the dough should be rolled between two $\frac{1}{2}''$ bars. This will guarantee uniformity in height.

Linzer Spritz Cookies

2 lbs. 12 ozs. butter	$1\frac{3}{8}$ cups butter
1 lb. 12 ozs. powdered sugar	$1\frac{3}{8}$ cups powdered sugar
5 eggs	2 eggs
15 egg yolks	4 egg yolks
4 lbs. 8 ozs. pastry flour	$4\frac{1}{2}$ cups pastry flour
1 orange rind, grated	$\frac{1}{4}$ orange rind, grated
vanilla	vanilla

Method

Cream together butter, sugar, and flavoring. Add eggs and yolks slowly. Blend in sifted flour. Dough will be too firm for pastry bag, so must be pressed through a meat grinder with *spritz* cooky attachment. Cookies are then formed into desired shapes and set on paper-lined pans. Bake at 300° F. When cold, dip ends in melted chocolate and sprinkle with chopped pistachios.

Sugar Cookies

1 lb. 4 ozs. sugar	$1\frac{1}{4}$ cups sugar
$1\frac{1}{2}$ lbs. butter	$\frac{3}{4}$ cup butter
7 eggs	2 eggs
$\frac{3}{4}$ pint milk	$\frac{3}{4}$ cup milk
1 oz. ammonium	3 tsp. ammonium
4 lbs. 6 ozs. pastry flour	$4\frac{1}{4}$ cups pastry flour (generous)
1 lemon rind, grated	$\frac{1}{4}$ lemon rind, grated
vanilla	vanilla

Method

Dissolve ammonium in milk. Cream butter, sugar, and flavoring. Add ammonium-milk mixture. Mix in sifted flour. Knead to smooth dough. Roll dough $\frac{1}{8}''$ thick. Cut with cooky cutters. Egg wash. Dip cookies into granulated sugar. Set on paper-lined pans. Bake at 350° F.

Note: Let dough rest for a few minutes before rolling. Currants or raisins may be added if so desired.

Lemon Cookies

1 lb. 7 ozs. sugar	1¼ cups sugar
10 ozs. lard	½ cup lard (generous)
2 lbs. 14 ozs. pastry flour	5¾ cups pastry flour
8 eggs	4 eggs
1 oz. ammonium	4 tsp. ammonium
3 lemon rinds, grated	3 lemon rinds, grated

Method

Process formula as directed under "Sugar Cookies." (*See Index.*) Ice baked cookies with lemon fondant.

Royal Butter Snaps

3 lbs. sugar	1½ cups sugar
1 lb. 4 ozs. shortening	¾ cup shortening
3 lbs. butter	1½ cups butter
10 eggs	2 eggs
6 lbs. pastry flour	6 cups pastry flour
2 lemon rinds, grated	½ lemon rind, grated
vanilla	vanilla

Method

Cream fats, sugar, and flavoring. Add eggs slowly. Continue beating until creamy smooth. Blend in sifted flour. Using a pastry bag with large star tube, dress mounds on greased, floured pans. Bake at 300° F.

Note: Decorate cookies with cherries, jam, or cocoanut before baking.

Ginger Snaps

1 lb. 5 ozs. brown sugar	scant 2 cups brown sugar
1 quart molasses	2 cups molasses
½ pint water	½ cup water
8 ozs. butter	½ cup butter
8 ozs. lard	½ cup lard
1 oz. baking soda	3 tsp. baking soda
⅓ oz. ammonium	2 tsp. ammonium
⅛ oz. salt	¾ tsp. salt
1½ ozs. ginger	3 tbsp. ginger
½ oz. allspice	3 tsp. allspice
6 lbs. pastry flour	12 cups pastry flour

Method

Cream fats, molasses, and sugar. Add spices. Dissolve ammonium in water and add to cream mixture. Blend in flour. Let dough stand for several hours before making up. Cut cookies with cooky cutters and set on paper-lined pans. Dampen cooky tops freely with wet cloth. Bake at 300° F.

German Springerle

2 lbs. 6 ozs. pastry flour	3¾ cups pastry flour
2 lbs. 14 ozs. sugar	2¾ cups sugar (generous)
8 eggs	4 eggs
½ oz. ammonium	4 tsp. ammonium
½ oz. anis seed	4 tsp. anis seed
1 lemon rind, grated	½ lemon rind, grated

Method

Beat eggs and sugar well. Add anis seed. Sift together the flour, ammonium, and lemon rind. Work into egg mixture. Roll dough very thin and press into the carved, wooden *springerle* forms. Set on lightly greased pans. Let dry completely. Bake at 275° F.

Chocolate Chip Cookies

1 lb. flour	4¼ cups flour
6 ozs. brown sugar	½ cup brown sugar
12 ozs. granulated sugar	1 cup granulated sugar
12 ozs. butter	1 cup butter
4 eggs	2 eggs
¼ oz. baking soda	1 tsp. baking soda
⅛ oz. salt	1 tsp. salt
1 oz. water	½ tsp. water
1 lb. 8 ozs. chocolate chips	12 ozs. chocolate chips
8 ozs. walnuts, chopped	1 cup walnuts, chopped
vanilla	vanilla

Method

Cream butter and sugar, adding water and eggs slowly. Sift dry ingredients together and blend into creamed mixture. Fold in chocolate chips. Dress mounds onto greased pans. Bake at 375° F.

Oatmeal Cookies

3 lbs. 4 ozs. sugar	1½ cups sugar (generous)
1 lb. 10 ozs. shortening	1 cup shortening
1¾ ozs. baking soda	2½ tsp. baking soda
¾ oz. ammonium	2½ tsp. ammonium
¾ oz. salt	2½ tsp. salt
3 lbs. 4 ozs. pastry flour	3¼ cups pastry flour
2 lbs. rolled oats	3 cups rolled oats
2 lbs. raisins	1¾ cups raisins
1½ pints water	¾ cup water
vanilla	vanilla

Method.

Cream shortening, sugar, and vanilla. Dissolve soda and ammonium in water, and add to fat mixture. Blend in sifted flour and oats. Add raisins. Knead to form smooth dough. Cut cookies and set on paper-lined pans. Bake at 350° F.

Almond Butter Cookies

2 lbs. sugar	1 cup sugar
1 lb. almond paste	4 ozs. almond paste
12 ozs. shortening	6 tbsp. shortening
12 ozs. butter	⅜ cup butter
1 lb. 8 ozs. eggs	4 eggs
3 lbs. 8 ozs. flour	scant 3 cups flour
vanilla	vanilla

Method

Soften almond paste gradually by adding shortening. Add butter, sugar, and vanilla. Cream mixture slowly, adding eggs one at a time. Blend in sifted flour. Using pastry bag with round tube, dress mounds on greased, floured pans. Sprinkle with sliced almonds. Bake at 325° F.

Butter Nuts

2 lbs. 4 ozs. butter	1⅛ cups butter
2 lbs. 4 ozs. shortening	1¼ cups shortening (generous)
2 lbs. 4 ozs. sugar	1⅛ cups sugar
1 oz. salt	1½ tsp. salt
2 lbs. 4 ozs. walnuts, ground	2 cups walnuts, ground
12 ozs. eggs	2 eggs
6 lbs. pastry flour	6 cups pastry flour
vanilla	vanilla

Method

Cream butter, sugar, shortening, and vanilla. Add eggs and salt. Blend in sifted flour and nuts. Form long roll ¾″ in diameter. Cut pieces ½″ wide and set on paper-lined pans. Bake at 350° F. Roll while still hot in vanilla-flavored, powdered sugar.

Fruit Bars

2 lbs. sugar	1 cup sugar
1 lb. shortening	½ cup shortening
1 pint molasses	½ cup molasses
1 pint milk	½ cup milk
2 ozs. baking soda	¾ tsp. baking soda
½ pint eggs	2 eggs
4 lbs. pastry flour	4 cups pastry flour
1 lb. 8 ozs. raisins	1¼ cups raisins
8 ozs. mixed fruits	¼ cup mixed fruits

Method

Cream shortening and sugar, adding eggs slowly. Stir in molasses. Dissolve soda in milk and add to cream mixture. Blend in sifted flour and fruits. Form strips 1½″ thick the full length of the greased and floured pans. Egg wash. Bake at 350° F. Cut bars when cold.

Brownies

4 lbs. 8 ozs. sugar	2¼ cups sugar
1 lb. 12 ozs. shortening	1 cup shortening
1½ ozs. salt	¾ tsp. salt
vanilla	vanilla
1 lb. honey	⅓ cup honey
18 eggs	4 eggs
2 lbs. pastry flour	2 cups pastry flour
8 ozs. nuts, chopped	½ cup nuts, chopped
12 ozs. bitter chocolate, melted	3 squares bitter chocolate, melted
¾ pint warm water	⅜ cup warm water

Method

Cream shortening, sugar, and salt, adding the eggs slowly. Mix in melted chocolate and honey. Add warm water. Blend in sifted flour and nuts. Grease pan and line bottom and sides with paper. Fill pan three-quarters full with mixture. Bake at 325° F. to 350° F. When cold, turn out and remove paper. Ice with chocolate fudge. Cut cubes or slices. (To fill standard bakery pan, 8 lbs. 12 ozs. batter is needed.)

Santa Claus Cookies

12 ozs. butter	1½ cups butter
1 lb. brown sugar	3 cups brown sugar (generous)
2 eggs	2 eggs
4 ozs. almonds, ground	1 cup almonds, ground
2 tsp. baking soda	2 tsp. baking soda
4 tsp. cinnamon	4 tsp. cinnamon
4 tsp. nutmeg	4 tsp. nutmeg
2 tsp. cloves	4 tsp. cloves
1 lb. 8 ozs. pastry flour	2 tsp. cloves
½ tsp. salt	6 cups pastry flour
	½ tsp. salt

Method

Cream butter and sugar. Add rest of ingredients and knead to smooth dough. Cut cookies of desired shapes. Place half almonds in center. Egg wash. Bake at 325° F.

Lady Fingers

1 lb. 3 ozs. pastry flour	1 cup pastry flour (generous)
1 lb. 3 ozs. sugar	¾ cup sugar
24 egg whites	6 egg whites
24 egg yolks	6 egg yolks
vanilla	vanilla
½ lemon rind, grated	1 tsp. lemon rind, grated

Method

Add a little of the sugar to the flavoring and egg yolks. Blend with a few swift strokes (don't whip). Whip the egg whites, adding remaining sugar gradually, until stiff. Fold yolk mixture into whites and blend in the sifted flour carefully. Using a pastry bag with medium round tube, dress lady fingers onto paper sheets in pans. Dust tops with powdered sugar. Bake at 350° F. Professional formula yields approximately 400 pieces.

IV

CAKES

Method for Warm Sponge Cakes

In preparing a sponge cake, care must be taken that the equipment is perfectly clean and free of grease. A speck of grease on the beater or mixing bowl may be the deciding factor in having a success or a failure. If it is necessary to use an aluminum or copper bowl, it should first be cleaned by scrubbing it with a half of a lemon and a little salt. This will remove the black mineral deposits.

The eggs, yolks, and sugar are beaten in the bowl over hot water until very warm and liquid. Remove from hot water and continue beating by machine until the mixture has cooled completely. The batter should be light and foamy. Cake flour must be sifted, and if the formula calls for cornstarch it is sifted with the flour. After it has been sifted several times, the flour is folded carefully by hand into the egg mixture (under no circumstances by machine). Then the warm, melted butter is added, and the batter is put into cake tins or on cake sheets. Those containers must be lightly greased or lined with paper.

The cakes are baked at 300° F. to 325° F. The proper baking time can only be determined by the hand test, as thick cakes require a longer period than thin layers. To see if the cake is baked, place hand on the browned top and press down gently. If the cake's own spring pushes back the finger impressions, remove the cake from the oven. Turn it upside down on a wire rack immediately. Allow to cool completely.

Vienna Sponge Cake (warm) 1

20 eggs (1 quart)	5 eggs
1 lb. 4 ozs. cake flour	1¼ cups cake flour
1 lb. 4 ozs. sugar	⅝ cups sugar
5 ozs. butter	⅛ cup butter
1 lemon rind, grated	¼ lemon rind, grated
1 orange rind, grated	¼ orange rind, grated
vanilla	vanilla

Vienna Sponge Cake (warm) 2

15 eggs	4 eggs
12 egg yolks	3 egg yolks
1 lb. sugar	½ cup sugar
8 ozs. cake flour	½ cup cake flour
8½ ozs. cornstarch	¼ cup cornstarch
8 ozs. butter	(generous)
1 lemon rind, grated	¼ cup butter
vanilla	¼ lemon rind, grated
	vanilla

Chocolate Sponge (warm)

20 eggs	5 eggs
1 lb. 3 ozs. sugar	¾ cup sugar
1 lb. 3 ozs. cake flour	1¼ cups cake flour
8 ozs. cocoa	9 tbsp. cocoa
6 ozs. butter	2½ tbsp. butter
1 orange rind, grated	¼ orange rind, grated
vanilla	vanilla

Almond Sponge Cake (warm)

20 eggs	5 eggs
24 egg yolks	6 egg yolks
2 lb. 8 ozs. sugar	1¼ cups sugar
10 ozs. almonds, ground	1 cup almonds, ground
8 ozs. butter	¼ cup butter
1 orange rind, grated	¼ orange rind, grated
1 lemon rind, grated	¼ lemon rind, grated
vanilla	vanilla

Marzipan Sponge Cake (warm)

20 eggs	5 eggs
20 egg yolks	5 egg yolks
1 lb. 8 ozs. sugar	¾ cup sugar
1 lb. 8 ozs. cake flour	1½ cups cake flour
12 ozs. almond paste	3 ozs. almond paste
1 lemon rind, grated	¼ lemon rind, grated
vanilla	vanilla

Vienna Sponge Cake (cold)

36 eggs	4 eggs
1 lb. 8 ozs. sugar	⅜ cup sugar
12 ozs. cake flour	⅜ cup cake flour
12 ozs. cornstarch	⅜ cup cornstarch
12 ozs. butter	3 tbsp. butter
1 lemon rind, grated	¼ lemon rind, grated
vanilla	vanilla

Method

Separate the eggs. Cream sugar, yolks, and flavoring well. Fold in stiffly beaten whites. Sift together the flour and starch, and blend slowly into the cream mixture. Add melted butter last. Bake at 300° F.

Note: In all formulas which have the egg whites beaten separately, one-third of the amount of sugar specified should be beaten with the egg whites to prevent them from getting smeary during the blending process.

Royal Honey Sponge (warm)

25 egg yolks	6 egg yolks
20 eggs	5 eggs
1 lb. 14 ozs. sugar	scant 1 cup sugar
12 ozs. butter	$\frac{3}{8}$ cup butter
1 lb. 2 ozs. cake flour	1 cup cake flour
12 ozs. cornstarch	$\frac{3}{8}$ cup cornstarch
$\frac{1}{4}$ pint honey	$\frac{1}{8}$ cup honey
$\frac{1}{4}$ pint water	$\frac{1}{8}$ cup water
$\frac{1}{2}$ tsp. salt	dash salt
1 lemon rind, grated	$\frac{1}{4}$ lemon rind, grated
vanilla	vanilla

Method

Beat over hot water until warm the eggs, yolks, sugar, honey, water, salt, and flavoring. Sift together flour and starch, melt butter. Proceed as directed under "Method for Warm Sponge Cakes."

Chocolate Butter Cake

4 eggs	1 egg
32 egg yolks	8 egg yolks
32 egg whites	8 egg whites
10 ozs. butter	$\frac{1}{4}$ cup butter (generous)
$8\frac{1}{2}$ ozs. filberts, toasted, ground	$\frac{1}{2}$ cup filberts, toasted, ground
$8\frac{1}{2}$ ozs. cocoa	$\frac{5}{8}$ cup cocoa
$8\frac{1}{2}$ ozs. cake flour	$\frac{1}{2}$ cup cake flour
$8\frac{1}{2}$ ozs. cake crumbs	$\frac{1}{2}$ cup cake crumbs
12 ozs. sugar	$\frac{3}{8}$ cup sugar
2 orange rinds, grated	$\frac{1}{2}$ orange rind, grated
1 lemon rind, grated	$\frac{1}{4}$ lemon rind, grated
vanilla	vanilla

Method

Whip the egg whites with one-third of the sugar until stiff. Cream together the butter, sugar, and flavoring. Add the eggs and yolks one at a time. Fold whites into creamed mixture. Sift together the flour, crumbs, and cocoa. Blend into first mixture. Bake in well-greased and floured pans at 325° F.

Rich Chocolate Sponge

15 eggs	4 eggs
10 egg yolks	2 egg yolks
1 lb. cake flour	1 cup cake flour
8 ozs. cocoa	$\frac{1}{2}$ cup cocoa (generous)
6 ozs. butter	3 tbsp. butter
1 orange rind, grated	$\frac{1}{4}$ orange rind, grated
vanilla	vanilla

Method

Follow the "Method for Warm Sponge Cakes." Bake at 325° F.

Almond Butter Cake

10 eggs	5 eggs
$\frac{1}{2}$ pint milk	$\frac{1}{2}$ cup milk
10 ozs. sugar	$\frac{5}{8}$ cup sugar
8 ozs. almond paste	4 ozs. almond paste
1 lb. cake flour	2 cups cake flour
$\frac{1}{3}$ oz. baking powder	1 tsp. baking powder
$6\frac{1}{2}$ ozs. butter	$\frac{3}{8}$ cup butter (generous)
1 lemon rind, grated	$\frac{1}{2}$ lemon rind, grated
vanilla	vanilla

Method

Soften almond paste with butter. Add sugar and flavoring, cream well. Add the eggs one at a time. Sift baking powder with flour and blend into cream mixture. Stir in milk. Bake at 400° F.

Note: Mixture is very rich, so bake in thin layers.

Almond Chocolate Cake

12 egg yolks	6 egg yolks
12 egg whites	6 egg whites
2 whole eggs	1 whole egg
10 ozs. sugar	$\frac{5}{8}$ cup sugar
5 ozs. cake crumbs	$\frac{2}{3}$ cup cake crumbs (generous)
$3\frac{1}{2}$ ozs. almonds, toasted, ground	$\frac{1}{2}$ cup almonds, toasted, ground
$2\frac{1}{2}$ ozs. cocoa	

3½ ozs. cake flour	5½ tbsp. cocoa
1½ ozs. water	scant ½ cup cake flour
¼ tsp. nutmeg	3 tbsp. water
1 orange rind, grated	dash nutmeg
vanilla	½ orange rind, grated
	vanilla

Method

Beat egg whites and one-third of the sugar until stiff. Beat together the rest of the sugar, yolks, eggs, flavoring, and water until foamy. Blend in crumbs and almonds, followed by the stiffly-beaten egg whites. Sift together flour and cocoa, add to above. Bake at 385° F.

Note: This formula contains no butter and is therefore considered very light. To toast nuts, place them on a baking sheet and brown swiftly in a hot oven, stirring frequently.

Filbert Cake (warm)

24 eggs	6 eggs
1 lb. 7 ozs. sugar	¾ cup sugar
1 lb. 3 ozs. filberts, toasted, ground	2⅛ cups filberts, toasted, ground
1 lb. 7 ozs. cake flour	1⅜ cups cake flour
10 ozs. cake crumbs	⅔ cups cake crumbs
3 ozs. butter	2 tbsp. butter
1 lemon rind, grated	¼ lemon rind, grated
½ tsp. cinnamon	⅛ tsp. cinnamon
vanilla	vanilla

Method

Beat eggs, sugar, vanilla, and rinds over water until hot. Sift together the flour, cinnamon, filberts, and crumbs. Melt butter. Proceed as directed under "Method for Warm Sponge Cakes."

Walnut Mocha Cake (warm)

24 eggs	6 eggs
1 lb. 3 ozs. sugar	⅝ cups sugar
1 lb. 8 ozs. cake flour	1½ cups cake flour
⅔ oz. baking powder	1 tsp. baking powder
5 ozs. butter	3 tbsp. butter
5 ozs. walnuts, ground	⅜ cup walnuts, ground
1½ tsp. instant coffee	¼ tsp. instant coffee
vanilla	vanilla
½ tsp. cinnamon	⅛ tsp. cinnamon
¼ tsp. nutmeg	dash nutmeg

Method

See "Walnut Cake."

Walnut Cake

12 egg yolks	3 egg yolks
8 egg whites	2 egg whites
6½ ozs. sugar	¼ cup sugar
3½ ozs. walnuts, ground	5 tbsp. walnuts, ground
3 ozs. cake crumbs	scant ⅓ cup cake crumbs
2 ozs. cake flour	⅛ cup cake flour
½ tsp. cinnamon	⅛ tsp. cinnamon
1 lemon rind, grated	¼ lemon rind, grated

Method (for above two formulas)

Cream the yolks, sugar, and rind. Sift together the flour, cinnamon, and nuts. Blend into first mixture. Fold in stiffly-beaten egg whites. Bake at 375° F.

Butter Layer Cake

12 eggs	3 eggs
1 lb. butter	½ cup butter
10 ozs. cake flour	⅝ cup cake flour
10 ozs. cornstarch	¼ cup plus 1 tbsp. cornstarch
⅙ oz. baking powder	¼ tsp. baking powder
1 lemon rind, grated	¼ lemon rind, grated
¼ tsp. nutmeg	dash nutmeg
vanilla	vanilla

Method

Cream butter, sugar, and rind. Add eggs one at a time. Sift together the dry ingredients and blend into the creamy butter mixture. Put into greased and floured cake forms to a depth no greater than ½″. Bake at 385° F to 400° F.

Note: This mixture is very rich and should be used as a cake base with a light sponge on top.

Butter Layer Cake Sponge

10 egg whites	5 egg whites
10 egg yolks	5 egg yolks
12 ozs. sugar	¾ cup sugar
13 ozs. cornstarch	¾ cup plus 1 tbsp. cornstarch
10 ozs. butter	⅝ cup butter
1 lemon rind, grated	½ lemon rind, grated
vanilla	vanilla

Method

Beat egg whites until stiff, adding approximately one-third of the sugar. Put rest of sugar plus sifted cornstarch on a baking sheet and warm gently in oven. Blend yolks and flavoring by hand into the stiff whites. Add warm sugar and starch mixture. Blend in the melted butter. Line cake tins with paper and bake swiftly at 400° F.

Dutch Cake

8 eggs	2 eggs
8 egg yolks	2 egg yolks
1 lb. 1 oz. sugar	½ cup sugar (generous)
1 lb. 1 oz. butter	½ cup butter (generous)
1 lb. 1 oz. cake flour	1 cup cake flour
10 ozs. almond paste	2½ ozs. almond paste
1 lemon rind, grated	¼ lemon rind, grated

Method

Cream almond paste, sugar, butter, and rind. Add eggs and yolks one at a time. Blend in sifted flour. Bake at 375° F. to 385° F.

Dobosh Cake

4 egg yolks	4 egg yolks
4 egg whites	4 egg whites
1 oz. butter, melted	2 tbsp. butter, melted
2½ ozs. sugar	¼ cup sugar (generous)
3 ozs. cake flour	¾ cup cake flour
½ lemon rind, grated	½ lemon rind, grated
vanilla	vanilla

Method

Beat egg whites with one-third of the sugar until stiff. Cream yolks, remaining sugar, and flavoring. Add yolk mixture to whites. Fold in sifted flour and melted butter. Grease pans and flour them lightly. Draw rings in the floured surface, using a cake tin of the desired size for the pattern. Spread the cake mixture inside the drawn rings to a depth of no more than ¼″. Bake at 300° F. Remove from pan while still hot. Join six or eight layers with butter cream for one cake.

SACHER CAKES

Sacher cakes are named after the famed Hotel Sacher in Vienna. They are the finest of chocolate cakes and an historic Viennese speciality. We present here several recipes, all excellent in flavor. However, some are more expensive than others.

The mixing procedure varies slightly, depending upon the eggs. If whole eggs are used, or yolks, these will be added slowly to the creamed butter and sugar, as in mixing pound cake. If egg whites are to be beaten separately, they will be folded into the cream mixture carefully. In the latter case some of the sugar should be whipped with the whites to assure a firmer stand.

Bitter chocolate, which makes the batter finer, may be used instead of cocoa. The chocolate is to be melted and creamed with the butter, sugar, and eggs. If the formula calls for flour, nuts, crumbs or baking powder, these materials should be sifted together. The mixing sequence will then be as follows: blend whites into cream mixture, and add flour mixture last.

The mixing bowl should be scraped frequently during the mixing process to assure a perfect blending of the materials, otherwise the cakes might become streaky. It is equally important to blend the whites into the cream mixture perfectly to avoid holes in the cake body. The baking process is to be watched carefully. Heavier cakes must be baked more slowly than light ones. The approximate temperatures are given along with the formulas.

Sacher Torte 1

16 egg yolks	4 egg yolks
10 egg whites	3 egg whites
6½ ozs. butter	¼ cup butter
8 ozs. sugar	¼ cup sugar
6½ ozs. cake crumbs	scant ⅔ cup cake crumbs
4 ozs. cocoa	3½ tsp. cocoa
1½ ozs. almonds, ground	2 tbsp. almonds, ground
¼ tsp. cinnamon	dash cinnamon
vanilla	vanilla
1 lemon rind, grated	¼ lemon rind, grated
1 orange rind, grated	¼ orange rind, grated

Method

Bake at 400° F.

Sacher Torte 2

12 egg whites	3 egg whites
16 egg yolks	4 egg yolks
8 ozs. sugar	¼ cup sugar
8 ozs. butter	¼ cup butter
3½ ozs. cocoa	3 tbsp. cocoa
¼ tsp. cinnamon	dash cinnamon
vanilla	vanilla
1 lemon rind, grated	¼ lemon rind, grated
6½ ozs. cake crumbs	scant ⅔ cup cake crumbs

Method

Formula one and two do not call for flour. Bake at 400° F.

Sacher Torte 3

20 egg yolks	5 egg yolks
4 eggs	1 egg
16 egg whites	4 egg whites
6½ ozs. sugar	¼ cup sugar
6½ ozs. sugar (with whites)	¼ cup sugar (with whites)
6½ ozs. butter	¼ cup butter
6½ ozs. bitter chocolate, melted	1½ ozs. bitter chocolate, melted
5 ozs. cake flour	¼ cup cake flour
6½ ozs. almonds, ground, toasted	⅜ cup almonds, ground, toasted
1½ ozs. cake crumbs	2 tbsp. cake crumbs
½ tsp. cinnamon	⅛ tsp. cinnamon
¼ tsp. cloves	dash cloves
2 lemon rinds, grated	½ lemon rind, grated
vanilla	vanilla

Method

Bake at 350° F.

Sacher Torte 4

18 egg whites	4 egg whites
14 egg yolks	4 egg yolks
8½ ozs. butter	¼ cup butter (generous)
8½ ozs. bitter chocolate, melted	2¼ squares bitter chocolate, melted
8 ozs. sugar	¼ cup sugar
5 ozs. cake flour	¼ cup cake flour
4 ozs. almond paste	1 oz. almond paste
vanilla	vanilla
1 lemon rind, grated	¼ lemon rind, grated
1 orange rind, grated	¼ orange rind, grated

Method

Bake at 350° F.

Sacher Torte 5

10 egg yolks	10 egg yolks
2 eggs	2 eggs
8 egg whites	8 egg whites
6½ ozs. sugar	¾ cup sugar (generous)
3½ ozs. butter	scant ½ cup butter
3 ozs. bitter chocolate, melted	3 squares bitter chocolate, melted
2½ ozs. cake flour	⅝ cup cake flour
½ oz. cake crumbs	¼ cup cake crumbs
3 ozs. almonds, toasted, ground	¾ cup almonds, toasted, ground
⅛ tsp. cinnamon	⅛ tsp. cinnamon
dash cloves	dash cloves
1 lemon rind, grated	1 lemon rind, grated
vanilla	vanilla

Method

Bake at 325° F.

The Glazing of Sacher Torten

Cool the cakes. Spread the top and sides of each cake with hot apricot jam—a thin layer only. Top with chocolate fondant or semi-sweet chocolate.

If a layer cake is desired, use raspberry jam for filling. Then finish with the traditional glaze given above.

Canadian Chocolate Cake

24 egg whites	6 egg whites
24 egg yolks	6 egg yolks
1 lb. 8 ozs. sugar	¾ cup sugar
8 ozs. almond paste	2 ozs. almond paste
4 ozs. filberts, ground	⅜ cup filberts, ground
10 ozs. bitter chocolate, melted	2½ squares bitter chocolate, melted
1 lb. 8 ozs. cake flour	1½ cups cake flour
8 ozs. hot water	¼ cup hot water
1 lemon rind, grated	¼ lemon rind, grated
6 ozs. butter, melted	2 tbsp. butter, melted

Method

Beat egg whites with a little of the sugar until stiff. Cream yolks, remaining sugar, and flavoring. Melt chocolate, add hot water to it and blend into yolk mixture. Blend whites into the mixture. Sift flour and nuts. Fold into batter. Add melted butter. Bake in greased and floured pans, at 350° F.

Parisienne Cake

16 egg whites	4 egg whites
16 egg yolks	4 egg yolks
8 ozs. sugar	¼ cup sugar
6½ ozs. butter	scant ¼ cup butter
6½ ozs. nougat	1½ ozs. nougat
12 ozs. cake flour	¾ cup cake flour
1½ ozs. cocoa	1½ tbsp. cocoa
1 lemon rind, grated	¼ lemon rind, grated

Method

Cream butter, nougat (see Index) sugar, and flavoring. Add yolks, one at a time. Beat whites with part of sugar until stiff and blend into cream mixture. Sift flour and cocoa together and fold into batter. Bake in layers of batter not more than $\frac{1}{2}''$ in depth. Bake at 400° F.

Macaroon Layer Cake

6 egg whites	3 egg whites
$1\frac{1}{2}$ ozs. cornstarch	2 tbsp. cornstarch
$3\frac{1}{2}$ ozs. cake crumbs	$\frac{2}{3}$ cup cake crumbs
13 ozs. almond paste	$6\frac{1}{2}$ ozs. almond paste
13 ozs. sugar	$\frac{3}{4}$ cup sugar (generous)
8 egg whites	4 egg whites
pink coloring	pink coloring
vanilla	vanilla
1 orange rind, grated	$\frac{1}{2}$ orange rind, grated

Method

Soften almond paste with second amount of egg whites, blend in sugar, and cream until smooth. Beat first amount of whites until stiff, and whip in cornstarch swiftly. Blend egg white mixture into almond paste. Add coloring, flavoring, and cake crumbs. Bake in paper-lined pans filled to a depth of three-quarters of an inch at 375° F. After baking, cakes will be stuck on the paper. To remove paper, set cakes on a wet table top for a few minutes. Paper will come off easily.

Light Fruit Cake (Christmas Cake)

Note: The recipe for home use is different from the professional formula, and thus the ingredients do not correspond to each other.

9 lbs. butter	1 lb. butter
10 lbs. sugar	2 cups sugar
1 lb. almond paste	9 eggs
100 eggs	5 cups flour
10 lbs. flour	1 tsp. baking powder
1 oz. salt	$\frac{1}{2}$ tsp. salt
2 lbs. light raisins	3 cups light raisins
3 lbs. glazed cherries	1 cup glazed cherries
2 lbs. 8 ozs. almonds, blanched, chopped	2 cups almonds, blanched, slivered
1 lb. 8 ozs. filberts	2 cups seedless raisins
1 lb. walnuts	1 cup citron peel
2 lbs. citron peel	$\frac{1}{2}$ cup wine or brandy
2 lbs. candied lemon peel	
3 lbs. candied orange peel	
2 lbs. crushed pineapples	
1 oz. cinnamon	

1 oz. allspice	
$\frac{1}{2}$ oz. nutmeg	
$\frac{1}{2}$ oz. cloves	
$\frac{1}{4}$ pint orange water	
1 oz. vanilla	

Method

Bake at 275° F. Mixing directions are given under "Dark Fruit Cake."

Dark Fruit Cake

10 lbs. butter	$1\frac{1}{2}$ cups butter
8 lbs. brown sugar	$1\frac{1}{2}$ cups brown sugar
96 eggs	$\frac{3}{4}$ cup honey
1 oz. salt	$\frac{1}{4}$ cup molasses
1 lb. honey	2 tbsp. *couleur*
1 quart molasses	1 tsp. salt
9 lbs. 8 ozs. flour	5 eggs
2 lbs. dates	$3\frac{1}{2}$ cups flour
2 lbs. raisins	$1\frac{1}{4}$ tsp. baking powder
3 lbs. cherries	$\frac{1}{2}$ cup stewed prunes
5 lbs. almonds, blanched, chopped	$\frac{1}{4}$ cup citron peel
	$\frac{1}{2}$ cup light raisins
2 lbs. candied orange peel	$\frac{1}{2}$ cup dark raisins
3 lbs. candied lemon peel	$\frac{1}{4}$ cup crushed pineapple
2 lbs. crushed pineapple	$\frac{1}{2}$ cup cherries
1 lb. stewed prunes	$\frac{1}{4}$ cup walnuts
1 oz. cinnamon	$\frac{1}{4}$ cup filberts
1 oz. allspice	$\frac{1}{4}$ cup candied lemon peel
$\frac{1}{2}$ oz. nutmeg	$\frac{1}{4}$ cup candied orange peel
$\frac{3}{4}$ oz. cloves	1 tbsp. vanilla
$\frac{1}{2}$ pint rum	$\frac{1}{2}$ cup rum
1 oz. vanilla	$\frac{1}{2}$ tsp. cloves
3 ozs. *couleur*	$\frac{1}{4}$ tsp. cardamom
	$\frac{1}{2}$ tsp. nutmeg
	1 tsp. allspice
	1 tsp. cinnamon

Method

Cut cherries in quarters, chop nuts and peel. Combine all fruits and pour rum over the mixture. Let stand several hours, preferably overnight.

Put butter, sugar, and salt in a bowl and cream well. Add eggs two at a time until all are used, blending well after each addition. When making the dark cake, put the mixer on low speed and blend in the honey and molasses. Sift flour and spices together several times. Blend flour by hand into creamy butter mixture, stirring only as long

62

Porcupine cake glazed with chocolate fondant

Latticed *Linzer Torte* sprinkled with almond slices

Angel food cake, iced and decorated.

Cherry cake with buried, black cherries.

Pineapple upside-down cake glazed with sugar syrup

Hawaiian cheese cake

as necessary to get a smooth dough. Add the fruits and stir them thoroughly into the dough by hand.

Line the bottoms and sides of the cake tins with brown paper, making sure that the side paper extends ½″ above the top of the tins. Put the dough into the tins. Make the tops smooth by dipping the fingers frequently into milk and patting the cakes. If the cakes are not to be iced, decorate them with glazed fruits and blanched almonds. Bake at 275° F. Place a pan of water inside the oven to assure moist baking. Approximate baking time is from two and one-half to three hours. After baking, glaze the tops with rum-flavored sugar syrup or a gum arabic solution.

Note: Illustrations for decorated Christmas cakes are under "Christmas Season." (*See Index.*)

Krokant Cake

12 egg whites	3 egg whites
15 egg yolks	4 egg yolks
10 ozs. sugar	¼ cup sugar (generous)
5 ozs. krokant	¼ cup krokant
(See Index.)	(See Index.)
3¾ ozs. cake flour	¼ cup cake flour (generous)
5 ozs. cake crumbs	⅓ cup cake crumbs
4 ozs. almonds, balnched, ground	⅜ cup almonds, blanched, ground
¼ tsp. cinnamon	dash cinnamon
vanilla	vanilla

Method

Beat whites stiff with part of the sugar. Cream the remaining sugar, yolks, and vanilla. Add whites to cream mixture. Sift flour and cinnamon. Mix with almonds, chopped krokant, and cake crumbs. Blend carefully into egg mixture. Bake at 350° F.

Royal Chocolate Cake

20 eggs	5 eggs
5 lbs. sugar	2½ cups sugar
2 lbs. shortening	1 cup shortening
½ tsp. salt	dash salt
red food coloring	red food coloring
vanilla	vanilla
2 quarts buttermilk	1 pint buttermilk
4 lbs. cake flour	4 cups cake flour
12 ozs. cocoa	scant 1 cup cocoa
2 ozs. baking soda	1 tbsp. baking soda

Method

Cream the sugar, shortening, salt, and vanilla. Add a few drops of red coloring. Add eggs one at a time, creaming thoroughly after each addition. Scrape sides of bowl frequently during creaming process. Dissolve the soda in one-quarter of the buttermilk. Add to cream mixture. Sift together flour and cocoa. Put mixer on low speed and stir in flour. Add remaining buttermilk, scrape bowl, and mix thoroughly. Put batter in greased cake tins. Bake at 300° F. Remove cakes from tins immediately after baking.

Frenchipan

2 lbs. 8 ozs. almond paste	10 ozs. almond paste
2 lbs. 8 ozs. sugar	1½ cups sugar
2 lbs. 8 ozs. butter	1¼ cups butter
25 eggs	6 eggs
4 ozs. bread flour	¼ cup bread flour
1 lb. cake flour	1 cup cake flour
vanilla	vanilla
dash nutmeg	pinch nutmeg

Method

Blend sugar with almond paste. Add butter and cream slightly. Add eggs one by one, beating after each addition. Fold in flour. Bake in cake tins or on baking sheets at 300° F.

Note: This cake is very rich and will stay moist for a considerable time.

UNDECORATED CAKES

This section contains formulas for cakes which are ready for sale or consumption when they are taken from the oven. They require no fillings and little, if any, decoration.

Angel Food Cake

1½ quarts egg whites	15 egg whites
2 lbs. 13 ozs. sugar	1¼ cups sugar
1 lb. 4 ozs. cake flour	1¼ cups cake flour
4 ozs. cornstarch	⅛ cup cornstarch
juice of ½ lemon	juice of ¼ lemon
½ tsp. cream of tartar	¼ tsp. cream of tartar
vanilla	vanilla

Method

If a metal bowl is used, clean thoroughly with salt and lemon juice. Rinse well. Whip egg whites with lemon juice and cream of tartar. As soon as whites become stiff, beat sugar in slowly. Continue beating until firm peaks form. Fold in the sifted flour and starch. Use ungreased tube pans for the cakes. Bake at 375° F. Turn tins upside down onto a wire screen and allow to cool completely. Remove from tins.

Angel food cake can be made with different flavors. Some of the most popular combinations are given here. These additional ingredients are stirred into the cake batter after the cake tins are filled.

(1) Pineapple: four tablespoons crushed pineapple for each cake
(2) Chocolate chip: a half-cup chipped chocolate for each cake
(3) Strawberry: five tablespoons sweetened, chopped strawberries for each cake
(4) Cherry: a half-cup chopped, glazed cherries for each cake
(5) Filbert: a half-cup chopped, toasted filberts for each cake
(6) Cherry Walnut: a quarter-cup glazed, chopped cherries and a quarter-cup chopped nuts for each cake.

Linzer Torte

10 ozs. butter	1¼ cups butter
10 ozs. powdered sugar	2 cups powdered sugar
1 egg	1 egg
2 egg yolks	2 egg yolks
10 ozs. almonds, toasted, ground	2½ cups almonds, toasted, ground
8 ozs. pastry flour	2 cups pastry flour
3 ozs. cake crumbs	1 cup cake crumbs
vanilla	vanilla
¼ tsp. cinnamon	¼ tsp. cinnamon
⅛ tsp. cloves	⅛ tsp. cloves
1 lemon rind, grated	1 lemon rind, grated

Method

Knead all ingredients together thoroughly to form a smooth dough. Let dough rest in a cool place for about fifteen minutes. Cover bottom of a lightly greased cake tin with dough ¼" thick. Spread raspberry jam ¼" thick in the center, leaving about 1" strip free from jam around the outer edge. Roll strips of dough to finger-thickness and form lattice work on the jam.

With remaining dough form a ring, and place it around the outer edge of the cake top. Apply egg wash and sprinkle with sliced almonds. Bake at 300° F. Turn out of tin and cool. Fill holes in lattice with hot jam. Sprinkle with powdered sugar.

Porcupine Cake

8 egg whites	8 egg whites
8 egg yolks	8 egg yolks
8 ozs. sugar	1 cup sugar
5½ ozs. butter	scant ¾ cup butter
5½ ozs. cake flour	1¼ cups cake flour (generous)
3 ozs. cocoa	¾ cup cocoa (generous)
¼ tsp. baking powder	¼ tsp. baking powder
1 orange rind, grated	1 orange rind, grated
1 lemon rind, grated	1 lemon rind, grated
3 ozs. almonds, chopped	¾ cup almonds, chopped
¼ tsp. cinnamon	¼ tsp. cinnamon

Method

Beat egg whites with part of the sugar until stiff. Cream butter, sugar, and flavoring. Add yolks one at a time. Sift together flour and cocoa, mix in nuts, and add to cream mixture. Pour batter into greased and floured half-round loaf tin. Bake at 350° F. to 375° F. Turn out on cake rack and cool. Glaze with chocolate fondant. Stick with almond slivers.

Cherry Cake

4 eggs	4 eggs
2 egg whites	2 egg whites
2 egg yolks	2 egg yolks
14 ozs. sugar	1¾ cups sugar
8½ ozs. cake flour	2 cups cake flour (generous)
6 ozs. butter	¾ cup butter
fresh cherries	fresh cherries
1 lemon rind, grated	1 lemon rind, grated
vanilla	vanilla

Method

Beat eggs, yolks, and one-half of the sugar, first warm and then cold as described under "Sponge Cake." (*See Index*.) Beat whites with rest of sugar until stiff. Add to first mixture. Blend in the sifted flour. Add melted butter last. Half fill a greased cake tin with the batter. Cover surface with stoned, black cherries. Pour remaining batter on top. Bake at 350° F. and cool. Sprinkle top with powdered sugar.

Diamond Cake

8 egg yolks	8 egg yolks
8 egg whites	8 egg whites
5 ozs. almond paste	5 ozs. almond paste
7 ozs. sugar	scant 1 cup sugar
5 ozs. cake flour	1¼ cups cake flour
3 ozs. butter	⅜ cup butter
5 ozs. walnuts, chopped	1 cup walnuts, chopped
2½ ozs. mixed fruits	½ cup mixed fruits
5 ozs. chocolate chips	5 squares chocolate chips
1 lemon rind, grated	1 lemon rind, grated
dash salt	dash salt
vanilla	vanilla

Method

Soften almond paste with yolks. Add butter and cream slowly. Beat whites with sugar until stiff, and add to first mixture. Blend in sifted flour. Add rest of ingredients. Stir only as much as necessary to assure the proper blending of the materials. Bake in greased, floured pan at 325° F.

Pineapple Upside-Down Cake

12 egg whites	6 egg whites
12 egg yolks	6 egg yolks
7 ozs. butter	¼ cup butter
1 lb. 3 ozs. sugar	scant 1¼ cups sugar
13 ozs. cake flour	1½ cups cake flour
6 ozs. crushed pineapple	¾ cup crushed pineapple
1 lemon rind, grated	½ lemon rind, grated
vanilla	vanilla

Method

Cream butter, half of sugar, vanilla, and rind. Add yolks, one at a time. Beat whites with remaining sugar until stiff. Blend into butter mixture. Blend in sifted flour and pineapple. Grease a cake tin well, spread brown sugar in the bottom. Form a decorative design with sliced pineapple and glazed cherries on bottom of tin. Fill tin with batter and bake at 350° F. After baking turn out onto cake rack immediately. Glaze top with sugar syrup. (*See Index.*)

Poppy Seed Cake

6 egg whites	3 egg whites
6 egg yolks	3 egg yolks
10 ozs. sugar	⅝ cup sugar
4 ozs. butter	¼ cup butter
8 ozs. ground poppy seed	¾ cup ground poppy seed
2 ozs. orange peel, candied	(generous)
½ lemon rind, grated	1½ tbsp. orange peel, candied
	¼ lemon rind, grated

Method

Cream butter and half of sugar, and add egg yolks one at a time. Add lemon rind, orange peel, and poppy seed. Beat whites with remaining sugar until stiff and fold into first mixture. Pour batter into greased, floured pans. Bake at 300° F. to 325° F. Sprinkle with sugar after baking.

Hawaiian Cheese Cake

Part 1

5 lbs. fine cottage cheese	1 lb. 4 ozs. fine cottage cheese
12 ozs. butter	
1 quart sour cream	⅜ cup butter
	½ pint sour cream

Part 2

20 egg yolks	5 egg yolks
12 ozs. sugar	⅜ cup sugar

Part 3

20 egg whites	5 egg whites
12 ozs. sugar	⅜ cup sugar

Part 4

5 ozs. cornstarch	3 tbsp. cornstarch
2 lemon rinds, grated	½ lemon rind, grated
1 orange rind, grated	½ orange rind, grated
vanilla	vanilla
6 ozs. raisins	¼ cup raisins
crushed pineapple	crushed pineapple
shortbread or cooky dough	shortbread or cooky dough

Method

Line bottom of cake tins with ¼″ thickness of cooky or shortbread dough. Use dry cottage cheese. If cheese is not dry, place inside of cloth and squeeze moisture from it. Press cheese through fine sieve. Soften butter at room temperature. Combine parts *1* and *4,* adding sour cream last. Blend ingredients well without creaming. Beat Part *2* together until foamy. Add to cheese mixture. Whip Part *3* until stiff and fold into cheese mixture. Cover cooky dough in tins with crushed, drained pineapple. Fill cheese mixture up to the top of the tins. Bake at 300° F.

A special baking procedure is followed when making cheese cake. After the cheese mixture has risen about ½″ above the edge of tin, remove it from oven. Take a sharp knife and make a cut around the top edge of the cake tin, holding the knife horizontally and letting the point of the knife penetrate the cake about ½″ toward the center. Let stand until mixture has dropped back noticeably. Then return cake to oven. The process of rising, cutting and dropping back is to be repeated two more times. This is referred to as "three times baking." Cheese cakes which are baked only once will always be very flat and heavy.

Viennese Cream Cheese Cake

4 egg yolks	4 egg yolks
¾ pint milk	1½ cups milk
9 gelatine leaves or	4½ tbsp. gelatine
(1½ ozs. crystallized	¾ cup sugar
gelatine)	1 lb. fine cottage cheese
6 ozs. sugar	½ cup raisins
1 lb. fine cottage cheese	1 cup whipping cream
2 ozs. raisins	1 lemon rind, grated
½ pint whipping cream	vanilla
1 lemon rind, grated	dash salt
vanilla	puff paste
dash salt	
puff paste	

Method

Use left-over puff paste and roll out two rounds, each 11″ in diameter and ⅛″ thick. Set on lightly greased, wet pan. Poke holes over surface of dough. Let rest about twenty minutes. Bake at 400° F. and cool. Trim to fit a 10″ cake tin. Place one in bottom of tin. Cut second round of pastry into desired number of pieces for the top of the cake. These are to be set on top of the cream filling. (Shortbread dough my be used if puff paste is not available.)

Prepare the cream as follows : Soak gelatine in cold water until softened. Put soft gelatine in double boiler. Add milk, sugar, yolks, salt, rind, and vanilla. Stir constantly until milk starts to boil. Allow mixture to boil for a few seconds. Set pan in cold water and let cool. Press cheese through sieve and blend into first mixture. Whip the cream until stiff and stir into cheese mixture carefully. Sprinkle raisins on bottom crust. Pour mixture into tin quickly. Smooth top with a knife, place cut pastry sections on top. Sprinkle with powdered sugar and refrigerate.

Note: If crystallized gelatine is used, cook it in milk without soaking.

Duchess Cake

10 egg yolks	10 egg yolks
10 egg whites	10 egg whites
5 ozs. sugar	⅝ cup sugar
6 ozs. cake flour	1½ cups cake flour
2 ozs. mixed fruits	⅓ cup mixed fruits
3 ozs. melted butter	⅜ cup melted butter
Filling	*Filling*
3 ozs. almonds, ground	¾ cup almonds, ground
3 ozs. sugar	⅜ cup sugar
rum	rum

Method

Cream yolks with one-half of the sugar. Beat whites with remaining sugar until stiff and fold into yolks. Add chopped, mixed fruits. Blend in sifted flour, followed by melted butter. Line cake tin with puff paste ⅛″ thick. Mix filling ingredients with a little rum to a smooth spread and and spread over puff paste. Pour cake mixture over it. Bake at 325° F. After baking, sprinkle with powdered sugar.

Brown Cherry Cake

12 egg yolks	6 egg yolks
8 egg whites	4 egg whites
7 ozs. sugar	⅜ cup sugar (generous)
5 ozs. butter	¼ cup butter (generous)
7 ozs. crumbs	¾ cup crumbs
½ pint milk	¼ pint milk
4 ozs. almond, ground	½ cup almonds, ground
1 oz. candied orange peel	2 tsp. candied orange peel

Viennese cream cheese cake

Bishop's cake

Hawaiian pineapple loaf decorated with cherries and pineapple rings

Marble cake loaf

1 oz. citron peel   2 tsp. citron peel
¼ oz. cinnamon   dash cinnamon
1 lemon rind, grated   ½ lemon rind, grated
vanilla   vanilla
1 lb. 10 ozs. firm, fresh   13 ozs. firm, fresh cherries
    cherries or glazed   or glazed cherries
    cherries

Method

Soak crumbs in milk. Cream together thoroughly all ingredients except cherries and whites. Add crumbs and milk to cream mixture. Beat whites until stiff and fold into batter. Fold in cherries. Bake in a greased pan at 375° F. Sprinkle with powdered sugar.

CAKES FOR DESSERTS, TEA, OR COFFEE

Viennese Cake-Gugelhopf 1

6 eggs   6 eggs
6 egg yolks   6 egg yolks
6 ozs. sugar   ¾ cup sugar
5 ozs. cake flour   1¼ cups cake flour
3 ozs. cornstarch   ⅜ cup cornstarch
4 ozs. butter   ½ cup butter
1 lemon rind, grated   1 lemon rind, grated
vanilla   vanilla

Method

Proceed as described under "Method for Warm Sponge Cakes." Pour cake batter into greased and floured cake tins. Bake at 325° F. Sprinkle with powdered sugar after baking.

Viennese Cake Gugelhopf 2

6 egg whites   6 egg whites
6 egg yolks   6 egg yolks
12 ozs. sugar   1½ cups sugar
8 ozs. butter   1 cup butter
1 lb. cake flour   4 cups cake flour
½ tsp. baking powder   ½ tsp. baking powder
½ pint milk   ½ pint milk
vanilla   vanilla
1 lemon rind, grated   1 lemon rind, grated

Method

Cream butter, two-thirds of the sugar, and flavoring. Add yolks, one at a time. When creamy, mix in the milk. Beat whites with remaining sugar until stiff. Stir into first mixture. Sift together the flour and baking powder, and blend into batter. Bake at 350° F. Sprinkle with powdered sugar after baking.

Bishop's Cake

24 egg whites   6 egg whites
28 egg yolks   7 egg yolks
1 lb. 7 ozs. cake flour   scant ½ cup cake flour
1 lb. 2 ozs. sugar   ½ cup sugar (generous)
14 ozs. melted butter   ⅜ cup melted butter
4 ozs. raisins   (generous)
12 ozs. mixed fruits   ¼ cup raisins
4 ozs. almonds, chopped   ½ cup mixed fruits
1 orange rind, grated   (generous)
1 lemon rind, grated   ¼ cup almonds, chopped
¼ tsp. nutmeg   ¼ orange rind, grated
vanilla   ¼ lemon rind, grated
     dash nutmeg
     vanilla

Method

Beat yolks with one-half of the sugar and vanilla. Beat egg whites until stiff, adding the remaining sugar slowly. Blend yolks into whites. Sift flour and blend into egg mixture. Mix together the raisins, mixed fruits, and rinds. Sprinkle with a little flour to keep separated. Add to egg mixture. Stir in melted butter quickly. Bake in half-round or rectangular loaf tin lined with paper. Bake at 300° F. When cold, glaze with hot apricot jam and wrap in thinly rolled, light-green marzipan, or sprinkle with powdered sugar.

Blitzkuchen

12 egg yolks   12 egg yolks
12 egg whites   12 egg whites
1 lb. 3 ozs. sugar   2¼ cups sugar (generous)
13 ozs. cake flour   3¼ cups cake flour
7 ozs. melted butter   ⅞ cup melted butter
1 lemon rind, grated   1 lemon rind, grated
vanilla   vanilla

Method

Beat yolks with one-half of the sugar, vanilla, and rind. Beat whites with remaining sugar until stiff. Blend yolks into whites. Sift flour and fold into cake batter. Stir in melted butter. Grease and flour a round cake tin. Line outer edge of tin with almond halves. Pour in cake batter. Bake at 325° F. Dust with powdered sugar.

Oriental Tea Bread

12 eggs	3 eggs
1 lb. 4 ozs. sugar	⅝ cup sugar
1 lb. 4 ozs. cake flour	1¼ cups cake flour
1 lb. 4 ozs. butter	⅝ cup butter
2 lemon rinds, grated	½ lemon rind, grated
vanilla	vanilla

Method

Cream together the butter, sugar, and flavoring. Add eggs one at a time, and continue creaming after each addition. Scrape bowl frequently. Blend in sifted flour. Pour into greased, floured loaf tin. Bake at 300° F. Sprinkle with powdered sugar after baking.

Italian Lemon Bread

6 eggs	2 eggs
1 lb. 8 ozs. sugar	1 cup sugar
1 lb. 2 ozs. cake flour	1½ cups cake flour
¾ pint milk	½ cup milk
¾ lb. butter	½ cup butter
½ oz. baking powder	1 tsp. baking powder
2 lemon rinds, grated	½ lemon rind, grated
juice of 2 lemons	juice of 1 lemon
6 ozs. sugar	¼ cup sugar

Method

Cream butter, larger amount of sugar, and rinds. Add eggs, one at a time. Stir in milk and vanilla. Sift together the flour and baking powder, fold into creamed mixture. Pour batter into greased, floured loaf tin. Bake at 350° F. After baking and while still hot, top with a mixture of the lemon juice and smaller amount of sugar.

Milan Anis Bread

8 eggs	4 eggs
8 egg yolks	4 egg yolks
3½ ozs. sugar	½ cup sugar
8½ ozs. cake flour	1 cup cake flour
4 ozs. butter	¼ cup butter
1 oz. anis seed	2½ tsp. anis seed

Method

Proceed as described under "Method for Warm Sponge Cakes." Bake in greased, floured loaf tin at 375° F. Sprinkle with powdered sugar after baking. To increase the fine flavor, sprinkle the individual slices with anis liqueur before serving.

Banana Cake

1 lb. 7 ozs. sugar	¾ cup sugar
10 ozs. butter	⅓ cup butter
4 large eggs	1 large egg
¾ pint butter milk	⅓ cup butter milk
6 medium bananas	2 medium bananas
1 lb. 4 ozs. cake flour	1¼ cups cake flour
5 ozs. nuts, chopped	⅓ cup nuts, chopped
2½ tsp. baking powder	½ tsp. baking powder
2 tsp. soda	½ tsp. soda
2 tsp. salt	½ tsp. salt

Method

Cream butter, sugar, and salt, adding eggs slowly. Add strained bananas and chopped nuts. Sift together dry ingredients and blend into creamed mixture. Stir in milk gently. Put mixture into paper-lined loaf tin and bake at 350° F.

Walnut Kirsch Bombe

10 eggs	5 eggs
12 ozs. sugar	¾ cup sugar
14 ozs. butter	⅞ cup butter
10 ozs. cake flour	1¼ cups cake flour
7 ozs. cornstarch	scant ½ cup cornstarch
⅓ oz. baking powder	1 tsp. baking powder
5 ozs. nuts, ground	⅝ cup nuts, ground
2½ ozs. kirsch liqueur	1¼ ozs. kirsch liqueur
1 lb. 4 ozs. glazed cherries	1¾ cups glazed cherries
¼ tsp. salt	dash salt
vanilla	vanilla
1 lemon rind, grated	½ lemon rind, grated

Method

Soak cherries and nuts in kirsch liqueur. Cream together the butter, sugar, salt, vanilla, and rind. Add eggs one at a time, beating after each addition. Sift together the flour, starch, and baking powder. Blend into cream mixture. Add the nut and cherry mixture to the batter. Pour batter into a greased, floured baking tin and bake at 300° F. When cold, ice with sweet chocolate and decorate with almond slivers and cherries.

Hawaiian Pineapple Loaf

9 eggs	4 eggs
5 ozs. sugar	$\frac{1}{4}$ cup sugar (generous)
5 ozs. almond paste	$2\frac{1}{2}$ ozs. almond paste
$8\frac{1}{2}$ ozs. cake flour	1 cup cake flour
$\frac{3}{4}$ tsp. baking powder	$\frac{1}{4}$ tsp. baking powder (generous)
5 ozs. pineapple cubes	$\frac{1}{2}$ cup pineapple cubes
$1\frac{1}{2}$ ozs. maraschino liqueur	$\frac{3}{4}$ oz. maraschino liqueur
1 lemon rind, grated	$\frac{1}{2}$ lemon rind, grated
$\frac{1}{4}$ tsp. salt	dash salt

Method

Cream slightly the butter, sugar, almond paste, liqueur, rind, and salt. Blend in the sifted flour and baking powder. Stir in pineapple quickly. Pour dough into paper-lined loaf tin. Bake at 300° F. When cold, glaze with hot apricot jam. Apply a thin layer of fondant icing and decorate with cherries and pineapple rings.

Tea Loaf a la Tosca

9 eggs	4 eggs
8 ozs. sugar	$\frac{1}{2}$ cup sugar
10 ozs. butter	$\frac{5}{8}$ cup butter
4 ozs. almonds, ground	$\frac{1}{2}$ cup almonds, ground
4 ozs. almond paste	2 ozs. almond paste
6 ozs. krokant (*See Index*)	3 ozs. krokant (*See Index*)
6 ozs. cake flour	$\frac{3}{4}$ cup cake flour
6 ozs. cornstarch	$\frac{3}{8}$ cup cornstarch
$\frac{1}{2}$ oz. baking powder	2 tsp. baking powder
$\frac{1}{4}$ tsp. salt	dash salt
1 lemon rind, grated	$\frac{1}{2}$ lemon rind, grated
$\frac{1}{4}$ tsp. nutmeg	dash nutmeg
vanilla	vanilla

Method

Cream together the butter, almond paste, sugar, and flavoring. Add eggs one at a time, stirring continuously. Sift together the flour, cornstarch, and baking powder. Fold carefully into creamed batter. Blend in chopped krokant and ground almonds. Pour into greased, floured tins and bake at 325° F. After baking, sprinkle with finely ground krokant.

Date Loaf

4 lbs. pitted dates	1 lb. pitted dates
$1\frac{1}{3}$ ozs. baking soda	2 tsp. baking soda
4 lbs. boiling water	2 cups boiling water
8 ozs. shortening	4 tbsp. shortening
8 ozs. butter	$\frac{1}{4}$ cup butter
3 lbs. 4 ozs. brown sugar	$3\frac{1}{2}$ cups brown sugar
12 eggs	3 eggs
4 lb. cake flour	4 cups cake flour
$\frac{3}{4}$ oz. salt	1 tsp. salt
vanilla	vanilla

Method

Pour boiling hot water over the dates and baking soda and allow to soak over night. Cream together the butter, shortening, and brown sugar. Add eggs, one at a time. Add vanilla and salt, then add date mixture to the dough. Blend in sifted flour. Bake in paper-lined loaf tins at 325° F. Decorate with glazed cherries.

Note: To keep the loaves moist for any length of time, wrap in foil or cellophane.

Cherry Loaf

10 eggs	5 eggs
1 lb. butter	1 cup butter
1 lb. 14 ozs. sugar	$1\frac{7}{8}$ cups sugar
$\frac{3}{4}$ pint milk	$\frac{3}{4}$ cup milk
1 lb. 13 ozs. cake flour	$1\frac{3}{4}$ cups cake flour
$\frac{1}{2}$ oz. baking powder	$1\frac{1}{2}$ tsp. baking powder
$\frac{1}{2}$ oz. salt	$1\frac{1}{2}$ tsp. salt
1 lemon rind, grated	$\frac{1}{2}$ lemon rind, grated
1 orange rind, grated	$\frac{1}{2}$ orange rind, grated
juice of $\frac{1}{2}$ lemon	juice of $\frac{1}{4}$ lemon
vanilla	vanilla
$1\frac{1}{2}$ lbs. glazed cherries	2 cups. glazed cherries

Method

Cream together the butter, sugar, salt, juice, and vanilla. Add eggs one at a time, beating after each addition and scraping the bowl frequently. Roll cherries in flour to cover lightly. Using a mixer on low speed, add milk to cream mixture. Blend in the sifted flour and baking powder, followed by the cherries. Mix thoroughly. Bake in paper-lined loaf tins at 300° F. After baking place three cherry halves on top. Wrap as described under "Date Loaves" *(see Index)* to preserve moistness.

Marble Cake Loaf

Use the cherry loaf formula without the cherries. Add three ounces ($1\frac{1}{2}$ squares) semi-sweet, melted chocolate to one-half of the cake batter. Instead of chocolate, two ounces cocoa (4½ tbsp.) may be mixed with a little warm sugar syrup and used in its place. For a beautiful marble effect, pour the dark and light batter in alternating layers into a container. Then pour desired amount into paper-lined loaf tins. Bake at 300° F.

Arancini Loaf

27 eggs	7 eggs
17 egg yolks	4 egg yolks
1 lb. 10 ozs. sugar	¾ cup sugar (generous)
1 lb. 13 ozs. cake flour	1¾ cups cake flour (generous)
10 ozs. butter	¼ cup butter (generous)
12 ozs. cubed, candied orange peel	½ cup cubed, candied orange peel
vanilla	vanilla

Method

Proceed as described under "Method for Warm Sponge Cakes." (*See Index*.) Add chopped orange peel last. Bake in paper-lined loaf tins at 350° F. Decorate with candied orange peel.

CREAM-FILLED CAKES FOR DESSERTS AND PARTIES

Mocha Cake

Slice a Vienna sponge cake into three layers. Spread first layer with apricot jam topped with mocha butter cream. Set second layer on top. Drench with rum-flavored sugar syrup and spread with mocha butter cream. Top with third layer. Spread top with hot apricot jam and glaze with thin layer of mocha fondant. Spread sides of cake with cream and cover thoroughly with sliced, toasted almonds.

Mocha Walnut Cake

Slice a walnut cake into three layers. Drench bottom and second layer with coffee liqueur. Join layers with walnut butter cream. Spread sides and top with walnut butter cream and decorate with chopped nuts and walnut halves.

Cherry Walnut Cake

Slice a walnut cake into four layers. Drench every layer with cherry-flavored syrup. Spread each layer with cherry butter cream. On bottom layer cover cream with chopped, tart cherries. When layers are joined, spread top and sides with butter cream and decorate with glazed cherries and walnut halves.

Cherry Almond Cake

Slice an almond butter cake into several layers and drench each layer with maraschino liqueur. Spread each layer with lemon butter cream sprinkled with chopped, glazed cherries. Outside of cake is spread with the butter cream. Sides are decorated with macaroons.

Venetian Cake

Cut an almond sponge cake into several layers. Join layers with lemon and orange cream alternately. Cover a bottom layer of shortbread with butter cream and mixed fruits. Set almond sponge layers on top. Cover outside of cake with a thin layer of cream followed by a thin layer of marzipan. Gondolas are of chocolate.

Lemon Cream Cake

Cut a Vienna sponge cake into several layers. Join the layers with lemon butter cream and whipped cream alternately. Spread jam on top. Glaze with white, lemon-flavored fondant icing. Decorate with almond halves and lemon slices.

Orange Cream Cake

Slice a royal honey sponge cake into several layers and drench each with sweetened orange juice. Join with orange butter cream and whipped cream alternately. Spread top with jam. Ice with orange-colored and orange-flavored fondant. Glazed orange sections are used as the basic decorating medium.

Diplomat Cake

Use two layers of white sponge cake and three layers of puff paste. Join the layers alternately with custard cream. For finer flavor add whipped cream to the custard. Drench the sponge layers with rum-flavored sugar syrup. Decorate sides with butter cream and toasted nuts. Ice top with lemon fondant.

Mocha cake decorated with almonds and cherries

Mocha walnut cake

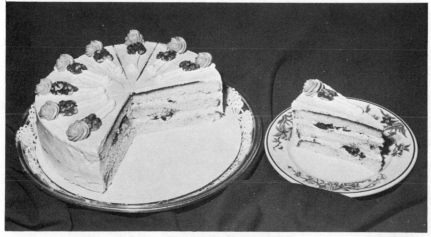

Cherry walnut cake

Cherry almond cake decorated with macaroons

Venetian cake decorated with chocolate gondolas

Lemon cream cake decorated with almond halves and lemon slices

Cherry Krokant Cake

Two layers of chocolate cake and two layers of white sponge cake are joined alternately as follows. Spread *krokant* butter cream on two bottom layers and kirsch-flavored butter cream on two top layers. Make a round of chopped cherries in the center of each layer, and put more butter cream in the center of each layer than is used on the outer edges. In this way the cake will form a dome shape. The sides and top of the dome are spread with apricot jam and covered with green marzipan. The cake is then glazed with chocolate and decorated with cherries.

Praline Nougat Cake

Sprinkle two layers of Sacher cake and two layers of macaroon cake with Jamaica rum. Join the first with raspberry jam to form the base, and top with the remaining layers joined with nougat butter cream. Ice with milk chocolate and decorate with nougat pralines.

Pineapple Cake

Join six thin layers of almond cake with pineapple butter cream. Wrap cake in a thin layer of marzipan. Decorate with glazed, sliced pineapple and finish sides with chocolate truffles.

Florentine Cake

Join three or four layers of sponge cake with almond butter cream. Glaze with semi-sweet chocolate. Bake one layer of *Florentiner (see Index)* the same size as the cake. Divide into the desired number of pieces and place on top of the cake.

Chocolate Macaroon Cake

Join two layers of macaroon cake and two layers of chocolate sponge cake. Drench the chocolate layers with curacao liqueur, and spread each layer with rum butter cream. Wrap cake in thin layer of marzipan. Ice semi-sweet or milk chocolate. Decorate with macaroons wholly or partially dipped in chocolate.

Dobosh Torte

Join six or eight layers of dobosh cake with rum nougat butter cream. Cover outside of cake as well. Glaze top layer separately with caramel. Cut into desired number of pieces and place on top of cake. Chocolate may be substituted for caramel or a combination of the two may be used.

Strawberry Cake à la Romanoff

Place a thick ring of rose-colored butter cream around the outside edge of a baked round of puff paste. Fill center with the following mixture: Whip one-quarter pint of whipping cream until stiff. Fold in chopped strawberries, fresh or frozen. Cover the filling with a layer of sponge cake. Spread top and sides of cake with more whipped cream. Decorate with marzipan strawberries.

Malakoff Torte

Use a $\frac{1}{2}$" high chocolate layer cake and sprinkle with curaçao liqueur. Top with four layers of lady fingers, alternating with four layers of Parisienne cream. Decorate with lady fingers, whipped cream, and chocolate chips.

Berlin Meringue Cake

Join four thin layers of Butter Cake with hot apricot jam, and cover the top layer with apricot halves. Cover top and sides generously with meringue. Using a pastry bag with medium star tube, form spiral on top of cake. The bands of the spiral should be about $\frac{1}{4}$" apart. Fill in open spaces with raspberry jam. Sprinkle cake with powdered sugar. Brown slightly in hot oven with over-heat only.

Chocolate Cream Cake

Slice a chocolate cake into three layers. Join the first two layers with raspberry jam, and the second and third layers with vanilla-flavored whipped cream. Ice with chocolate fondant. Decorate with marzipan flowers.

Chestnut Cake

Slice a ½″ high Parisienne cake into two layers. Spread a thin layer of jam on the first layer. Cover thinly with chestnut fudge. Spread fudge with jam and top with second cake layer. Wrap cake in pale green marzipan. Decorate with chestnuts molded from fudge.

Belvedere Torte

Join three layers of walnut cake with the following cream: Beat whipping cream until stiff. Flavor with toasted, ground filberts. Ice with lemon fondant and decorate with mignon desserts. (*See Index.*)

Madeira Roulade Cake

Use a ½″ Dutch cake as base, and drench with maraschino-flavored sugar syrup. Spread top with apricot jam. Cut ¼″ thick slices of Madeira Roulade *(see Index)* and place on top of cake. Glaze with neutral, transparent jelly.

Rum Punch Cake

Slice a sponge cake into three layers. Remove center layer. Spread jam on inside of top and bottom layers. Put center layer with leftover cake pieces in a bowl and sprinkle with Jamaica rum and sugar syrup. Mix loosely but do not mash. Put the mixture between the two cake layers and spread the top and sides with apricot jam. Ice with rum fondant.

Note: To obtain an attractive marble effect, put a little melted chocolate in a small paper tube. Cut a small opening at the end. Use warmed fondant to ice the cake, then make diagonal lines with the chocolate over the cake's surface. With a toothpick trace horizontal lines across the chocolate lines in alternate directions. Serve cake with vanilla sauce.

Royal Cocoanut Cake

Slice a Royal Honey sponge cake into two layers. Fold a little whipped cream into vanilla custard and flavor with rum. Spread mixture between layers. Cover cake with cooked marshmallow topping. (*See Index.*) Sprinkle sides and top with shredded cocoanut.

Truffle Cake

Split a chocolate cake into four layers. Join with two layers of rum-flavored chocolate butter cream and one layer of white butter cream mixed with little truffles. Ice with semi-sweet chocolate. Decorate sides with chocolate decorettes. Decoration on top consists of marzipan balls dipped in milk chocolate and rolled in decorettes.

Almond Cream Cake

Slice an almond butter cake into four layers, sprinkle with maraschino liqueur. Join the layers with marzipan butter cream (soften a little marzipan with egg yolks and blend into butter cream). Wrap cake in a thin layer of marzipan. Decorate with whipped cream-filled *canolli* rolls. (*See Index.*)

Wine Cream Cake

Bake a shortbread shell in a cake tin of desired size. Put a thin layer of sponge cake in the bottom of the shell. Fill shell with wine cream *(see Index)*. Cover top with alternating rings of green and blue grapes. Glaze with wine jelly. Decorate sides with toasted almond slivers.

Peach Cake

Bake a 10″ round of puff paste. Spread with jam and place a thin layer of cake on top. Add fresh peach halves and glazed cherries. Top with jelly.

Mandarin Cake

Slice an almond sponge cake into three layers. Mix finely chopped oranges and a little orange juice into butter cream. Spread this mixture between the layers and on the top and sides of the cake. Decorate top with mandarin orange sections, grapes, and cherries. Top with jelly.

Cherry Jubilee Cake

Thicken the juice of black cherries with cornstarch (¼ teaspoon for two cups of juice). Let boil. Add a few drops of almond extract and grated lemon rind. Pour mixture into a baked puff paste shell. Decorate with whipped cream.

Orange cream cake with glazed orange sections

Diplomat cake decorated with butter cream and toasted nuts

Cherry, dome-shaped *krokant* cake.

Praline nougat cake

Pineapple cake

Florentine cake

Chocolate macaroon cake

Dobosh cake

Strawberry cake *a la* Romanoff

Malakoff *Torte* topped with lady fingers and shredded chocolate

Berlin meringue cake

Chocolate cream cake decorated with marzipan flowers

Chestnut cake decorated with fudge chestnuts

Belvedere *Torte* decorated with mignon desserts

Madeira roulade cake

Rum punch cake

Royal coconut cake

Truffle cake

Almond cream cake decorated with *canolli* rolls

Wine cream cake decorated with grapes and almonds

Peach cake

Mandarin cake decorated with orange sections, grapes, and cherries.

Cherry jubilee cake

Checkerboard cake

Lemon cream cheese cake

Whipped cream cake decorated with cherries

Apple Cake

Line the bottom and sides of a cake tin with cooky dough or puff paste. Prick holes in dough. Fill with a mixture of sliced apples, a few raisins, grated orange peel, cinnamon, and sugar. Sprinkle a little melted butter on top. Bake at 350° F. for about ten minutes.

Meanwhile prepare the following topping: Blend together one and one-half ounces sugar, one ounce cornstarch, one ounce melted butter, a quarter-pint milk, and vanilla. Fold in two stiffly beaten egg whites. Pour mixture on top of cake. Sprinkle with sliced almonds. Continue baking until topping is cooked. When cold, sprinkle with powdered sugar.

Apple Meringue Cake

Line the bottom and sides of a cake tin with cooky dough or puff paste and bake. Cook the following filling: sliced apples, raisins, sugar, cinnamon, grated lemon rind, candied orange peel, and a little butter. Fill the baked shell with the mixture. Form a lattice on top with stiffly beaten egg whites. Sprinkle with sliced almonds or filberts, and brown in hot oven.

French Apple Cake

Line a cake tin with cooky dough and bake. Fill to a depth of $\frac{1}{4}''$ with cinnamon-flavored custard cream. Cover custard with a thin layer of sponge cake. Place apple slices on top. Place a second tin under the first to prevent burning and bake until the apples are soft.

Checkerboard Cake

Use two layers of Sacher *torte* and two layers of almond butter cake. (*See Index.*) Cut into strips. Assemble the strips with almond butter cream, alternating the colors. Form checkerboard design on top with either fondant or butter cream.

Lemon Cream Cheese Cake

2 qts. milk	2 cups milk
4 eggs	1 egg
4 ozs. cornstarch	2 tbsp. cornstarch
1 lb. sugar	$\frac{1}{2}$ cup sugar (generous)
2 lbs. cream cheese	8 ozs. cream cheese
dash salt	pinch salt
vanilla	vanilla
3 lemon rinds, grated	1 lemon rind, grated
juice of 2 lemons	juice of $\frac{1}{2}$ lemon
6 gelatine leaves or	scant tbsp. gelatine
1 oz. crystallized gelatine	

Method

Place gelatine in a saucepan with a little of the milk and heat until dissolved. Set aside. Blend together the eggs, salt, cornstarch, rind, juice, and vanilla. Liquify the mixture with a little milk and whip in the gelatine. Bring the remaining milk and sugar to a boil and swiftly stir in the egg-gelatine mixture. Continue boiling until mixture thickens.

Place cream cheese in mixer and soften slowly with the custard until all ingredients are well blended. In the bottom of a cake tin place a 1″ layer of sponge cake. Pour cheese mixture over it and chill. Decorate with whipped cream. Mixture yields two 9″ cakes.

Whipped Cream Cake

Line a cake tin with shortbread and bake. Top shortbread with layers of sponge cake joined with kirsch-flavored butter cream. Decorate with vanilla-flavored whipped cream, cherries, and chocolate decorettes.

INTRODUCTION TO CAKE DECORATING

The cake is the queen of international cuisine. The wide range of materials available for decorating gives us an infinite variety from which to choose.

The public's taste in art has changed throughout the years, and to a certain extent this change has affected culinary art as well. In the past, cakes decorated with the complex loops and whirls typical of the Roccoco period were considered artistically acceptable. Although it is still in use on some occasions, this old-fashioned style has

73

been replaced with modern designs. European professionals have adopted the modern methods, whereby decorating lines have become finer and straighter, eliminating the thick curves which often create a clumsy appearance.

I shall always remember my first encounter with modern cake decoration during a culinary art exhibition at a Viennese vocational school. While most entries were decorated in the usual old-fashioned manner, one chef entered a cake not more than ½″ high, iced flawlessly with white icing. On the left side was one thin straight line drawn vertically, crossed by another line horizontally near its lower end. On the opposite side was one dark red caramel rose with a green stem and three slightly curved leaves. The writing was in pencil-thin chocolate lines, with letters slightly abstract in design. The effect of that one rose left other entries with up to a dozen roses far behind.

A word should also be said about coloring. Many decorated cakes that I have seen over the years would have deserved an A *1* classification if the colors had not been used so freely. Colors should be treated very carefully. It is absolutely unnecessary to have cream leaves as green as nature grows them. There is hardly anything more irritating to a civilized eye than a cake displaying all the colors of the rainbow at the same time.

The following section contains a variety of ideas, and shows the different styles in decorating. Most decorations utilize a little of the traditional method and a little of the modern style to suit the average person's taste.

The modern influence is extremely noticeable wherever marzipan animals are used. Years ago, these figures were molded in cast-iron forms which showed every hair, leaving absolutely nothing to the imagination. Modern animals would represent motion rather and tend to display a certain humorous characteristic which seldom fails to impress a customer or guest. For example, in the body of a rabbit the exact placement of its hairs is unimportant. The emphasis is put on the animal's motion and ears.

Whenever flowers are used, both systems are workable. Replicas of real flowers as well as plants and blossoms in modern style are acceptable.

The following section presents a large variety of decorated cakes in traditional as well as in modern style. The materials are explained in the accompanying descriptions.

THE ART OF WRITING

The appearance of a cake is greatly influenced by the quality of the inscription. The writing style and letters must be in harmony with the general style of the decorations.

The following illustrations show the most common types of inscriptions. The samples are written in such a way that even the most inexperienced writer should be able to master them after a short period of practice. The creation of the many different writing types depends upon the tools and materials used. Next to the all-important paper tube we might use an icing bag with a small tube or a set of cutters for marzipan lettering. The list of materials is headed by the most commonly used white royal icing and black royal chocolate icing. (*See Index,* "Icings.") After these two mediums are all kinds of creams, piping jelly, and chocolate plastic. All writing substances which are to be pressed through a small opening must be perfectly smooth and free of sugar crystals or other clogging materials.

The distribution of an inscription depends upon the size of cake and type of decoration. The following examples show what is right and what is wrong.

The illustration on the left shows a wrong arrangement which is unfortunately very often seen in pastry or bake shops. The letters are too big and clumsy, thus crowding the rest of the decorations on the extreme outside edge.

To obtain fine, delicate writing as previously mentioned. the paper tube is very important. The following illustrations show how to make a durable, sharp-pointed tube.

The Basic Technique of Writing

Method 1

The paper tube is held with the right hand, which also applies the necessary pressure to

74

Telegram-styled Sacher cake. The fine print has been done with a brush using chocolate color. The large letters from white and chocolate icings. Sides decorated with almond macaroons.

This anniversary cake is made of Sacher *Torte,* iced with fondant. Flowers of pale-yellow butter cream and side decorated with almond macaroons.

RIGHT

WRONG

An inscription improperly and properly placed.

The preparation and manipulation of writing materials

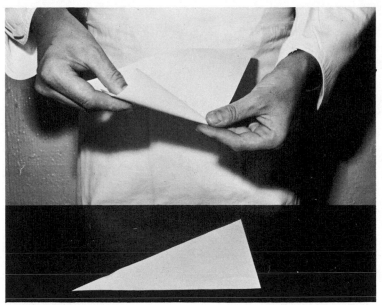

Use a triangular-shaped piece of parchment or waxed paper, and begin turning.

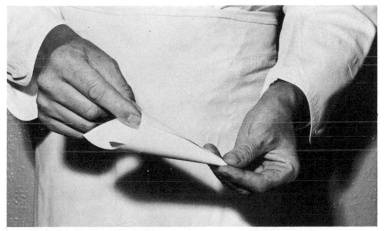

The end must be closed tight, to prevent the paper from uncoiling.

The tube is filled and closed tightly.

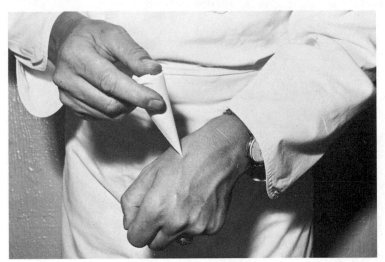

At this point, the writing end of the tube must be needle-sharp.

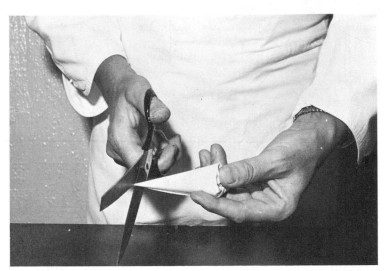

The opening is cut with a pair of scissors. The hole should be just large enough to allow a free and even flow.

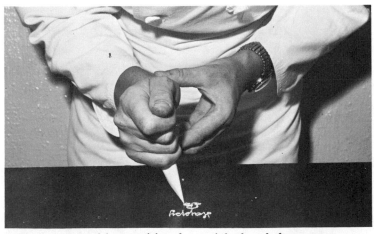

Correct writing position for a right-handed person.

guarantee an even flow of the writing material. The left hand lends support to steady and lead the right hand. This procedure, of course, is reversed with left-handed persons. The arms are kept close to the body and the hands held directly above the writing surface.

Method 2

This time the tube is held between the index and middle finger, while the thumb applies the pressure. The right hand rests on top of the left hand. This method is used when writing with white royal icing, and it is particularly advised for the old-fashioned Pearl Script.

Writing Exercises

Some writing exercises may be practiced with almost any kind of writing medium. Once the simple forms run evenly and smoothly from the tube, the real writing will cause no more problem than writing with a pen.

Decorative Cake Designs

Block Printing

Block printing must be executed very correctly with straight, fine lines. Double lines may be used at the first letter of every word, or those letters may be written slightly higher than the following letters.

Cursive Writing

The beginner with a cursive style writing, is advised to use very thin lines (marked with a knife) in order to get an equal height in all letters. The letters are not joined together as they would be in writing with a pencil. Instead, every letter is rounded individually, leaning slightly to the right. The fine lines may be combined with heavy up and down strokes.

Script Writing

Script writing looks very attractive, but requires much practice. Once mastered, however, it will enhance the appearance of any cake decorated in the traditional fashion.

Modern Style Printing

Modern style printing is neither bound to any specific group, nor does it have to be executed in a special manner. It is subject to fancy. Following are several combinations that will suit a number of different decorating styles.

Marzipan Letters

Marzipan letters are either cut or molded from differently colored marzipan.

Pre-Fabricated Inscriptions

Inscriptions that are pre-fabricated have various advantages. For the beginner, it is much easier to re-write a small strip of marzipan than having to re-ice the whole cake in the event of an error. For the busy professional it means fast service.

Since marzipan dries out quickly and thus becomes inedible, glycerine must be added before rolling. This will slow the drying time considerably. The signs should be shaped to suit the general appearance of the decorations.

HOW TO MAKE BUTTER CREAM FLOWERS

Butter Cream Roses

For making roses, a special rose tube is needed. Place tube inside of a waxed paper or pastry bag, and fill with smooth, colored butter cream. Hold flower stem in left hand and form the petals around the rosebud as illustrated. If roses in various shades are desired, put differently colored cream in layers inside the cream bag.

Apple Blossoms

Apple blossoms can be made right on the cake top. They consist of five petals which are overlapped in small rounds from the center. Use three-quarters of the bag's width for pink and the remaining quarter for white butter cream. Thus both colors will come from the bag simultaneously.

Daisy Blossoms

White butter cream is used for dressing the main flower and yellow cream for the flower's center.

Miscellaneous Flowers

Miscellaneous flowers can be made with differently shaped tubes. Experimenting with a variety of tubes will unfold many decorating possibilities.

V

ICINGS CREAMS AND FLAVORING MEDIUMS

Icings - Basic Formulas for Icings - The Creams - Custard Creams - Cooked Whipping-Cream Mixtures - Flavoring Mediums

ICINGS

The beautiful appearance of a cake, pastry, or dessert piece depends largely upon the quality of the icing. Icings may be colored as desired and must be applied very thinly. Pastel colors will look more elegant than brightly-colored icings. Properly iced pieces will have a high shine which will last for several hours. In order to obtain this shine it is necessary to study the pastry or dessert to determine its type of surface. If the top is dry it will naturally absorb the moisture from the icing. This will cause dullness a few minutes after application. To prevent this from happening, dry surfaces must be coated with a thin layer of hot apricot jam. The insulating jam layer will also serve another purpose. There are usually crumbs on top of cakes which will mix into the icings, especially when the icing is a little too cool or stiff. The jam will bind these loose pieces to make a smooth surface upon which the icing will flow easily.

Icings which have to be warmed before using, such as fondant, chocolate icing, and so forth, should never be heated directly over the open flame, as the sugar on the bottom will melt, which in turn will cause crystallization. This will destroy the shine of even the most expensive glaze. Icings should be warmed in a double boiler or in a bowl over hot water. If repeated warmings are necessary it is advisable to add a little fresh icing, as sugar will lose part of its shining and binding power during the repeated process.

Non-fat icings will harden very fast in dry climates or under hot summer conditions. Stirring a few drops of glycerine or egg whites into the icing before applications will help retain a smooth, flexible texture.

The flavoring of icings is just as important as the flavoring of cakes and creams. All icings which are to be flavored with fruit aromas should contain a few drops of lemon acid, lemon juice, or orange juice. This will give a delicate, piquant flavor to the icing. In the following chart some basic combinations are suggested.

Type of Icing	Color	Extracts and Flavoring	Uses
Fondant	white	maraschino, almond	french pastries, cakes
Water	white	vanilla or arrack	danish and puff pastries
Egg White	white	vanilla, almond	cookies and macaroons
Egg White	white	vanilla, lemon juice	cakes, writing medium
Fondant	yellow	vanilla	french pastries, cakes, desserts
Water	yellow	vanilla, lemon + juice	danish and puff pastries
Fondant	yellow	lemon, lemon juice	candies, pastries, etc.
Fondant	pink	rum or brandy	candies, pastries, etc.
Fondant	rose	rose water	fine petits fours
Fondant	red	strawberry, raspberry, lemon juice	fruit cakes, fruit pastries
Fondant	orange	orange or apricots, lemon juice	orange, apricot, peach desserts
Fondant	mocha	coffee, rum, nutmeg	mocha cakes, pastries
Fondant	pale green	pistachios, chartreuse	french pastries, cakes
Fondant	brown	chocolate, rum cocoa	french pastries, cakes

BASIC FORMULAS FOR ICINGS

Fondant

10 lbs. sugar	10 cups sugar
2 lbs. glucose	1¼ cups glucose
few drops blue coloring	few drops blue coloring

Method

Boil all ingredients together to the medium-ball stage, 242° F., as described under the "Boiling of Sugar." (*See Index.*) Pour sugar onto a wet marble slab. In places where a marble slab is not available, pour syrup into a steel bowl or saucepan and cool in ice water. Sprinkle top with

79

cold water to prevent formation of crust. Allow sugar to cool down to a luke-warm degree. Take a wooden spatula and mix, in a circular motion, until the sugar turns to a milky-white color and begins to harden. Scrape fondant together and cover with a hot, wet cloth. Let stand until sugar softens, then knead well and put fondant into a container. Cover with a wet cloth to keep the fondant soft and place lid on tightly. Avoid using aluminum utensils, as they will turn fondant gray.

If the fondant hardens unreasonably fast during the mixing process, it indicates that the sugar was boiled to too high a degree. Since there is a considerable difference between the various thermometers, the suggested 242° F. is to be taken as a basic degree.

When no thermometer is available use the following method to determine the degree. Form a loop ½″ in diameter at one end of a piece of wire. Dip the wire frequently into the boiling sugar solution. When the loop will hold a thin film of sugar, blow through it. If the sugar flies away in large bubbles (similar to soap bubbles) the approximate degree has been reached.

If the sugar has not been processed carefully enough from the start, crystallization may take place. As it is impossible to dispose of the crystals any other way, the whole boiling process must be repeated.

How to Warm Fondant

Put desired amount of fondant into a small saucepan, add flavoring and spices, and place container in hot water. Stir frequently until fondant becomes very warm. For a creamier consistency, liquify with sugar syrup. Blend in coloring and pour over cake, or dip French pastries into the fondant and set on a wire screen.

Note: Excess fondant which has been collected from the screens may be saved and cooked with five percent of its weight of glucose as described under "Fondant." (*See Index.*) The mixture thus obtained can be used for chocolate icing only.

Chocolate Icing 1

2 lbs. sugar	2¼ cups sugar
1 lb. water	1 cup water
5 ozs. cocoa	3½ tbsp. cocoa

Method

Mix all ingredients together and boil to 221° F., or crystal stage. Remove from heat and mix well with a wooden spoon until icing thickens. Ice the individual pieces and place them on a screen to allow the excess icing to run off. Then place them for a few minutes into a hot oven. This will help to make the icing dry with a high shine.

Chocolate Icing 2

6½ ozs. semi-sweet chocolate	3 squares semi-sweet chocolate
2 lbs. sugar	2¼ cups sugar
1 lb. water	1 cup water
vanilla	vanilla

Method

Melt chocolate and add other ingredients. Proceed as described in "Chocolate Icing *1*."

Egg-White Icing 1

egg whites	egg whites
powdered sugar	powdered sugar
vanilla	vanilla

Method

Put a few egg whites into mixer, using low speed. Slowly add sifted powdered sugar until icing becomes very creamy. Add flavoring. This type of icing is often applied before baking the goods and provides a crispy brown, shiny glaze. It is excellent for danish pastries, puff pastry, macaroons, sweet yeast doughs, et cetera.

Egg-White Icing 2

4 egg whites	4 egg whites
8 ozs. powdered sugar	¾ cup powdered sugar
1½ ozs. vinegar	⅛ cup vinegar
2 ozs. cornstarch	¼ cup cornstarch

Method

Beat all ingredients, except starch, together in a double boiler until hot. Continue beating until cold and stiff. Mix starch with a little water and add to above. Stir in two tablespoons of sugar syrup for a better shine. Dip the baked goods into the icing and set on trays. Dry them in a warm oven for a few minutes.

Chocolate icing. Flower arrangement made from butter cream. Writing in white royal icing.

White, lemon-flavored butter cream icing. Pale-green marzipan strip across center. Butter cream roses and hearts cut from marzipan filled with strawberry jelly. Writing in royal chocolate icing.

Pale pink, rum-flavored butter cream icing decorated with three dark-red marzipan roses with green leaves. Writing in royal chocolate icing. Side decorations are corrugated marzipan.

Pale yellow fondant icing. Butter cream flower arrangement. The writing and ornaments are royal chocolate icing and side decorations are white butter cream.

Pale green, almond-flavored butter cream. Ornamental flowers from éclair dough and writing in chocolate butter cream.

Orange fondant icing. Butter cream rosettes. Disks cut from plastic chocolate. Writing and ornamental design in royal chocolate icing.

Pale-blue fondant icing and plastic chocolate ornaments. The writing is royal chocolate icing.

This cloth-like effect is obtained by cutting a thin sheet of marzipan with different cooky and vegetable cutters and placing it on a chocolate-iced cake top. The flowers are also made of marzipan. Side decoration is butter cream and the writing is royal chocolate icing.

Cake decorated with marzipan flowers and animals. The merry-go-round is prefabricated.

Pale-blue fondant icing. The writing and ornaments are white and chocolate royal icing.

Pale-pink fondant icing. Carriage and side decoration made from marzipan, flower arrangement from cherries, angelica, and almonds. Writing in royal chocolate icing.

Pale-pink fondant icing. Hearts made from red caramel sugar and ornamental decorations from white royal icing. Flower, with cherry in center, is cut from marzipan and dried over a rolling pin.

Pale-green fondant base. Flowers modelled from marzipan and birds and writing from royal icing.

Cake covered with a thin layer of marzipan. Rings and hearts modelled from
marzipan and birds and writing from royal icing.

White fondant icing. Ornaments are marzipan and royal chocolate icing.

Water Icing

Add sifted powdered sugar to hot sugar syrup until a creamy paste is obtained. Add desired flavoring. Use a metal spatula to ice cold items, or a pastry brush for hot goods. Dry goods in a warm oven.

Lemon and Orange Icing

2 lemons or 2 oranges	2 lemons or 2 oranges
powdered sugar	powdered sugar

Method

Grate the rinds of the fruits into a small saucepan. Add a little water and the fruit juice. Blend in powdered sugar and whip until creamy. Proceed as in "Water Icing."

Marshmallow Topping (Cream)

1 qt. egg whites	5 egg whites
5 lbs. sugar	$1\frac{1}{3}$ cup sugar
juice of two lemons	juice of $\frac{1}{4}$ lemon
$\frac{1}{2}$ tsp. cream of tartar	pinch of cream of tartar
vanilla	vanilla

Method

Put sugar and lemon juice in sauce pan. Add enough water to moisten sugar thoroughly. Boil swiftly to 242° F. Whip whites with cream of tartar to medium-stiff froth. Pour hot sugar syrup into whites, continuing to beat at medium speed until marshmallow feels lukewarm to the touch. Add flavoring.

Royal Chocolate Icing

Place the desired amount of melted semi-sweet or bitter chocolate into a cup. Gradually add cold sugar syrup (see Index) or plain water until the chocolate becomes soft but firm enough to be used for writing or decorating. This type of icing is seldom used for any other purpose.

Royal Icing

4 egg whites	4 egg whites
1 lb. powdered sugar, approx.	$2\frac{1}{4}$ cups powdered sugar, approx.
pinch cream of tartar	pinch cream of tartar
drop of blue coloring	drop of blue coloring

Method

Use a non-corroding mixing bowl. Beat whites and cream of tartar until they begin to stiffen. Add sifted powdered sugar a little at a time. Add coloring. Continue beating and adding sugar until the mixture is creamy and stiff. Royal icing will dry quickly when exposed to air. Keep icing covered at all times with a wet rag. Royal icing is excellent for wedding cakes or ornamental purposes. When white royal icing is desired, a few drops of blue coloring will increase the whiteness.

Note: The amount of sugar recommended in the list of ingredients may vary with the size of the eggs used.

Cream Caramel Icing

1 lb. 8 ozs. sugar	$2\frac{3}{4}$ cups sugar
8 ozs. butter	1 cup butter
$\frac{3}{4}$ pint whipping cream	$\frac{3}{4}$ pint whipping cream
vanilla	vanilla

Method

Boil all ingredients together to 240° F. or medium-ball stage. Continue as described under "Fondant." (See Index.)

Fruit Icing

Use any amount of desired fruit juice. Strain juice through a cloth to remove the pulp. Add one tablespoon of lemon juice for each pint of juice. Blend in enough powdered sugar to get a smooth, fine paste. Spread icing with metal spatula onto pastries.

THE CREAMS

In the following section different formulas are given for butter and custard creams. These recipes can be easily altered to suit the individual's needs. In some parts of the country it is not economical to use one hundred percent butter, in which case, high-ratio vegetable shortening may be substituted. However, it must be emphasized that this will definitely affect the flavor of the cream. In many cases the few cents saved will result in lost dollars when the discriminating customers pass by the cheaper product.

I have purposely refrained from giving detailed

formulas on the flavoring of butter cream, as it is mainly a matter of individual taste. In all the formulas where cream is mentioned, as in "French Pastries and Cakes," it should be understood that the basic formula is used with the appropriate flavor medium. For example :

(1) Chocolate cream — butter cream with melted chocolate
(2) Nougat cream — butter cream with nougat
(3) Mocha cream — butter cream with strong coffee
(4) Krokant cream — butter cream with crushed krokant
(5) Chestnut cream — butter cream with mashed chestnuts

How to obtain the flavoring mediums is described in the section immediately following "The Creams."

Practical Suggestions Concerning Creams

Since butter's ability to absorb moisture is very limited, care must be taken that colors or flavors are of a thick or creamy consistency rather than liquid. In other words, coffee, tea, et cetera should be prepared with very little water, giving enough flavor to the cream without causing the baker to face the almost impossible task of beating liquid into fat. If the butter cream is too cold to begin with, trouble may develop even with the thickened flavors. In this case the cream should be warmed just enough to allow the substances to bind. When warming butter cream, take into consideration that the mixing bowl will stay warm for some time. It is therefore important not to warm it too much.

Butter cream should always be mixed in non-corrosive bowls. The cream will turn gray in aluminum utensils.

When mashed fruits are used in butter cream, it is advisable to use fewer eggs in order to ensure the smooth binding of all ingredients.

Custard Creams

Some general rules apply to the formulas for creams or puddings. The sugar and approximately two-thirds of the milk should be boiled together.

The rest of the ingredients are mixed into the remaining one-third of milk with a hand beater. The latter is then quickly poured into the boiling milk and removed from the heat as soon as it has thickened. A double boiler is a good investment, as it completely eliminates the danger of burning the mixture.

When stored away, custard cream will form a crust or skin on top. In order to prevent this, a sheet of buttered paper should be placed over the entire surface of the cream.

Butter Cream 1

1 lb. butter	1 cup butter
13 ozs. powdered sugar	1 cup powdered sugar
8 eggs	4 eggs
flavoring	flavoring

Method

Cream butter with one-half of sugar. Beat eggs with remaining sugar until fluffy. Blend into first mixture. Flavor as desired. The cream will be very light and excellent for fillings.

Butter Cream 2

1 lb. 8 ozs. butter	1½ cups butter
10 ozs. powdered sugar	¾ cup powdered sugar
2½ ozs. cornstarch	⅛ cup cornstarch
4 egg yolks	2 egg yolks
1 quart milk	1 pint milk
vanilla	vanilla

Method

Mix cornstarch in a little of the milk. Boil together the starch, milk, egg yolks, sugar, and vanilla. Stir constantly until thick. Remove from heat and let cool completely. Cream butter. Slowly add the milk mixture.

French Butter Cream

15 ozs. sugar	1 cup sugar
1½ ozs. glucose	1 tbsp. glucose
1 lb. 1 oz. butter	1¼ cups butter
4 eggs	2 eggs

Method

Boil sugar and glucose with a little water to 232° F. or soft-ball stage. Beat eggs, adding sugar

82

Ornaments rest on heavy fruit-cake bases, iced with white and pink royal icing.

Dark fruit cake wrapped in marzipan and iced white with royal icing. The top is made from sugar plastic and the vase from casted sugar.

Dark Christmas cake base with corrugated marzipan on the side. Other decorations entirely from white sugar plastic.

Base of Sacher *Torte* and a second layer of pound cake. Ornaments from white and pink royal icings and plastic sugar.

Lemon fondant icing. Flowers are modelled from pale-pink marzipan with cherry centers. Leaves cut from honey dew melon and writing in royal chocolate icing.

Heart-shaped sponge cake, iced with pink, rum-flavored fondant. Flowers made from differently colored royal icing and leaves cut from angelica.

Yellow fondant icing, vanilla-flavored with a pale-green marzipan strip across center. Flowers and leaves modelled from marzipan and decorated with royal chocolate icing. Cake base, decorated with silver dragées.

Cake covered with pastel marzipan. Basket cut from pound cake, fondant iced. Remaining decorations are royal chocolate icing. Flower petals from colored butter cream.

Pale orange-flavored fondant icing. Hearts molded from strawberry jelly. Marzipan flowers. Side decoration are corrugated marzipan.

Pink rum-flavored fondant icing. Hearts made from strawberry jelly. Pale-pink
marzipan strip laid across center and ornaments and writing are royal chocolate
icing.

Semi-sweet chocolate icing. Three roses modelled from red-colored caramel sugar.

Heart-shaped cake, marzipan covered. Royal chocolate icing used for stems and leaves as well as for writing.

Pale-blue fondant icing. Vase, stems, and flowers are made from marzipan. Writing is royal chocolate icing.

mixture slowly. Beat until cool. When fruit cream is desired, mix without eggs and add fruit purée to equal the amount of eggs left out. Stir in butter and cream well.

Butter Cream—Custard Combination

1 lb butter	1 cup butter
7 ozs. powdered sugar	¾ cup powdered sugar
1 pint custard cream	1 cup custard cream
flavoring	flavoring

Method
Cream butter and sugar well. Slowly add custard cream with wooden spoon. Add flavoring and blend thoroughly.

Butter Cream—Marshmallow Combination

12 egg whites	4 egg whites
1 lb. 3 ozs. sugar	¾ cup sugar
1 lb. 8 ozs. butter	1 cup butter
vanilla	vanilla

Method
Boil sugar with a little water to 242° F. or soft-ball stage. Add it to stiffly-beaten egg whites. Continue beating until cold, adding the vanilla. Cream butter and add to the first mixture. Blend well.

Tea Butter Cream

5 ozs. sugar	⅓ cup sugar
8 egg yolks	4 egg yolks
1 oz. cornstarch	1 tbsp. cornstarch
½ oz. gelatine	2 tsp. gelatine
½ pint strong tea	½ cup strong tea
salt	salt
3 lbs. butter	3 cups butter

Method
Brew strong tea and dissolve gelatine in it. Mix starch in a little water. Add starch, yolks, sugar, and salt to tea. Boil until thickened. Cool mixture and add it to creamed butter.

CUSTARD CREAMS

Standard Custard

1 quart milk	1 pint milk
5 ozs. sugar	⅓ cup sugar
3 ozs. cornstarch	scant ¼ cup cornstarch
6 egg yolks	3 egg yolks
vanilla	vanilla

Method
Mix starch into a little milk, blend all ingredients together and boil until thickened, stirring constantly. Let cool.

Light Custard

1 quart milk	1 pint milk
5 ozs. sugar	⅓ cup sugar
3 ozs. cornstarch	scant ¼ cup cornstarch
10 egg yolks	5 egg yolks
10 egg whites	5 egg whites

Method
Mix starch into a little milk. Boil the starch, milk, yolks and vanilla until thickened. Beat egg whites with sugar until stiff. Blend whites quickly into hot custard. This cream must be used for fillings immediately after cooking.

Vanilla Cream

1½ quarts milk	3 cups milk
12 ozs. sugar	¾ cup sugar
4½ ozs. flour	½ cup flour
2 ozs. cornstarch	⅛ cup cornstarch
12 egg yolks	6 egg yolks
12 egg whites	6 egg whites
½ oz. gelatine	2 tsp. gelatine
vanilla	vanilla

Method
Soften gelatine in a little milk. Stir starch into a little milk. Boil together milk, one-half of the sugar, flour, starch, yolks, and gelatine until thickened. Beat egg whites with remaining sugar until stiff. Add one-half of the whites to boiling cream. Mix well. Blend in second half of whites. Use the cream hot.

Wine Cream

1 pint white wine	1 pint white wine
juice of 2 lemons and 1 orange	juice of 2 lemons and 1 orange
6 ozs. sugar	¾ cup sugar
8 egg yolks	8 egg yolks
5 egg whites	5 egg whites
¾ oz. gelatine	2 tbsp. gelatine

Method

Dissolve gelatine in a little milk. Over the heat, beat the wine, juices, sugar, yolks, and gelatine until hot and stiff. Remove from heat and beat until cold. Whip egg whites stiff. Blend into first mixture.

COOKED WHIPPING-CREAM MIXTURES

Parisienne Cream

1 quart whipping cream	1 pint whipping cream
2 lbs. semi-sweet chocolate	1 lb. semi-sweet chocolate
8 ozs. butter	½ cup butter
vanilla	vanilla

Method

Sliver chocolate with a knife. Boil the cream and vanilla. Add the chocolate and remove from heat. Allow chocolate to melt, stirring occasionally, then cool completely. Before using, cream the mixture thoroughly and blend in the butter. Jamaica rum will increase the fine flavor of the cream. Do not add more than two or three ounces of rum to the above formula.

Canache

16 ozs. sugar	1 cup sugar (generous)
13 ozs. whipping cream, heated	¾ cup whipping cream, heated
1 lb. butter	1 cup butter
vanilla	vanilla

Method

Melt sugar to caramel stage. Add hot cream slowly. When caramel is blended in well, add butter. Let cool completely. Cream well before using.

FLAVORING MEDIUMS

The well-known flavoring mediums in the food industry are divided into two groups.

(1) Natural flavors—fruits, et cetera.
(2) Chemically processed extracts.

It should be made clear at this point that artificial flavors are, in spite of the advances of chemistry, a far cry from the natural flavors.

Fruit purées are excellent for flavoring fine creams, pralines, puddings, and various sauces. No artificial flavor will ever be able to compete seriously with them. Fruit purées are easily prepared, and when stored away in a cool place, will last almost indefinitely.

Lemon and Orange Flavors

These flavors, combined with vanilla, are commonly used in cakes, cookies, yeast doughs, and so forth. The grated peel is mixed with the same amount of granulated sugar, put in a closed jar, and stored.

Strawberry Purée

Press berries through a sieve, then add one and one-half pound of sugar for each pound of berries. Cook berries and sugar for a few minutes. It is not necessary to add liquid, as most berries contain enough juice. Fill glass jars with the purée and cover tightly. The older the purée gets, the stronger the aroma and flavor will become.

Pineapple Purée

Peel the pineapple and cut into small pieces. Cook with sugar to equal the weight of the pineapple until tender. Do not sieve the pineapple, as this would result in a great loss of fruit. Store in glass jars.

Apricots and Peaches, Puréed

Remove stones from the fruit. Add sugar to equal half the weight of the fruit. Cook until tender and press through a sieve. Fill glass jars. Set covered jars on a wooden rack in a boiler containing a little water. Cover the jars with rags and allow to steam for approximately twenty minutes. Let cool before removing from boiler to prevent cracking of the glass.

Cherry Purée

Use ripe cherries. Proceed as directed.

Chocolate Syrup

1 quart water	1 pint water
2 lbs. sugar	2¼ cups sugar

White fondant icing. Basket and fruits made from marzipan and the grain and stems are ornamented with pale yellow and royal chocolate icings. Fruits are polished with sugar syrup.

Top of cake is covered with white marzipan. Ornaments are a combination of differently colored icings. Side decoration of toasted macadamia nuts.

Horn of plenty. Fruit and vegetables are free-modelled from marzipan. Writing in royal chocolate icing.

Dark orange-colored fondant icing. Ornaments made from chocolate icing. Witch cut from thin layer of chocolate plastic.

Dark orange-colored fondant. Ornaments from chocolate fondant. Pumpkins are modelled from orange marzipan. Side decorations are chocolate decorettes.

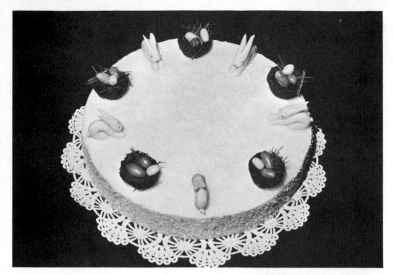

Cake covered with pale yellow marzipan. Nests molded from chocolate and shredded cocoanut. Eggs and rabbits are from marzipan. Grass is imitated with thinly chopped, dried marzipan. Side decorated with fine nuts.

Pale-green fondant icing. Chicks and hen molded from marzipan and flowers from cherries and angelica.

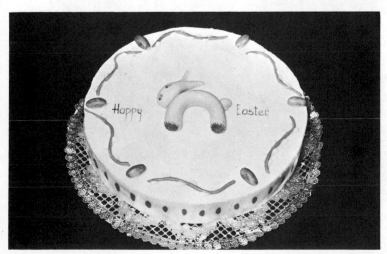

Pussy willows and rabbit made from marzipan set on fondant iced cake.

Pale-green fondant icing, overlapped with marzipan. Trees cut from green, pepper-mint-flavored jelly. The star is cut from marzipan. Royal chocolate icing.

White fondant icing. Trees painted with vegetable colors. Ornaments and writing from royal chocolate icing.

Pale-green fondant icing. Sheet music and bells cut from marzipan. Ornamenting and writing from royal chocolate icing.

Royal chocolate icing ornaments and writing on white fondant icing. Window's shadow is painted with vegetable colors.

Pale-blue fondant icing. Clock and dice made from marzipan, dotted with royal chocolate icing.

Pale-green fondant icing. Ornaments and writing in royal chocolate icing. Pigs modelled from pink marzipan.

1 lb. bitter chocolate	8 squares bitter chocolate
½ lemon	¼ lemon
½ orange	¼ orange
bay leaf	bay leaf
3 cloves	2 cloves
4 tbsp. rum	2 tbsp. rum

Method

Bring all ingredients except chocolate to a boil. Cook about five minutes, then strain. Add chopped chocolate. Store in glass jars in a cool place.

Coffee Syrup

2 lbs. sugar	1 cup sugar (generous)
1 pint strong, fresh coffee	1 cup strong, fresh coffee

Method

Cook sugar to *couleur*. *(See Index.)* Use the coffee to dilute the *couleur* instead of water. This will prevent the syrup from becoming too weak. Store in bottles.

Brown Nougat Purée

1 lb. filberts, toasted	1½ cups filberts, toasted (generous)
1 lb. sugar	1 cup sugar (generous)
8 ozs. bitter chocolate	4 squares bitter chocolate
vanilla	vanilla

Method

Roll the toasted filberts between two towels to remove skins. Cook sugar to light brown caramel. Add filberts, and cool. Grind mixture several times through a fine meat grinder until oily and soft. Add melted chocolate and vanilla. Store in jars until needed. If nougat becomes too hard, work it by hand until it becomes rollable.

White Nougat Purée

1 lb. almonds, blanched	2 cups almonds, blanched
1 lb. sugar	1 cup sugar
10 ozs. cocoa butter or hardened vegetable shortening	1¼ cups cocoa butter or hardened vegetable shortening

Method

Boil sugar with little water to 264° F. or light-crack stage. Add white almonds, and cool. Grind mixture several times through a fine meat grinder until oily and soft. Add melted fat. Store in a closed jar.

Liqueur

Liqueur may be used to increase the delicate flavors of fine creams and sauces. However, in different areas the commercial use of such liqueurs is restricted. A special permit must be obtained if the beverage used contains a certain percentage of alcohol.

These designs may be made with any kind of icing. They appear very difficult at first, but as soon as some simple combinations are mastered the rest is merely practice.

A B C D E F G
H I J K L M N
O P Q R S T U
V W X Y Z

A sample of block-printing style.

HAPPY BIRTHDAY
or
HAPPY BIRTHDAY

A sample of festive script writing.

Happy
Birthday

Happy   Merry
Birthday Christmas

Very thin lines characterize a cursive style.

Lettering in a modern style.

Marzipan letters.

Marzipan signs overlaid with script.

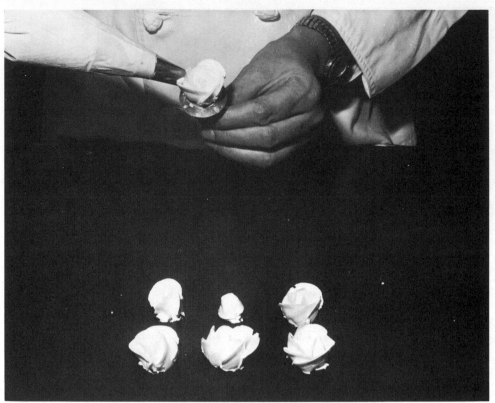

Designing cream roses.

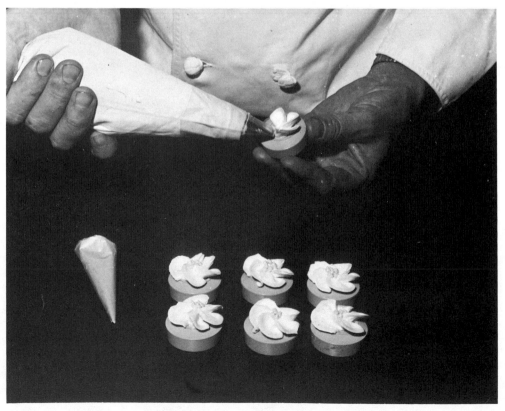

Apple blossoms made from butter cream.

Daisy blossoms made from butter cream.

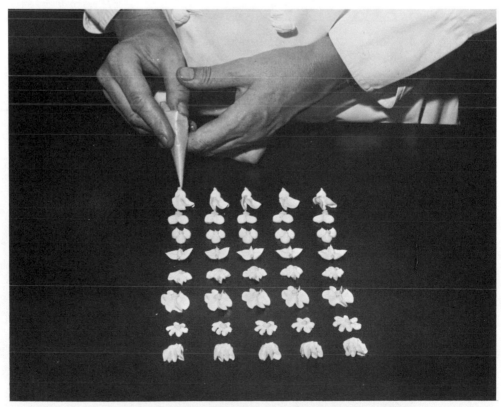

Blossoms made from butter cream.

VI

DESSERTS

Strudels - Cooked Sweet Desserts - Fritters - Soufflés, Omelettes, Pancakes - Ice Cream Desserts - Iced Drinks - Ice Cream *Bombes* - Ice Cream Cakes - Baked Accompaniments for Ice Cream Dishes - Pies - Fruit Cocktails - Sauces - Puddings

Strudels are a specialty which originated in Central Europe. They may be made of yeast dough, puff paste, or the Viennese pulled strudel dough. The first two types have been thoroughly covered in their respective sections in this book. Viennese strudel dough is made as follows:

Basic Strudel Dough

1 lb. bread flour	2 cups bread flour
1 oz. lard or shortening	1 tsp. lard or shortening
1 tsp. salt	¼ tsp. salt
¼–½ pint warm water	¼–½ cup warm water
2 egg yolks	1 egg yolk
1 tbsp, vinegar	½ tbsp. vinegar

Illustrated method for basic strudel dough

Vienna Apple Strudel

6 lbs. apples, peeled, cored, sliced	6 lbs. apples, peeled, cored, sliced
10 ozs. bread crumbs	2½ cups bread crumbs
3 ozs. butter	⅜ cup butter
8 ozs sugar	1 cup sugar
4 ozs. almonds, chopped	1 cup almonds, chopped
3 ozs. raisins	½ cup raisins
1 lemon rind, grated	1 lemon rind, grated
1 orange rind, grated	1 orange rind, grated
1 tsp. cinnamon	1 tsp. cinnamon

Method

Brown crumbs in butter and let them cool slightly. Sprinkle onto the pulled strudel dough. Distribute apples, raisins, and almonds evenly over dough. Sprinkle with sugar and cinnamon. Grate orange and lemon rinds over apples. Roll strudel and place on baking sheet. If strudel is too long, place it in horseshoe shape. Brush top with melted butter. Bake at 325° F. Serve hot or cold with apricot sauce.

Cherry Strudel

Use pulled strudel dough. Proceed as directed under "Vienna Apple Strudel." Use black, stoned cherries in place of apples.

Apricot Strudel

Proceed as described under "Vienna Apple Strudel," using stoned apricots instead.

Sour Cream Strudel

Prepare pulled strudel dough. Spread with filling given below. Roll the strudel and place in round cake tin. Brush top with melted butter. Bake at 325° F. to 350° F.

Filling

⅓ quart sour cream	1⅓ cups sour cream
1½ ozs. butter	3 tbsp. buter
1½ ozs. sugar	3 tbsp. sugar
1½ ozs. bread crumbs	⅜ cup bread crumbs
1 tbsp. flour	1 tbsp. flour
2 egg yolks	2 egg yolks
2 egg whites	2 egg whites
2 ozs. raisins	½ cup raisins
1 lemon rind, grated	1 lemon rind, grated
½ orange rind, grated	½ orange rind, grated

Method

Cream well the butter, one-half of the sugar, egg yolks, and flavoring. Mix in sour cream, followed by bread crumbs and flour. Beat egg whites stiff with remaining sugar. Blend into cream mixture. Spread filling on dough and sprinkle raisins over it. Bake as directed. Serve with vanilla sauce.

Cottage Cheese Strudel

8 ozs. cottage cheese, strained	1¼ cups cottage cheese, strained
2 ozs. butter	¼ cup butter
2 ozs. sugar	¼ cup sugar
4 egg yolks	4 egg yolks
½ lemon rind, grated	½ lemon rind, grated
4 egg whites	4 egg whites
2 tbsp. sour cream	2 tbsp. sour cream
2 ozs. raisins	scant ½ cup raisins
2 ozs. cake crumbs	⅔ cup cake crumbs

Method

Cream butter, sugar, and egg yolks. Add lemon rind, sour cream, raisins, and crumbs. Blend in stiffly-beaten egg whites. Spread filling on pulled strudel dough and roll. Place in round cake tin.

Brush top with melted butter. Bake at 325° F. to 350° F. Serve with caramel or vanilla sauce.

Farina Strudel

4 egg whites	4 egg whites
4 egg yolks	4 egg yolks
10 ozs. farina	1⅔ cups farina
7 ozs. butter	⅞ cup butter
6 ozs. sour cream	⅔ cup sour cream
dash salt	dash salt
3 ozs. bread crumbs	scant ¾ cup bread crumbs
1 lemon rind, grated	1 lemon rind, grated

Method

Cream half of the butter with sugar. Add egg yolks one at a time, beating after each addition. Add salt and lemon rind. Stir farina into sour cream and add to butter mixture. Blend in stiffly-beaten egg whites. Spread filling on pulled strudel dough and roll. Cut pieces 2″ to 3″ wide. Pinch together cut edges tightly. Boil in water with a little salt for fifteen minutes. Drain well. Brown crumbs in remaining butter and sprinkle over strudel pieces. Serve with plum compote.

Poppy Seed Strudel

2 ozs. sugar	¼ cup sugar
8 ozs. bread flour	2 cups bread flour
3 ozs. butter	⅜ cup butter
3 egg yolks	3 egg yolks
½ oz. yeast	1 cake yeast
1 tsp. salt	1 tsp. salt
½ pint milk	1 cup milk
1 lemon rind, grated	1 lemon rind, grated

Filling

7 ozs. poppy seed, ground	1½ cups poppy seed, ground
3 ozs. butter	6 tbsp. butter
1 pint milk	2 cups milk
3 ozs. sugar	⅜ cup sugar
3 tbsp. honey	3 tbsp. honey
1½ ozs. rum	1½ ozs. rum
2½ ozs. raisins	½ cup raisins (generous)
2 ozs. orange rind, grated	⅓ cup orange rind, grated
dash cloves	dash cloves
dash cinnamon	dash cinnamon

Method

Cook milk, sugar, butter, and honey until thickened, stirring constantly. Blend in remaining ingredients and let cool.

Roll yeast dough ¼″ thick. Spread filling on dough and roll. Egg wash and let rise. Bake at 350° F.

Mix dough as described under "Yeast Dough." *(See Index.)*

Walnut Strudel

Filling

7 ozs. walnuts, ground	1¾ cups walnuts, ground
1 pint milk	2 cups milk
3 ozs. sugar	⅜ cup sugar
3 ozs. cake crumbs	1 cup cake crumbs
2 tbsp. honey	2 tbsp. honey
dash cinnamon	dash cinnamon
1½ ozs. rum	1½ ozs. rum

Method

Using same yeast dough, proceed as directed under "Poppy Seed Strudel."

Fruit Strudels of Puff Paste

Roll strip of puff paste (*See Index.*) 8″ wide, ⅛″ thick and the full length of the baking sheet. Sprinkle cake crumbs over dough and cover surface with the desired fruit. Sprinkle fruit with sugar, cinnamon, and grated lemon rind. Add few drops of lemon juice. Cover fruits entirely or decorate with dough strips. Before baking, brush top with egg wash. Bake at 350° F. to 375° F. When almost baked, remove from oven and sprinkle with powdered sugar. Continue baking until the sugar has melted. For variation, glaze some pieces with hot apricot jam. Strudels may be served with suitable sauce, whipped cream or just plain.

Note: Warm strudels slightly before serving.

COOKED SWEET DESSERTS

Yeast Dumplings

1½ lbs. flour	3 cups flour
⅜ oz. yeast	⅜ cake yeast
3 ozs. sugar	3 tbsp. sugar
1¼ pints milk	1¼ cups milk
3 eggs	2 eggs
2 egg yolks	1 egg yolk
1 lemon rind, grated	½ lemon rind, grated
vanilla	vanilla

1. Sift flour onto table. Add salt, fat, vinegar, yolks, and water. Knead until dough becomes elastic and smooth and loosens from the table. Flour a tablecloth and set the ball of dough in center. Sprinkle a little flour on the dough and cover with a warmed bowl.

2. Let rest about twenty minutes. Roll dough flat with a rolling pin and brush entire surface lightly with warm butter.

3. Lift up dough onto the backs of the hands and pull dough slowly, working with a circular motion. When dough is paper-thin, lay it on the table and cut off the thick outside edges.

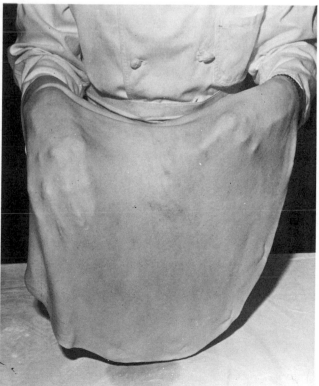

4. Add one of the fillings

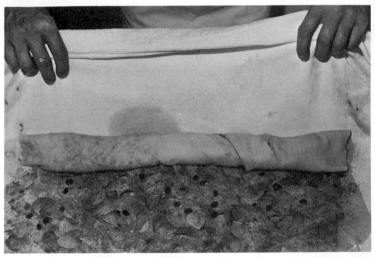

5. To roll strudel, lift up tablecloth on one end and roll up completely. Do not attempt to roll dough without cloth.

6. Place strudel on a lightly greased pan.

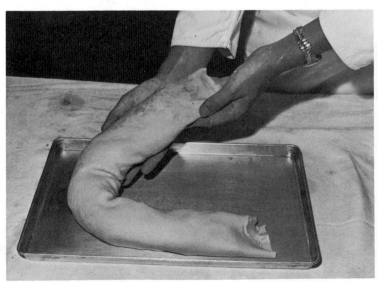

Baked poppy seed strudel.

Preparing poppy seed strudel.

Use firm, stoned apricot halves. Canned apricots must be dried thoroughly before placing on puff paste. Egg wash edges before securing top dough piece.

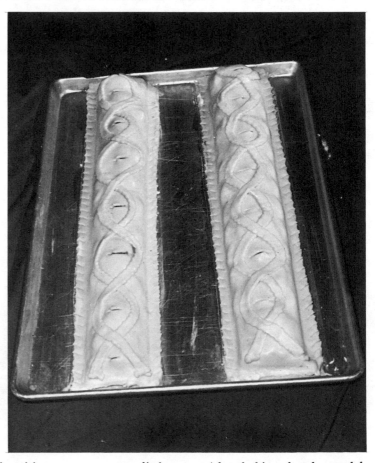

Sprinkle apples with raisins, currants, or a little rum. After baking, brush strudels with hot apricot jam.

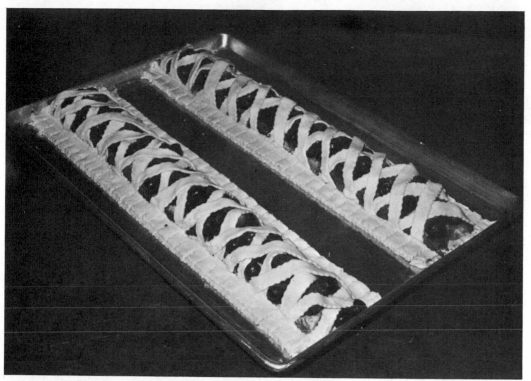

If canned cherries are used, drain fruits well. Sprinkle cherries with almond-flavored sugar syrup.

Cover strip of puff paste with strips of pineapple, papaya, and grapes. Decorate outside with dough strips. Brush with egg wash and bake at 300° F. to 325° F.

Apricot dumplings made with potato dough.

Apples in dressing gowns and decorated with rosettes.

Method

Prepare a firm dough according to general directions given under "Yeast Dough." (*See Index*.) Dough must be firm. Do not add all liquid at once.

Form smooth rolls of dough (1½ ozs. each). Flatten the individual pieces on floured table-top with rolling pin. Put plum jam in center. Fold dough ends over jam and form smooth balls by rolling them in floured hands. Set dumplings on board, cover with towel and let rise. Use a large utensil filled two-thirds with water. Add a little salt. Bring to a boil. Drop dumplings into the boiling water carefully. Boil, covered, for three or four minutes. Turn dumplings over in water and continue cooking for another three or four minutes. Prick with fork few times during cooking.

In another container prepare ground poppy seed, with sugar to taste, and melted butter. Roll dumplings into mixture, sprinkle with powdered sugar, and serve at once.

Note: To check proper cooking time, open one dumpling and test.

Apricot Dumplings of Potato Dough

2 lbs. potatoes	2 lbs. potatoes
1½ ozs. butter	3 tbsp. butter
1 egg	1 egg
8 ozs. bread flour	scant 2 cups bread flour
dash salt	dash salt

Method

Boil potatoes, peel, and press through strainer. Add rest of ingredients. Knead until dough becomes firm and smooth. Let rest about fifteen minutes. Form round balls, set on floured board, and flatten by hand. Remove stones from small apricots and replace with a sugar cube and a little cinnamon. Wrap apricots securely into flattened dough pieces. Roll dumplings smooth by hand and drop into boiling, salted water. Boil gently for four or five minutes. Drain, then rinse with luke warm water. Brown some bread crumbs in butter and roll dumplings in crumbs. Place finished dumplings in hot oven for a few minutes to crisp the surfaces. Dumplings may be rolled in ground poppy seed if so desired. Sprinkle with powdered sugar. Serve with vanilla sauce.

Plum Dumplings

Proceed as described under "Apricot Dumplings," using plums instead. For better flavor, sprinkle fruit with Jamaica rum before wrapping in dough.

Fruit Dumplings in Éclair Dough

¼ pint milk	1 cup milk
½ oz. sugar	1 tbsp. sugar
4 ozs. butter	½ cup butter
5 ozs. flour	1¼ cups flour
3-4 eggs	3-4 eggs
dash salt	dash salt

Method

Put the milk, salt, butter, and sugar in a saucepan and bring to a boil quickly. Stir in flour and cook until mixture clings together in a lump. Stir quickly and thoroughly. Remove from heat. Blend in eggs one at a time, stirring well after each addition. Dough should be firm. Let cool. Cut small pieces and wrap a plum or apricot in each piece. Drop dumpling in boiling, salted water. Let boil five or six minutes. Brown bread crumbs in butter and roll dumplings in crumbs. Sprinkle with powdered sugar.

Vienna Apple Charlotte

Brush charlotte form (small soup bowl) generously with melted butter. Line the inside of the form with white bread. Cut crusts off bread and allow the pieces to overlap. Fill with the following mixture:

Peeled, sliced apples, a few raisins, one-half lemon rind (grated), a dash cinnamon, three tablespoons apricot jam, a few drops of rum, five tablespoons sugar or to taste.

Cover top with two layers of white bread. Bake at 325° F. for three-quarters to one hour. When baked, the protective top layer will be burned. Remove the bread. Turn the charlotte upside down onto a serving platter. Glaze with icing or sprinkle with powdered sugar. Serve hot with apricot sauce and whipped cream in side dishes.

Apple Cromesky

Fry ten or twelve thin pancakes 8″ in diameter. Trim each cake to form two equal squares or rectangles. Prepare apple mixture with raisins, cinnamon, a little apricot jam, and a few drops of rum to suit taste. Spread apple mixture on pancakes and roll. Dip in dough mixture given below, and fry in hot butter. Serve desserts hot with vanilla sauce and whipped cream.

Dough Mixture

Dissolve one-third of an ounce of yeast ($\frac{2}{3}$ of a cake) in a little luke-warm water. Add a dash of salt and two tablespoons of sugar. Mix well and let rise for fifteen minutes. Blend in about seven ounces flour ($1\frac{1}{2}$ cups) and enough milk to make a thin batter. Blend in four egg whites (medium stiff) and allow to stand for a few minutes before using.

FRITTERS

Frying Batter 1

$\frac{3}{4}$ pint white wine	$\frac{3}{4}$ cup white wine
3 eggs	1-2 eggs
dash salt	dash salt
$\frac{1}{2}$ lemon rind, grated	$\frac{1}{4}$ lemon rind, grated
$\frac{3}{4}$ oz. sugar	$\frac{1}{2}$ tbsp. sugar
$8\frac{1}{2}$ ozs. flour	$1\frac{1}{8}$ cups flour

Method

Beat egg whites until stiff. Mix remaining ingredients well. Blend whites and other mixture together.

Frying Batter 2

$\frac{3}{4}$ pint milk	$\frac{3}{4}$ cup milk
3 eggs	1–2 eggs
$1\frac{1}{2}$ tbsp. sugar	$\frac{3}{4}$ tbsp. sugar
1 tbsp. rum	$\frac{1}{2}$ tbsp. rum
6 ozs. flour	$\frac{3}{4}$ cup flour
vanilla	vanilla

Method

Blend all ingredients together to make a smooth batter.

Frying Batter 3

$\frac{3}{4}$ pint beer	$\frac{3}{4}$ cup beer
3 egg whites	2 egg whites
3 egg yolks	1–2 egg yolks
dash salt	dash salt
$1\frac{1}{2}$ ozs. butter	1 tbsp. butter
$8\frac{1}{2}$ ozs. flour	$1\frac{1}{8}$ cups flour

Method

Mix all ingredients except egg whites until smooth. Blend in stiffly-beaten egg whites.

Apple Fritters

Peel and core apples. Cut slices $\frac{1}{3}$" thick. Rub slices in cinnamon-flavored sugar. Dip into desired batter and place in deep, hot frying fat. Bake golden brown. Serve at once with vanilla sauce.

Note: Fritters may be made with different fresh or canned fruits such as plums, pears, pineapple, apricots, et cetera. If canned fruit is used, it must be well drained and dried on a towel.

Apples in Dressing Gowns

Peel small cooking apples and remove core. Blanch apples in boiling water to which a little lemon juice has been added. When apples are slightly tenderized, remove from water and let dry. Roll puff paste *(see Index)* $\frac{1}{8}$" thick. Cut dough into equal squares, each large enough to cover an apple entirely. Place a few cake crumbs on each center and place apple over crumbs, right side up. Fill the opening with cinnamon-flavored sugar, raisins, and chopped almonds. Brush edges of dough with egg wash and overlap corners on top of apple. Decorate with rosettes and strips of dough. Egg wash and place on wet pans. Bake at 400° F. until lightly browned. Serve with apricot or wine sauce.

Baked Prunes in Chocolate

Cook dried prunes in water flavored with cinnamon, cloves, and one-half of a lemon until tender. Remove pits and replace with whole, blanched almonds. Dip prunes in a milk frying batter and deep fry in hot fat. Roll, while still hot, in shaved sweet chocolate.

Profiteroles

8 ozs. bread flour	2 cups bread flour
8 ozs. butter	1 cup butter
$\frac{1}{2}$ pint milk	1 cup milk
3 eggs	3 eggs
1 oz. sugar	$\frac{1}{8}$ cup sugar
dash salt	dash salt

Method

Process the above formula like éclair dough. *(See Index.)* Use pastry bag with small tube. Squeeze mounds the size of a dime onto greased pan. Egg wash. Bake at 400° F. When cold, fill with sweetened whipped cream. Serve with chocolate sauce.

Soufflés, Omelettes, Pancakes

General Directions for Soufflés

Unless otherwise directed, blend all ingredients except egg whites in mixing bowl, using a hand beater. Beat egg whites until stiff and blend into yolk mixture. Grease soufflé dish well with melted butter. Sugar inside of dish with granulated sugar. Fill container to top with soufflé batter. Bake at 325° F. to 350° F. Sprinkle with powdered sugar. Soufflés must be served at once. Most of the following formulas will serve four or five.

Coffee Soufflé

4 egg whites	4 egg whites
4 egg yolks	4 egg yolks
3 ozs. sugar	scant $\frac{3}{8}$ cup sugar
1$\frac{1}{2}$ tsp. cornstarch	1$\frac{1}{2}$ tsp. cornstarch
$\frac{1}{2}$–$\frac{3}{4}$ oz. coffee extract, or strong coffee	$\frac{1}{2}$–$\frac{3}{4}$ oz. coffee extract, or strong coffee

Serve with vanilla sauce.

Chocolate Soufflé

4 egg whites	4 egg whites
4 egg yolks	4 egg yolks
2 ozs. sugar	$\frac{1}{4}$ cup sugar
1$\frac{1}{2}$ tsp. cornstarch	1$\frac{1}{2}$ tsp. cornstarch
1$\frac{1}{2}$ ozs. semi-sweet chocolate	1$\frac{1}{2}$ ozs. semi-sweet chocolate
$\frac{1}{4}$ orange rind, grated	$\frac{1}{4}$ orange rind, grated
vanilla	vanilla

Serve with rum-flavored chocolate sauce.

Banana Soufflé

4 egg whites	4 egg whites
4 egg yolks	4 egg yolks
4 ozs. sugar	$\frac{1}{2}$ cup sugar
2 bananas, mashed	2 bananas, mashed
1$\frac{1}{2}$ tsp. cornstarch	1$\frac{1}{2}$ tsp. cornstarch
$\frac{1}{4}$ lemon rind, grated	$\frac{1}{4}$ lemon rind, grated
vanilla	vanilla

Serve with vanilla sauce.

Orange Soufflé

4 egg whites	4 egg whites
2 egg yolks	2 egg yolks
4 ozs. sugar	$\frac{1}{2}$ cup sugar
1$\frac{1}{2}$ tsp. cornstarch	1$\frac{1}{2}$ tsp. cornstarch
2 orange rinds, grated	2 orange rinds, grated
vanilla	vanilla

Serve with orange-flavored sauce.

Macadamia Nut Soufflé

4 egg whites	4 egg whites
4 egg yolks	4 egg yolks
3 ozs. sugar	$\frac{3}{8}$ cup sugar
1$\frac{1}{2}$ tsp. cornstarch	1$\frac{1}{2}$ tsp. cornstarch
$\frac{1}{2}$ lemon rind, grated	$\frac{1}{2}$ lemon rind, grated
1$\frac{1}{2}$ ozs. nuts, chopped	$\frac{3}{8}$ cup nuts, chopped
vanilla	vanilla

Serve with maraschino sauce.

Soufflé Rothschild

4 egg whites	4 egg whites
4 egg yolks	4 egg yolks
1$\frac{1}{2}$ ozs. sugar	3 tbsp. sugar
1$\frac{1}{2}$ tsp. cornstarch	1$\frac{1}{2}$ tsp. cornstarch
$\frac{1}{4}$ lemon rind, grated	$\frac{1}{4}$ lemon rind, grated
3 ozs. mixed fruit	$\frac{1}{2}$ cup mixed fruit
vanilla	vanilla

Serve with rum sauce.

Apricot Soufflé

4 egg whites	4 egg whites
4 egg yolks	4 egg yolks
4 ozs. sugar	$\frac{1}{2}$ cup sugar
4 ozs. apricot jam	$\frac{1}{3}$ cup apricot jam
3 ozs. almonds, blanched, chopped	$\frac{3}{4}$ cup almonds, blanched, chopped
vanilla	vanilla

Serve with apricot sauce.

Wine Soufflé

4 egg whites	4 egg whites
4 egg yolks	4 egg yolks
2½ ozs. sugar	¼ cup sugar
1½ ozs. cake crumbs	⅜ cup cake crumbs
2¼ ozs. white wine	¼ cup white wine
¼ lemon rind, grated	(generous)
dash cloves	¼ lemon rind, grated
	dash cloves

Serve with wine chateau.

Rice Soufflé

2 egg whites	2 egg whites
2 egg yolks	2 egg yolks
1 pint milk	2 cups milk
4 ozs. rice	½ cup rice
2 ozs. sugar	¼ cup sugar
2 ozs. butter	¼ cup butter
dash salt	dash salt
½ lemon rind, grated	½ lemon rind, grated
1 tbsp. raisins	1 tbsp. raisins

Method
Place washed rice in milk and salt and boil slowly for thirty minutes. Let cool. Beat rest of ingredients except egg whites until creamy. Add to rice. Fold in stiffly-beaten egg whites. Serve with raspberry sauce.

Lemon Soufflé

4 egg whites	4 egg whites
2 egg yolks	2 egg yolks
4 ozs. sugar	½ cup sugar
1½ tsp. cornstarch	1½ tsp. cornstarch
2 lemon rinds, grated	2 lemon rinds, grated
juice of ¼ lemon	juice of ¼ lemon
vanilla	vanilla

Serve with vanilla sauce.

Cheese Soufflé

3 egg whites	3 egg whites
3 egg yolks	3 egg yolks
2½ ozs. sugar	⅓ cup sugar
½ pint sour cream	1 cup sour cream
6 ozs. cottage cheese	¾ cup cottage cheese
1 oz. raisins	¼ cup raisins
½ lemon rind, grated	½ lemon rind, grated

Method
Press cheese through strainer. Add flavor, egg yolks, and sugar. Beat well. Add sour cream. Beat egg whites until stiff and fold into cheese mixture. Serve with caramel sauce.

Marzipan Soufflé

4 egg whites	4 egg whites
4 egg yolks	4 egg yolks
1 oz. sugar	⅛ cup sugar
3 ozs. almond paste, softened with yolks	3 ozs. almond paste, softened with yolks
1½ tsp. cornstarch	1½ tsp. cornstarch
¼ lemon rind, grated	¼ lemon rind, grated
vanilla	vanilla

Serve with almond sauce.

Omelette Soufflé

4 egg whites	4 egg whites
4 egg yolks	4 egg yolks
2½ ozs. sugar	¼ cup sugar (generous)
2 ozs. flour	½ cup flour
¼ lemon rind, grated	¼ lemon rind, grated

Method
Beat egg whites until stiff, adding the sugar slowly. Cream yolks and lemon rind. Add to egg whites. Blend in sifted flour. Bake in large, greased pan at 350° F. Turn onto cloth. Brush quickly with hot apricot jam. Fold over twice. Sprinkle with powdered sugar. Serve at once with vanilla sauce and whipped cream.

Bohemian Omelette

8 ozs. cake flour	2 cups cake flour
1 tbsp. sugar	1 tbsp. sugar
dash salt	dash salt
1 oz. melted butter	⅛ cup melted butter
3 eggs	3 eggs
milk	milk
vanilla	vanilla

Method
Blend all ingredients together, adding enough milk to get smooth batter. Let rest fifteen minutes. Heat a little butter in frying pan. Pour omelette

Pineapple surprise set in spun sugar.

Grouping of *Coups*.

Glasses filled with different sherbets and topped with stuffed oranges. The stuffing consists of whipped cream, chopped nuts, and diced oranges. Glasses are covered with spun sugar.

Glasses filled with a mixture of ice cream and chopped, glazed fruits. Decoration consists of spun sugar, angelica, and royal-icing birds.

batter in it to cover bottom thinly. Bake light brown on both sides. Spread surface with jam of desired kind. Roll omelette in jelly roll fashion. Sprinkle with powdered sugar. Serve hot with sauce to complement the filling.

Crêpes Suzettes

3 eggs	3 eggs
¾ pint milk	1½ cups milk
3 ozs. sugar	⅜ cup sugar
4½ ozs. cake flour	1 cup cake flour
¾ tsp. salt	(generous)
1½ tsp. baking powder	¾ tsp. salt
1 tbsp. cognac	1½ tsp. baking powder
vanilla	1 tbsp. cognac
	vanilla

Filling

6 ozs. butter	¾ cup butter
10 ozs. sugar	1¼ cups sugar
juice of 1 orange	juice of 1 orange
2 orange rinds, grated	2 orange rinds, grated
2 tbsp. lemon juice	2 tbsp. lemon juice

Put all ingredients of filling together and cream well.

Method

Pour liquid ingredients into mixing bowl. Beat eggs and sugar with lemon rind. Add to liquids. Sift flour, salt, and baking powder. Blend into liquid mixture. Combine all ingredients with a few swift strokes. Pour small amount of batter into hot, buttered frying pan. Dip pan to allow batter to spread well. Bake light brown on both sides. Spread the above filling on cakes and roll up. Set desired amount of rolls in serving dish. *Note:* Mix cognac and white wine in proportions of two to one and pour around suzettes. Light liquor with match. Serve at once.

ICE CREAM DESSERTS

Peach Melba

Put one peach-half, inside up, into champagne glass. Pour thickened raspberry juice over it. Set one scoop of vanilla ice cream in center. Decorate with cherry and whipped cream.

Coup Royal Hawaiian

Line dish with vanilla ice cream and let harden in freezer. Place piece of sponge cake on bottom. Add chopped pineapple. Fill two-thirds with pineapple juice and remaining third with cognac. Top with whipped cream and decorate with almond macaroons.

Coup Ali Baba

Mix macaroon crumbs with a little whipped cream. Place in daiquiri glass. Add coffee liqueur. Fill with soft vanilla ice cream and decorate with strawberry sherbet.

Galaxy of Sherbet

Place chopped, fresh fruits with a little juice in daiquiri glass. Flavor with Jamaica rum. Put three small scoops of different sherbets in center, topped with fourth scoop. Decorate with lady fingers and whipped cream.

Coup Marron Glacé

Mix chocolate chips with marron fudge *(see Index, "Chestnut Fudge")* and half fill a dish Fill dish to top with a mixture of vanilla ice cream, maraschino liqueur and whipped cream. Decorate with three glazed marrons. (Form marrons from marron fudge and dip in caramel sugar. Set on buttered pan.)

Coup de Ville

Fill half of dish with chocolate ice cream. Add one layer of skinned orange sections. Flavor with curaçao liqueur. Fill glass with whipped cream. Decorate with chocolate ornaments and cherries.

Coup de Romain

Strawberry ice cream is mixed with orange juice. Fill high glass two-thirds full. Add a few fresh strawberries, flavored with cognac. Decorate with whipped cream.

Cherry Jubilee

Line glass dish with thin layer of sponge cake. Sprinkle with cherry brandy. Add one scoop of vanilla ice cream and mold it to form a half-shell. Thicken the juice of black cherries slightly by bringing it to a boil with approximately one-quarter teaspoon cornstarch and one-quarter grated lemon rind. Stir in cherries. Place mixture in separate dish. When serving, pour cognac on cherries and light with match. Pour over ice cream.

Coup Vienna

Use high glass or silver cup. Fill first third with lemon sherbet and second third with orange sherbet. Sprinkle some macaroon crumbs on top. Fill cup completely with white wine château. *(See Index.)*

Coup Canadienne

Set one large scoop of vanilla ice cream in center of daiquirí glass. Surround it with a ring of small scoops of butterscotch ice cream alternating with watermelon balls. Mix a little cognac with maple syrup and pour on top. Decorate with whipped cream and maple leaves baked from shortbread dough.

Coup Ile de France

Line bottom of cup with small piece of cake. Place one scoop of mint sherbet in center. Arrange sliced pears around sherbet. Flavor with *apéritif*. Decorate with whipped cream and cherries.

Coup Cologna au Kirsch

Soak sweet, stoned cherries in rum-flavored sugar syrup. Drain well. Wrap each cherry in thin, pink colored marzipan. Mix a scoop of vanilla ice cream with chopped, blanched almonds. Set in center of champagne glass. Make ring of whipped cream around ice cream. Set prepared cherries on top. Pour kirsch liqueur over cherries.

Strawberry Romanoff

Half fill a cup with vanilla ice cream. Cover with a thin layer of sponge cake. Sprinkle with maraschino liqueur. Fill cup with mixture of fresh strawberries and whipped cream. Sprinkle with toasted, chopped almonds.

Coup South Seas

Set three scoops of sherbet (papaya, guava, pineapple) in champagne glass. Set papaya slices around sherbet. Top with whipped cream, flavored with cocoanut syrup. Sprinkle with toasted, shredded cocoanut.

Pineapple Surprise

Use small pineapple with greenery on it. Cut top off to use as lid. Carve a hole the size of a cup into the pineapple and freeze the shell. Place a few cubes of pound cake on bottom of pineapple and sprinkle with rum. Fill half of remaining space with a lemon and whipped cream mixture. Fill top space with a raspberry and whipped cream mixture. Sprinkle top with cherries and replace lid. Decorate plate around pineapple with spun sugar. *(See Index.)*

Coup Marie Antoinette

Mix chopped, toasted almonds into vanilla ice cream. Set one scoop in center of serving dish. Flavor raspberry sauce with vanilla liqueur and pour over ice cream. Place four meringue shells around center and decorate with whipped cream and nuts.

Coup Oriental

Cook desired quantity of rice pudding. *(See Index.)* Let cool completely. Mix with vanilla ice cream and whipped cream. Pour ginger ale over mixture. Decorate with candied ginger.

Coup Espresso

Line serving dish with thin layer of chocolate or white cake. Mix one portion of strong *espresso* coffee with one portion of coffee ice cream. Pour into cup. Decorate with vanilla-flavored whipped cream.

Coup Mignon

Mix together one portion of vanilla custard and one portion of vanilla ice cream. Blend in a few whole cherries, some cherry juice and cognac. Pour into champagne glass. Decorate with whipped cream and chopped krokant.

Note: The above mentioned Coups may be decorated with spun sugar if so desired.

Outside shell made from orange sherbet. Center, vanilla ice cream mixed with fresh fruits and macaroon pieces. Decoration, chocolate and éclair dough ornaments.

Outside shell made from pineapple sherbet; second layer, lemon sherbet. Center, creamed mixture of vanilla ice cream, whipped cream, chopped cherries, and cognac. Decoration, fruit ornaments and marzipan flowers.

Outside shell made from cocoanut ice cream. Center, pineapple sherbet, pineapple cubes, whipped cream, and arrack. Decoration, crown of marzipan, whipped cream, cherries, and lady fingers.

Outside shell made from chocolate ice cream. Second shell, vanilla ice cream. Center, macadamia-nut ice cream mixed with whipped cream and rum. Decoration, éclair dough ornament and whipped cream.

Outside shell made from orange sherbet. Center, vanilla ice cream mixed with chopped oranges, whipped cream, and cognac. Decoration, *canolli* rolls filled with whipped cream or butter cream.

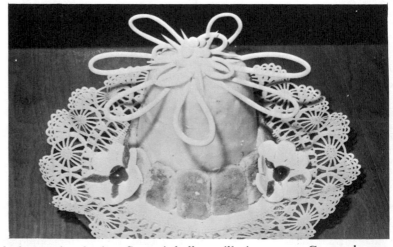

Outside shell made from mint sherbet. Second shell, vanilla ice cream. Center, lemon sherbet mixed with chopped apricots and gin. Decoration, flowers of plastic sugar and lady fingers.

Ice Cream Parfaits

Parfaits may be made ahead of time if the filled glasses are kept in the refrigerator. The following section suggests a number of different flavor combinations. As the processing is the same regardless of ingredients, the method will be given only once.

High, narrow glasses are to be used. Chill glasses before filling. Place two small scoops of ice cream in glass. Add sauce, liqueur, syrups, and so forth. Set another scoop of ice cream on top, pressing down to fill in spaces. Decorate top with whipped cream, nuts, cherries, or whatever is indicated.

(1) Vanilla Parfait : vanilla ice cream, raspberry sauce (*see Index*), vanilla liqueur

(2) Mocca Parfait : coffee ice cream, rum, coffee syrup

(3) Chocolate Parfait : chocolate ice cream, curaçao liqueur, chocolate sauce (see Index)

(4) Cocoanut Parfait : cocoanut ice cream, cocoanut syrup

(5) Macadamia Parfait : vanilla ice cream, chopped macadamia nuts, vanilla sauce (*see Index*)

(6) Orange Parfait : orange sherbet, chopped candied peel, orange syrup

(7) Pineapple Parfait : pineapple sherbet, pineapple sauce with lemon flavoring (*see Index*)

(8) Rainbow Parfait : different layers of sherbets, starting with the lightest color.

(9) Strawberry Parfait : vanilla and strawberry ice cream, strawberry sauce (*see Index*), cognac

(10) Cherry Parfait : lemon sherbet, chopped cherries, kirsch liqueur

(11) Wine Parfait : lemon sherbet, blue grapes, red wine

(12) Krokant Parfait : vanilla ice cream, chopped krokant (*see Index*), caramel sauce (*see Index*), rum

(13) Nougat Parfait : chocolate and vanilla ice cream, maraschino liqueur, nougat sauce (*see Index*)

Coffee Ice

Mix one scoop of vanilla ice cream into one-half glass of strong, black coffee. Add one or two tablespoons of whipped cream.

Chocolate Ice

Half fill a cup with cold chocolate. Add one scoop vanilla ice cream and curaçao liqueur. Stir in one spoon of whipped cream.

Pineapple Sorbet

Mix one-quarter bottle of champagne into three-quarters of a quart of pineapple sherbet. Serve in glasses.

Peach Sorbet

Put one scoop of peach sherbet in glass and add cognac to taste. Fill glass with sparkling water.

Raspberry Sorbet

Dilute raspberry sherbet with red wine to suit taste.

Arrack Punch

Mix together eight ounces sugar (1 cup), juice of three lemons, grated rind of one lemon, a quarter-pint arrack ($\frac{1}{2}$ cup). Place a scoop of lemon sherbet in glass and add shaved ice. Fill with first mixture.

Ice Cream Bombes

Hotels, restaurants, and fine pastry shops use special *bombe* forms which are made of corrugated metal. However, any dome-shaped objects such as bowls or large cups may be used. The forms must be kept under refrigeration before filling. Usually the inside wall is lined with a $\frac{1}{2}$" thickness of solid ice cream of any kind supported by a second wall of different colored ice cream. The center can be a mixture of fruits, nuts, or ice cream diluted to half its stiffness with either liqueur, whipped cream, or another suitable medium. When making large *bombes,* it is advised to use thin cake-strips between ice cream layers so the *bombes* will not be too rich. One should try to avoid clashing colors and flavors. The decorating possibilities are without limit. Follow the same rule as for cakes and do not over-decorate.

Bombe Jaqueline

The outside shell is lemon sherbet, and the center is vanilla ice cream, mixed fruits, and one glass cointreau liqueur. Decorate with whipped cream and éclair dough ornaments.

Bombe Ambassador

The outside shell is mocha ice cream mixed with chopped *krokant,* and the center is vanilla ice cream mixed with toasted, ground filberts, whipped cream, curaçao liqueur. Decorate with royal icing ornaments, candied violets, and angelica.

Bombe Jeanette

The outside shell is strawberry sherbet, and the center is vanilla ice cream mixed with chopped cherries, vanilla liqueur, and whipped cream. Decorate with marzipan flowers, royal chocolate icing ornaments, and angelica.

Cherry Bombe

The outside shell is vanilla ice cream, and the center is lemon sherbet, chopped cherries, macaroons, and cherry brandy. Decorate with marzipan cherries, royal-chocolate icing ornaments, cooky rosettes half-dipped in sweet chocolate.

Bombe Sunrise

The outside shell is mocha ice cream, and the center is milk ice, whipped cream, and chocolate chips. Decorate with sunrise made of yellow-colored sugar plastic, white-royal icing ornaments, and lady fingers.

Bombe à la Bohème

The outside shell is almond ice cream, and the center is almond ice cream mixed with chopped macaroons and mixed fruit. Decorate with small macaroons, half-dipped in sweet chocolate and royal-chocolate icing ornaments.

ICE CREAM CAKES

Italian Cassatta

Line cake tin with paper. Place ¼″ layer of sponge cake on bottom and sides and spread with apricot jam. Add a layer of vanilla ice cream. Fill cake with a mixture of stiffly-beaten whipped cream mixed with diced fruit and rum. Freeze. Decorate with whipped cream and glazed fruit.

Viennese Mocha Ice Torte

Prepare cake tin as above, using a layer of Sacher cake. Spread with raspberry jam or jelly, followed by a thin layer of vanilla ice cream. Fill cake with stiffly-beaten whipped cream flavored with strong coffee, rum, and macaroon pieces. Freeze. Decorate top with whipped cream and coffee beans made of marzipan.

Waikiki Ice Cake

Prepare cake tin as above, using baked shortbread as bottom lining. Spread with apricot jam and set thin layer of sponge cake on top. Sprinkle with maraschino-flavored sugar syrup. Divide stiffly-beaten whipped cream into two bowls. Mix first part with chopped pineapple and cover with sponge layer. Mix second part with fresh, shredded cocoanut and pink coloring. Put mixture in cake form. Freeze. Decorate with pineapple rings and whipped cream.

Ice Torte a la Tosca

Prepare cake tin lined with paper, followed by layer of Sacher cake on bottom. Sprinkle with cherry brandy. Mix chopped cherries into vanilla ice cream and blend in a few spoons of whipped cream. Fill cake and freeze. Make a small jelly roll *(see Index)* and cut pieces ½″ thick. Set cut side on ice cream cake shortly before serving.

Note: Do not freeze roulade.

Outside shell made from papaya sherbet. Center, cocoanut ice cream mixed with chopped, fresh papaya. Decoration, birds of shortbread iced with fondant, royal-chocolate icing ornaments.

Outside shell made from vanilla ice cream. Second shell, lemon sherbet. Center, vanilla ice cream mixed with whipped cream, chopped apricots, and maraschino flavored. Dress made of whipped cream and fancy trimmings of colored marshmallow. Entire dress sprinkled with fine silver dragées.

This *cassatta* cake was decorated with roses and served on an ice piece lit from the bottom by a hidden battery. Flowers inside the vase were real and were put there shortly before serving.

Baked Alaska decorated with birds and glazed cherries.

Baked Alaska decorated for a wedding anniversary.

Ice cream dishes decorated with lady fingers, royal icings, and whipped cream.

Baked Alaska Flammé

A brick of ice cream is wrapped in a thin sheet of sponge cake, covered in a decorative manner with meringue and browned quickly in a hot oven or under a salamander. When serving, pour burning alcohol over it. Baked Alaskas may be decorated with glazed fruits, meringue roses, et cetera.

BAKED ACCOMPANIMENTS FOR ICE CREAM DISHES

Almond Rolls

8 ozs. almond paste	8 ozs. almond paste
8 ozs. powdered sugar	1½ cups powdered sugar
2¼ ozs. flour	(generous)
dash nutmeg	scant ½ cup flour
vanilla	dash nutmeg
4 egg whites	vanilla
milk	4 egg whites
	milk

Method

Mix almond paste with sugar by hand. Soften slowly with egg whites. Add flavoring and flour blending until perfectly smooth. Add enough milk to make a thin batter. Spread mixture almost paper thin on greased, floured pans. Bake at 400° F. Cut sheet quickly in equal squares. Leave pan on oven door to keep soft. Turn squares upside down onto table, set a round stick of wood on one side of square and roll up. Start rolling as soon as dough shows a little color, otherwise last ones will burn.

A metal stencil with an opening cut 4" x 2" may be used. The stencil may also be round. After rolls have cooled, dip ends in sweet or semi-sweet chocolate.

How to make Leaves

Obtain a leaf-shaped stencil. Hold on greased, floured pan. Spread on a thin layer of almond roll mixture. (*See Index,* "Almond Rolls.") Bake at 400° F. After baking, quickly remove from pan and place over rolling pin or other round object to give the leaves a natural appearance.

Fancy Ornaments from Almond Batter

Use formula for almond rolls, making batter a little thicker by using less milk. Place in a paper tube and cut a small opening. Have the desired ornaments marked on greased, floured pan and outline carefully with tube. Since these objects are very fine and delicate, they will burn easily. Watch oven carefully. Bake at 300° F.

Fancy Ornaments of Éclair Dough

Use the same procedure as for almond batter. Grease pan, but do not flour. Bake until light brown and remove from pan while still hot.

Fancy Ornaments from Royal Icings

See Index for white or chocolate royal icing. The designs are drawn on white paper, outlined with icing and left to dry. Chocolate icing is kept refrigerated.

Ice Cream Waffles

5 egg whites	5 egg whites
5 egg yolks	5 egg yolks
4 ozs. butter	½ cup butter
4 ozs. cake flour	1 scant cup cake flour
1 lb. 4 ozs. milk	2⅓ cups milk
¼ lemon rind, grated	¼ lemon rind, grated

Method

Cream together butter, half of the flour, lemon rind, and yolks. Beat whites until stiff. Blend second half of flour into the whites. Stir milk into yolk mixture and fold in whites. Bake in waffle irons.

Filling for Waffles

Almond Filling

¼ pint egg whites	½ cup egg whites
1¼ lbs. sugar	2½ cups sugar
¾ lb. ground, toasted almonds	3 cups ground, toasted almonds
2 ozs. rum	2 ozs. rum
vanilla	vanilla

Method

Beat egg whites, adding sugar slowly, until stiff. Blend in almonds, rum and vanilla. Join waffles in layers of four with the filling. Press overnight with heavy object. Cut to desired sizes.

Nougat Filling

8 ozs. brown nougat (*See Index*)	8 ozs. brown nougat
5 ozs. shortening	$\frac{5}{8}$ cup shortening
5 ozs. melted, sweet chocolate	5 squares melted, **sweet** chocolate
4 ozs. powdered sugar	$\frac{3}{4}$ cup powdered **sugar** (generous)
vanilla	vanilla
1 oz. rum	1 oz. rum

Method

Cream together fat, sugar, and flavoring. **Add** nougat. Pour in melted, warm chocolate. Spread quickly between waffles. Press tightly **and cut**.

Lemon Filling

1 lb. shortening	$1\frac{1}{4}$ cups shortening
$1\frac{1}{2}$ lbs. powdered sugar	$2\frac{1}{2}$ cups powdered sugar
$\frac{3}{4}$ oz. cornstarch	scant $\frac{1}{8}$ cup cornstarch
3 lemon rinds, grated	$1\frac{1}{2}$ lemon rinds, grated
juice of 1 lemon	juice of $\frac{1}{2}$ lemon

Method

Mix all ingredients together until creamy. Add color if desired. Spread between waffles and press overnight.

Note: Different fruits may be used, such as oranges, strawberries, cherries, et cetera.

Ice Cream Imitations

Since it is extremely difficult to display ice cream desserts over long periods of time even under refrigeration, these articles may be imitated with plastic sugar. (*See Index.*) For this purpose plastic sugar is rolled $\frac{1}{4}''$ to $\frac{1}{2}''$ thick, depending upon size of the object. It is placed over or in an ice bombe form and left to dry. The sugar must be colored exactly as the real bombe would be. Outside decorations, such as whipping **cream**, are re-created with white royal icing. The finished object is then glazed with shellac. It will **have a** startling resemblance to real ice cream. If a dessert piece is to be advertised showing a **cut**, the inside must be filled in realistically. If fruits are used, they may be real glazed fruits or imitations.

Basic Pie Crust Formulas

Formula 1

$\frac{3}{4}$ oz. salt	2 tsp. salt
2 lbs. 2 ozs. pastry flour	$4\frac{1}{4}$ cups pastry flour
1 pint water	1 cup water
1 lb. 11 ozs. shortening	2 cups shortening

Formula 2

2 lbs. 8 ozs. pastry flour	$2\frac{1}{2}$ cups pastry flour
1 lb. 8 ozs. shortening	$\frac{3}{4}$ cup shortening
$\frac{1}{2}$ pint water	$\frac{1}{4}$ cup water
$\frac{1}{2}$ oz. salt	$\frac{3}{4}$ tsp. salt

Formula 3

2 lbs. 4 ozs. pastry flour	$2\frac{1}{4}$ cups pastry flour
1 lb. shortening	$\frac{1}{2}$ cup shortening
$\frac{2}{3}$ oz. salt	1 tsp. salt
1 pint boiling water	scant $\frac{1}{2}$ cup boiling water

Method

Sift flour and salt together. Rub shortening into flour until mixture forms coarse **crumbs**. Sprinkle water over mixture a section at a time. Stir gently until all parts are moistened evenly. Chill dough in refrigerator. Form smooth **ball** and set on lightly floured board or cloth. Roll dough to correct size with a rolling pin.

Note: When making fruit pies, fruit **juice may** be substituted for the water.

Crumb Crust Formulas

Crumb Crust 1

$2\frac{1}{2}$ lbs. zwieback crumbs	1 cup zwieback crumbs
1 lb. 7 ozs. sugar	$\frac{3}{4}$ cup sugar
15 ozs. butter, melted	3 tbsp. butter, melted
1 lemon rind, grated	1 tsp. lemon rind, grated

Crumb Crust 2

2 lbs. 13 ozs. graham crumbs	$1\frac{1}{2}$ cups graham crumbs
1 lb. 4 ozs. sugar	$\frac{1}{4}$ cup sugar
1 lb. 10 ozs. butter, melted	$\frac{1}{3}$ cup butter, melted
1 lemon rind, grated	1 tsp. lemon rind, grated

Crumb Crust 3

2 lbs. zwieback crumbs	1 cup zwieback crumbs
12 ozs. almonds, chopped, toasted	$\frac{1}{2}$ cup almonds, chopped, toasted
1 lb. 4 ozs. sugar	$\frac{1}{4}$ cup sugar
1 lb. 10 ozs. butter, melted	$\frac{1}{3}$ cup butter, melted
1 lemon rind, grated	1 tsp. lemon rind, grated

For variation use shredded cocoanut instead of almonds.

Method

Blend all ingredients well and press into pie plate. Set smaller plate on crumbs and apply pressure to distribute crumbs evenly. Crumb crusts may be chilled or baked at 350° F. for extra crispness and flavor.

Meringue Topping

Beat together the whites of three eggs and one-half a tablespoon of lemon juice until stiff. Add six tablespoons of sugar, slowly beating until sugar has dissolved. This formula makes one pie.

Cheese Crust

2 lbs. 8 ozs. flour	$2\frac{1}{2}$ cups flour
2 lbs. 8 ozs. shortening	$\frac{3}{4}$ cup shortening
$\frac{1}{2}$ pint water	$\frac{1}{4}$ cup water
$\frac{1}{2}$ oz. salt	$\frac{3}{4}$ tsp. salt
8 ozs. grated cheese	$\frac{1}{2}$ cup grated cheese

Method

Follow method for basic pie crust, mixing cheese into flour.

Royal Cocoanut Chiffon Pie

$2\frac{1}{2}$ quarts milk	$2\frac{1}{4}$ cups milk
$7\frac{1}{2}$ ozs. cornstarch	scant $\frac{1}{4}$ cup cornstarch
8 eggs	2 eggs
1 lb. 14 ozs. sugar	1 cup sugar
$1\frac{1}{4}$ pints egg whites	$\frac{1}{2}$ cup egg whites
vanilla	(generous)
12 ozs. shredded cocoanut	vanilla
	$\frac{3}{4}$ cup shredded cocoanut

Method

Mix starch, eggs, and vanilla with a little of the milk. Beat whites and sugar until stiff. Bring remaining milk to a boil, stir in starch mixture, and continue boiling until thickened. Remove from heat. Blend in whites and cocoanut with a few swift strokes. Pour into baked pie crust and chill. Spread top with whipped cream and shredded cocoanut.

Apple Pie

35–40 cooking apples	7 cooking apples
2 lbs. 8 ozs. sugar	1 cup sugar
$\frac{1}{2}$ oz. salt	dash salt
$4\frac{1}{2}$ tsp. cinnamon	$\frac{3}{4}$ tsp. cinnamon
1 tsp. nutmeg	$\frac{1}{4}$ tsp. nutmeg
1 lemon rind, grated	$\frac{1}{4}$ lemon rind, grated
1 orange rind, grated	$\frac{1}{4}$ orange rind, grated
5 ozs. butter	2 tbsp. butter
2 ozs. flour	1 tbsp. flour

Method

Peel, core, and slice apples. Add sugar and heat well. Cool apples and add rest of ingredients. Fill unbaked pie shell and cover with crust. Seal edges and egg wash. Sprinkle top with granulated sugar and prick holes in top. Bake at 400° F.

Blueberry Pie

1 quart blueberries	2 cups blueberries
dash salt	dash salt
12 ozs. sugar	$1\frac{1}{2}$ cups sugar
$\frac{1}{2}$ oz. cornstarch	1 tbsp. cornstarch
$1\frac{1}{2}$ ozs. butter	$1\frac{1}{2}$ tbsp. butter
$\frac{1}{2}$ lemon rind, grated	$\frac{1}{4}$ lemon rind, grated
1 tbsp. lemon juice	$\frac{1}{2}$ tbsp. lemon juice

Method

Mix sugar and starch together, blend into rest of ingredients. Fill unbaked pie shell and adjust top crust. Seal edges. Egg wash and bake at 375° F.

Peach Pie

Peel and slice peaches. Sprinkle unbaked bottom shell with cake crumbs. Cover with tightly packed layer of peaches. Sprinkle with cinnamon sugar. Add a layer of lady fingers and fill to top with peaches. Again sprinkle with cinnamon sugar. Sprinkle juice of one-half lemon on top. Adjust top crust. Seal edges. Egg wash and bake at 375° F.

Cherry Pie

3½ lbs. cherries, stoned	3 cups cherries, stoned
1½ lbs. sugar	1 cup sugar
dash salt	dash salt
7 ozs. butter	1 tbsp. butter
1 lemon rind, grated	¼ tsp. lemon rind, grated
juice of ½ lemon	juice of ¼ lemon

Method

Mix all ingredients and place in unbaked pie shell. Form lattice with dough strips. Egg wash and bake at 375°F.

Note: If canned cherries are used, thicken juice by adding a little cornstarch and allowing to boil for a few seconds, stirring constantly.

Rhubarb Pie

5 lbs. rhubarb	4 cups rhubarb
3 lbs. sugar	1¼ cups sugar
8 ozs. butter	3 tbsp. butter
⅓ oz. salt	dash salt
4 ozs. flour	3 tbsp. flour
1 orange rind, grated	½ orange rind, grated
½ lemon rind, grated	¼ tsp. lemon rind, grated

Method

Combine rhubarb, flour, sugar, and flavoring. Fill a pastry-lined pie pan. Sprinkle melted butter over filling. Adjust top crust. Egg wash and sprinkle with granulated sugar. Bake at 400°F. for 45 to 55 minutes.

Cherry Rhubarb Pie

6 ozs. butter	2½ tbsp. butter
4 ozs. flour	3¼ tbsp. flour
4 quarts rhubarb, diced	4 cups rhubarb, diced
1 lb. 8 ozs. sour cherries	1 cup sour cherries
3½ lbs. sugar	1¼ cup sugar
½ tsp. salt	⅛ tsp. salt
1 lemon rind, grated	¼ tsp. lemon rind, grated

Method

Sprinkle cake crumbs on bottom of unbaked pie shell. Mix together flour, sugar, salt, and rind. Place rhubarb on the bottom and sprinkle one-half of the flour mixture over it. Add cherries and remaining flour mixture. Dot with butter. Secure top crust with egg. Egg wash top. Prick holes to allow steam to escape. Bake at 400°F. Serve with whipped cream.

Raspberry Pie with Meringue

1½ lbs. raspberries	1¼ cups raspberries
1 lb. 15 ozs. sugar	1 cup sugar
2½ lbs. milk	1 cup milk
5½ ozs. cornstarch	3¼ tbsp. cornstarch
10 egg yolks, beaten	2 egg yolks, beaten
3 ozs. butter	1¼ tbsp. butter
8 ozs. orange juice	⅜ cup orange juice
4½ ozs. salt	¼ tsp. salt
1 lemon rind, grated	¼ lemon rind, grated
vanilla	vanilla

Method

Bring to a boil the milk, sugar, salt, and lemon rind. Make a smooth mixture of the orange juice and starch, and pour into milk, stirring constantly. Cook until thickened. Add the beaten yolks with a few swift strokes and remove from heat. Add remaining ingredients, stirring in raspberries gently. Let cool. Pour into baked pie shell. Top with meringue and brown in hot oven.

Pumpkin Pie

5 lbs. 15 ozs. canned pumpkin	1½ cups canned pumpkin
1 lb. 6 ozs. brown sugar	¾ cup brown sugar
1¼ pints milk	½ cup milk
15 egg yolks, beaten	3 egg yolks, beaten
2½ tsp. salt	½ tsp. salt
5 tsp. cinnamon	1 tsp. cinnamon
2½ tsp. nutmeg	½ tsp. nutmeg
5 tbsp. gelatine	1 envelope gelatine
½ pint water	¼ cup water

Method

Soften gelatine in cold water. Combine remaining ingredients and boil for ten minutes in double boiler, stirring constantly. Add gelatine mixture. Chill until it begins to set. Pour into unbaked pie shell. Bake at 450°F. for fifteen minutes. Reduce heat to 300°F. and continue baking for another twenty-five minutes. Serve cold with whipped cream.

Chocolate Chiffon Pie

10 ozs. water	¼ cup water
1¼ ozs. gelatine	1 tbsp. gelatine
1 lb. 4 ozs. milk	½ cup milk
15 ozs. sugar	½ cup sugar

Macadamia nut cream pie (*left*) and butterscotch pie with chocolate chips (*right*).

Carved pineapple filled with chopped, tropical fruits and sprinkled with kirsh-flavored sugar syrup. Serve chilled.

Carved basket-shaped cantaloupe lined with lettuce leaves, filled with mixed fruits, and flavored with maraschino liqueur. Serve chilled.

8 ozs. cocoa
2¼ quarts whipped cream
¼ oz. salt
vanilla
1 orange rind, grated
1½ ozs. rum

6½ tbsp. cocoa
2 cups whipped cream
¼ tsp. salt
vanilla
¼ tsp. orange rind, grated
½ oz. rum

Method

Soften gelatine in cold water for a few minutes. Heat milk and add sugar, cocoa, salt, and flavoring. Blend well. Stir in gelatine. Cook until mixture thickens. Cream until cool. Fold in stiffly-beaten whipping cream and rum. Pour into pre-baked crumb shell. Let chill. Serve cold with vanilla sauce.

Lemon Chiffon Pie

20 egg whites
20 egg yolks
1 lb. 5 ozs. sugar
¾ oz. lemon rind, grated
1¼ pints lemon juice
½ oz. salt
1¼ ozs. gelatine
8 ozs. water
1 lb. 2 ozs. sugar
vanilla

4 egg whites
4 egg yolks
½ cup sugar
1¼ tsp. lemon rind, grated
½ cup lemon juice
¼ tsp. salt
1 tbsp. gelatine
scant ¼ cup water
½ cup sugar
vanilla

Method

Soak gelatine in cold water. Beat sugar, yolks, lemon juice, rind, and salt in hot-water bath until creamy. Put mixture in double boiler and bring close to a boil. Stir in gelatine. Whip smooth and cool. When mixture starts to set, fold in beaten whites to which remaining sugar has been added. Pour into baked crumb-shell. Chill and serve with whipped cream.

Wine Chiffon Pie

16 eggs
1 lb. 12 ozs. sugar
½ tsp. salt
juice of one lemon
¼ orange rind, grated
3¾ quarts milk
⅔ pint cream
2 ozs. gelatine
1¾ pints white wine

3 eggs
¾ cup sugar
⅛ tsp. salt
juice of ¼ lemon
⅛ orange rind, grated
3 cups milk
¼ cup cream (generous)
1½ tsp. gelatine
¾ cup white wine

Method

Soak gelatine in white wine. Beat eggs, sugar, lemon juice, and orange rind in double boiler until hot. While stirring constantly, pour scalded milk over it. Strain mixture and let cook until creamy and thick. Add wine and gelatine solution. Whip well. Let cool. When mixture begins to set, fold in whipped cream. Chill. Top with whipped cream or marshmallow.

Lemon Cheese Pie

1 pint lemon custard
8 ozs. cream cheese

1 pkg. instant lemon
pudding
2 cups milk
8 ozs. cream cheese

Method

Soften cheese at room temperature. Use cold custard and blend in cheese. Chill. Serve with whipped cream.

FRUIT COCKTAILS

Pineapple Ruby

Use medium-sized, ripe pineapple. Cut off top plus greenery to form lid. Trim off part of bottom to secure firm stand. Separate fruit from skin with a sharp knife. leaving the wall about ⅜″ thick. Lift out fruit and remove core with a long metal tube. Put fruit back into shell and cut vertically to form long, narrow pieces. Sprinkle with brandy. Replace lid and serve chilled.

Apple Kirsch Coupé

Dice sweet apples and add some chopped, glazed cherries. Place mixture in glass and flavor with kirsch liqueur. Decorate with sliced, fresh fruit.

Orange Cocktail

Place chopped oranges and bananas in a glass. Sprinkle with lemon juice and add gin or orange juice. Decorate with orange sections and glaze with sugar syrup.

Tahitian Fruit Cocktail

Place mixed, fresh fruit in a glass. Add white wine. Decorate with papaya, banana, and pineapple slices. Serve chilled.

Cherry Almond Coupé

Use black, sweet, stoned cherries. Drain well, add a little starch to the juice, and bring to a boil. Let cool. Mix blanched almonds with cherries and add to juice mixture. Pour into glass and flavor with arrack liqueur.

Royal Fruit Cocktail

Mix together chopped apples, watermelon, bananas, honey dew melon, pears, and cherries. Moisten with rum-flavored cherry juice. Pour into glass and decorate with watermelon and honey dew melon balls.

Wine Cocktail

Cut seedless white and blue grapes in half. Place in glass and add dry, red wine. Decorate top with grapes and cherries.

SAUCES

Peach Sauce

1 quart peaches, mashed	2 cups peaches, mashed
¾ lb. sugar	scant 1 cup sugar
1 pint water	½ cup water
½ oz. cornstarch	1 tbsp. cornstarch
juice of one lemon	juice of ½ lemon

Method

Dissolve cornstarch in water. Bring to a boil the sugar, peaches and lemon juice. Stir in the starch mixture and let simmer until thickened. Sauce may be served hot or cold.

Chocolate Sauce

1 lb. sugar	1 cup sugar (generous)
1 pint water	½ cup water
vanilla	vanilla
8 ozs. semi-sweet chocolate	4 squares semi-sweet chocolate
2 ozs. rum	2 tbsp. rum

Method

Boil water and sugar until clear. Add chopped chocolate and vanilla. Stir frequently. Sauce is ready as soon as chocolate is dissolved.

Pineapple Sauce

1 pint pineapple, mashed	1 cup pineapple, mashed
1 lb. sugar	1 cup sugar (generous)
¼ pint water or pineapple juice	½ cup water or pineapple juice
1 pint white wine	1 cup white wine
juice of one lemon	juice of ½ lemon
1 oz. cornstarch	1 tbsp. cornstarch

Method

Dissolve cornstarch in water. Bring to a boil wine, juice, and sugar. Add starch mixture. Let simmer for a few minutes. Blend in pineapple.

Apricot Sauce

1 pint apricot pulp	1 cup apricot pulp
½ pint water	½ cup water
12 ozs. sugar	1 cup sugar (generous)
½ oz. cornstarch	½ tbsp. cornstarch
juice of one lemon	juice of one-half lemon
1 orange rind, grated	½ orange rind, grated

Method

Dissolve starch in water. Bring to a boil pulp, sugar, and flavoring. Stir in starch. Let boil for a few minutes. Strain. Serve hot or cold.

Note: Apricot sauce may also be made of apricot jam, in which case the jam is merely diluted with sugar syrup and heated.

Chocolate Cream Sauce

12 ozs. sugar	½ cup sugar (generous)
1 quart whipping cream	1 cup whipping cream
5 ozs. butter	2 tbsp. butter
7 ozs. chocolate	2 squares chocolate
1 oz. cornstarch	2 tbsp. cornstarch
8 egg yolks	2 egg yolks
vanilla	vanilla

Method

Heat cream and sugar. Dissolve starch in a little water and add with yolks to cream mixture. Let thicken, stirring constantly. Add chopped chocolate and butter. Blend well.

Note: Condensed milk may be substituted for one-half of the whipping cream.

Orange Cream Sauce

12 ozs. sugar	scant 1 cup sugar
1 pint white wine	1 cup white wine
1 pint water	1 cup water
5 egg yolks	3 egg yolks
5 egg whites	3 egg whites
1 oz. cornstarch	1 tbsp. cornstarch
juice of one orange	juice of one-half orange
1 orange rind, grated	$\frac{1}{2}$ orange rind, grated

Method

Bring to a boil the water, wine, juice, and rind. Dissolve starch in a little water. Add yolks and combine with boiling mixture. Blend the yolk mixture in with a few swift strokes and remove from heat. Strain the hot mixture and add the stiffly-beaten egg whites.

Strawberry Sauce

1 quart strawberries, mashed	2 cups strawberries, mashed
1 lb. sugar	1 cup sugar
juice of one orange	juice of one-half orange
1 lemon rind, grated	$\frac{1}{2}$ lemon rind, grated

Method

Combine berries with sugar and strain. Add juice and rind. Serve chilled.

Wine Sauce

12 ozs. sugar	$\frac{7}{8}$ cup sugar
1 pint white wine	1 cup white wine
$\frac{3}{4}$ pint water	$\frac{3}{4}$ cup water
juice and rind of 1 lemon	juice and rind of $\frac{1}{2}$ lemon
$1\frac{1}{4}$ ozs. cornstarch	1 tbsp. cornstarch
dash cinnamon	dash cinnamon
dash nutmeg	dash nutmeg

Method

Dissolve starch in a little of the water. Bring to a boil the remaining water and the sugar. Add starch and flavoring. Remove from heat and stir in wine. Serve hot.

Wine Chateau

1 pint white wine	1 cup white wine
6 egg yolks	3 egg yolks
2 whole eggs	1 whole egg
8 ozs. sugar	$\frac{1}{2}$ cup sugar (generous)
1 lemon rind, grated	$\frac{1}{2}$ lemon rind, grated
vanilla	vanilla

Method

Combine all ingredients in double boiler and beat until fluffy and hot. Serve at once.

Brandy Sauce

1 quart water	2 cups water
1 lb. 8 ozs. sugar	$1\frac{3}{4}$ cups sugar
2 ozs. cornstarch	2 tbsp. cornstarch
8 ozs. butter	scant $\frac{1}{2}$ cup butter
3 ozs. brandy	$1\frac{1}{2}$ ozs. brandy
juice and rind of one lemon	juice and rind of one-half lemon
dash nutmeg	dash nutmeg

Method

Dissolve starch in a little of the water. Bring to a boil the water, sugar, flavoring, and juice. Add starch mixture and boil two minutes. Strain, then add the brandy and butter. Mix well.

Cream Sauce with Rum

1 lb. sugar	1 cup sugar
1 pint wine	1 cup wine
$\frac{1}{4}$ pint rum	$\frac{1}{8}$ cup rum
1 oz. butter	1 tbsp. butter
8 egg yolks	4 egg yolks
1 oz. cornstarch	1 tbsp. cornstarch
juice and rind of one lemon	juice and rind of one-half lemon.

Method

Proceed as described under "Orange Cream Sauce." Add butter and rum.

Polonaise Sauce

12 ozs. sugar	$\frac{7}{8}$ cup sugar
1 pint white wine	1 cup white wine
$\frac{3}{4}$ pint water	$\frac{3}{4}$ cup water
juice and rind of one lemon	juice and rind of one-half lemon

1¼ ozs. cornstarch	1 tbsp. cornstarch
dash cinnamon	dash cinnamon
dash nutmeg	dash nutmeg
1½ ozs. chopped almonds	¼ cup chopped almonds
2 ozs. currants	¼ cup currants
1 oz. mixed fruit	½ cup mixed fruit
1 orange rind, grated	½ orange rind, grated

Method

Proceed as described under "Wine Sauce." Add fruits and let simmer until tender.

Hot Wine Foam

1 quart white wine	2 cups white wine
6 ozs. sugar	½ cup sugar (generous)
juice of three lemons	juice of 1½ lemons
1 lemon rind, grated	½ lemon rind, grated
6 egg yolks	3 egg yolks

Method

Put all ingredients into double boiler. Beat until hot and fluffy. Serve at once.

Vanilla Sauce

17 ozs. milk	2 cups milk
3½ ozs. sugar	½ cup sugar
5 egg yolks	5 egg yolks
1 tbsp. cornstarch	1 tbsp. cornstarch
vanilla	vanilla

Method

Put all ingredients in double boiler. Beat until thick and hot. Remove from heat and continue beating for another five minutes.

Swedish Sauce

4 ozs. sugar	scant ½ cup sugar
¼ pint water	½ cup water
⅛ pint brandy	¼ cup brandy

Method

Melt sugar until light brown. Dilute with water. When cold, add brandy.

Nougat Sauce

Prepare vanilla sauce. (*See Index.*) Stir enough nougat into the hot mixture to taste.

Raspberry Sauce

Prepare as directed under "Strawberry Sauce." (*See Index.*) Substitute raspberries for strawberries.

Caramel Sauce

8 ozs. sugar	1 cup sugar
1 oz. honey	⅛ cup honey
few drops red coloring	few drops red coloring
milk	milk

Method

Melt sugar, honey and coloring over heat, stirring constantly. When sugar crystals are dissolved and mixture is light brown, remove from heat. Dilute with hot milk, adding a little at a time until creamy thick. Let cool. Add a few spoons of rum if desired.

Sauce Zabayon

1 quart white wine	2 cups white wine
12 egg yolks	6 egg yolks
8 ozs. sugar	scant ½ cup sugar
1/16 pint rum	2 tbsp. rum
dash cloves	dash cloves

Method

Beat all ingredients together in double boiler until hot and slightly thickened. Serve at once.

Melba Sauce

½ quart fresh raspberry juice	2 cups fresh raspberry juice
½ pint red currant jelly	1 cup red currant jelly
8 ozs. sugar	scant ½ cup sugar
¼ oz. cornstarch	1 tsp. cornstarch

Method

Dissolve cornstarch in a little water. Bring to a boil the juice and jelly. Stir in sugar. Continue boiling for a few minutes, then add starch solution.

PUDDINGS

Puddings are custard-like desserts which are boiled or baked in forms. The forms must be well

An arrangement made from chocolate and vanilla pudding and lemon aspic triangles. The garnishes are cut truffles, parsley, and pale green butter cream.

Pudding *a la Rosenkavalier* resting in orchid blossoms.

The center is built from chestnut fudge decorated with whipped cream and topped with chestnuts made of fudge and chocolate. The plate is filled out with orange jelly.

Outside decoration is of *petits fours glacé*.

The gondola is constructed of pound cake and strawberry butter cream decorated with whipped cream and strawberries. Strawberry tarts set on a red jelly mirror complete the arrangement.

buttered and sugared to insure smooth separation of pudding from the form when it is turned out. Sugar is used rather than flour as sugar will not bind as solidly with butter, as flour and butter would. Because of this, the surface of the pudding will be softer and more absorbant.

Puddings may be served hot or cold, in the form, without the form, or sliced. They should always be accompanied by a properly seasoned sauce. The sauce may be poured over the pudding, or served in a side dish.

Warm puddings should be served as soon as they have been turned out of the molds. Otherwise they will fall and become watery. Cold puddings are creams to which gelatine has been added for better support, together with whipping cream or egg whites. Fruits may also be added. Puddings which are served in molds require less eggs than those which are turned out.

Puddings are baked in a water bath. The forms are placed in a large saucepan which has been half-filled with water. Bake in an oven with plenty of bottom heat to make sure that the water stays at the boiling point. The baking time is about one hour. However, it is better to bake puddings five minutes too long than two minutes too short.

Rice Pudding

3 ozs. rice	$\frac{3}{8}$ cup rice
1 pint milk	2 cups milk
3 ozs. sugar	scant $\frac{1}{2}$ cup sugar
$\frac{1}{2}$ oz. butter	1 tbsp. butter
4 egg yolks	4 egg yolks
dash salt	dash salt
vanilla	vanilla
4 egg whites	4 egg whites

Method

Bring rice to boil in water. Drain off water. Pour milk over rice and continue cooking until tender. Let cool. Cream butter, sugar, salt, and vanilla, adding yolks slowly. Blend in cooked rice. Beat whites until stiff and fold into rice mixture. Pour into buttered, sugared forms and bake as directed under "Puddings" for approximately one hour. Serve with wine foam.

Almond Pudding

3 ozs. sugar	scant $\frac{1}{2}$ cup sugar
3 ozs. marzipan or ground almonds	3 ozs. marzipan or $\frac{3}{4}$ cup ground almonds
5 egg yolks	5 egg yolks
4 egg whites	4 egg whites
3 ozs. flour	scant $\frac{3}{4}$ cup flour
$1\frac{1}{2}$ ozs. cake crumbs	$\frac{1}{2}$ cup cake crumbs
1 oz. melted butter	2 tbsp. melted butter
1 lemon rind, grated	1 lemon rind, grated
vanilla	vanilla

Method

Cream marzipan or almonds, sugar, flavoring, and yolks. Add stiffly-beaten whites. Blend in flour and crumbs. Stir in melted butter. Pour into buttered, sugared pudding forms and bake for approximately forty-five minutes. Serve with wine sauce.

Pudding Arrangement

Pudding à la Rosenkavalier

Pudding à la Rosenkavalier can be made from any kind of pudding in a cake tin. The one illustrated consists of layers of caramel pudding alternated with thin layers of almond butter cake. The decoration includes lady fingers, cherries, whipped cream, a marzipan rose, and angelica. (See Index.) Orchid blossoms and a silk ribbon complete the arrangement.

Pineapple Pudding

$1\frac{1}{2}$ ozs. macaroon crumbs	scant $\frac{1}{2}$ cup macaroon crumbs
$1\frac{1}{2}$ ozs. cake, diced	8–10 small cake cubes
3 ozs. pineapple cubes	$\frac{1}{2}$ cup pineapple cubes
3 egg yolks	3 egg yolks
$\frac{1}{4}$ pint whipping cream	$\frac{1}{2}$ cup whipping cream
$\frac{3}{4}$ oz. gelatine	$2\frac{1}{2}$ tbsp. gelatine
$1\frac{1}{2}$ ozs. sugar	scant $\frac{1}{4}$ cup sugar
vanilla	vanilla

Method

Sprinkle pineapple and cake crumbs with rum. Soften gelatine in a little cold water, add sugar, milk, and yolks. Bring to a boil, stirring constantly. Let cool. Shortly before the mixture becomes firm, add whipped cream. Blend in macaroon crumbs, pineapple and cake cubes. Pour into oiled pudding forms. Let chill. Serve with fruit sauce.

Chocolate Pudding 1

3¾ ozs. sugar	3½ cups sugar (generous)
1½ ozs. almonds, chopped	⅜ cup almonds, chopped
6 egg yolks	6 egg yolks
5 egg whites	5 egg whites
1½ ozs. flour	⅜ cup flour
2½ ozs. cake crumbs	¾ cup cake crumbs
1 oz. cocoa	(generous)
dash cinnamon	4½ tbsp. cocoa
dash cloves	dash cinnamon
vanilla	dash cloves
	vanilla

Method

Cream sugar, egg yolks, flavoring, and almonds. Add stiffly-beaten whites. Sift together the flour, cocoa, and crumbs. Blend into egg mixture. Pour into buttered and sugared pudding forms. Bake approximately one hour. Serve warm, with vanilla sauce or chocolate sauce.

Chocolate Pudding 2

½ pint milk	1 cup milk
4 egg yolks	4 egg yolks
4 egg whites	4 egg whites
½ oz. cornstarch	1 tbsp. cornstarch
¾ oz. cocoa	1¼ tbsp. cocoa
3¾ ozs. sugar	½ cup sugar (generous)
¾ oz. gelatine	2½ tbsp. gelatine
vanilla	vanilla

Method

Soften gelatine in little water. Add milk, starch, sugar, yolks, vanilla, and cocoa. Bring to a boil swiftly. Remove from heat and mix until almost cold. Blend in stiffly-beaten whites. Pour into oiled pudding forms. Serve with either chocolate or vanilla sauce.

Note: One-quarter of a pint whipped cream may be used instead of egg whites.

Apple Bread Pudding

Use sliced, toasted white bread without crust. Peel and slice apples. Put into buttered cake pan one layer of bread slices, soaked in standard custard cream *(see Index)* and one layer apple slices. Sprinkle raisins and cinnamon sugar on top. Alternate in this fashion until pan is three-quarters filled. Top layer must be bread. Pour more custard over bread-apple mixture until pudding will not absorb any more liquid. Place pan into larger sauce pan, filled to three-quarters with water and bake at 300° F. until apples are tender.

Almond Cherry Pudding

¾ oz. white bread, toasted	4–5 slices white bread, toasted
⅛ pint milk	¼ cup milk
2½ ozs. almonds, chopped	⅝ cup almonds, chopped
3½ ozs. sugar	½ cup sugar
2½ ozs. butter	¼ cup butter (generous)
6 egg yolks	6 egg yolks
3 egg whites	3 egg whites
1 lb. fresh or dried cherries	1 lb. fresh or dried cherries
dash cinnamon	dash cinnamon
dash cloves	dash cloves
1 lemon rind, grated	1 lemon rind, grated

Method

Cut bread into small pieces and soak in milk. Cream sugar, butter, yolks, flavors, and almonds. Add bread mixture. Beat whites until stiff and blend into first mixture. Add stoned cherries. Pour into buttered, sugared pudding forms. Sprinkle top with cake crumbs. Bake at 300° F. for approximately one hour. After baking sprinkle with cherry juice. Serve with almond, or cherry-flavored sauce.

English Pudding

4 ozs. butter	½ cup butter
5 ozs. sugar	scant ¾ cup sugar
6 ozs. flour	scant 1½ cups flour
4 eggs	4 eggs
4 ozs. currants	scant 1 cup currants
6 ozs. raisins	1¼ cups raisins
3 ozs. candied orange peel	½ cup candied orange peel
¾ oz. almonds, chopped	2 tbsp. almonds, chopped
dash baking powder	dash baking powder
dash cinnamon	dash cinnamon
1 tbsp. *couleur*	1 tbsp. *couleur*
½ oz. rum	½ oz. rum

Method

Cream eggs, butter, sugar, and flavoring. Soak fruits in rum and add to creamed mixture. Pour into buttered and sugared pudding forms. Bake at 300° F. for approximately three hours. Test pudding with tooth pick, which should stay clean when pulled out of pudding. Before serving, sprinkle with rum.

Lemon Cream Pudding

¼ pint white wine	1 cup white wine
juice of two lemons	juice of two lemons
5 ozs. sugar	scant ¾ cup sugar
3 eggs	3 eggs
½ oz. gelatine	1½ tbsp. gelatine
1 lemon rind, grated	1 lemon rind, grated

Method

Soften gelatine in wine. Add rest of ingredients. Put mixture into double boiler and beat until just about boiling hot. Continue beating until mixture is cool. Pour into buttered, sugared pudding form. Allow to chill completely. Decorate top with whipped cream and glazed fruits.

Orange Cream Pudding

3 ozs. sugar	scant ½ cup sugar
5 egg yolks	5 egg yolks
juice of four oranges	juice of four oranges
1 orange rind, grated	1 orange rind, grated
⅛ pint white wine	¼ cup white wine
½ oz. gelatine	1½ tbsp. gelatine
⅓ pint whipped cream	½ cup whipped cream

Method

Proceed as described under "Lemon Cream Pudding."

Cream Pudding Charlotte

¼ pint milk	½ cup milk
5 egg yolks	5 egg yolks
3½ ozs. sugar	½ cup sugar (generous)
vanilla	vanilla
¾ ozs. gelatine	2 tbsp. gelatine
¼ pint whipped cream	½ cup whipped cream

Method

Line bottom and sides of a cake tin or glass bowl with sponge cake. Sprinkle with rum. Soak gelatine in milk. Add yolks, sugar, and vanilla. Bring to a boil, stirring constantly. Continue mixing until cold. Blend in whipped cream shortly before cream hardens. Pour into prepared pudding form. Serve decorated with whipped cream and glazed fruits.

Caramel Pudding

5 egg whites	5 egg whites
5 egg yolks	5 egg yolks
2½ ozs. flour	½ cup flour
5½ ozs. sugar	scant ¾ cup sugar
½ pint milk	1 cup milk
2 ozs. butter	¼ cup butter
¼ lemon rind, grated	¼ lemon rind, grated
6 ozs. sugar	¾ cup sugar
1 tbsp. honey	1 tbsp. honey

Method

Melt six ounces sugar (¾ cup) with honey over slow fire until golden brown. Dilute with either water or sugar syrup until creamy thick. Pour into pudding forms. Let cool.

Boil milk, sugar, and butter. Add flour and continue boiling until thick. Let cool. Blend in yolks with few swift strokes and fold in stiffly-beaten whites. Pour into prepared pudding forms. Bake at 300° F. for approximately one hour. After baking, let cool and allow pudding to soften caramel before serving.

Coffee Mousse

½ pint strong coffee	1 cup strong coffee
dash salt	dash salt
½ tbsp. flour	½ tbsp. flour
4 egg whites	4 egg yolks
4 egg yolks	4 egg whites
8 ozs. sugar	1 cup sugar
½ pint milk	1 cup milk
1 pint whipping cream	2 cups whipping cream
½ lemon rind, grated	½ lemon rind, grated

Method

Heat milk, coffee, sugar, and salt. Stir in flour. Bring to a boil, stirring constantly. Remove from heat and stir in beaten yolks. Cook mixture in double boiler until thickened. Let cool. Beat whites until stiff and add to milk mixture. Fold in whipped cream. Freeze. Decorate with whipped cream and glazed fruits.

Lemon Mousse

4 egg whites	4 egg whites
4 egg yolks	4 egg yolks
pinch salt	pinch salt
1 pint whipping cream	2 cups whipping cream
¼ pint honey	½ cup honey
¼ pint lemon juice	½ cup lemon juice
1 lemon rind, grated	1 lemon rind, grated

Method

Beat yolks, honey, juice, and rind in double boiler until thickened. Let cool. Fold in stiff whites and whipped cream. Freeze. Decorate with whipped cream and glazed citron peel.

Jellied Puddings

To line a mold with jelly, use jelly when it is almost cold but still liquid. Wine jelly is a good choice. (*See Index.*) Pour jelly into mold and place in ice water. The jelly will start to set from the outside. Take molds from water and turn upside down to allow the liquid center to run out. The jelly wall should be about ⅛″ thick. Large molds should have a slightly thicker layer of jelly.

Method 1

Prepare a chocolate pudding, mixing some pieces of lady fingers into it and pour cold into jelly-lined molds. Close mold with layer of cake. Let set. Turn out of mold, decorate, and serve.

Method 2

Line molds with clear wine jelly. Warm strawberry sauce and add one ounce of dissolved gelatine to every one quart of sauce. Pour into molds just before it sets, alternating layers of sauce and lady fingers. Let cool completely. Turn out of mold and decorate with whipped cream and glazed fruits.

These examples suggest the great variety that may be obtained by using clear or colored jellies in combination with any desired pudding.

Basic Jelly

8 ozs. gelatine	¾ cup gelatine
4½ quarts water	2¼ quarts water
3 lbs. sugar	3½ cups sugar

juice of 10 lemons	juice of 5 lemons
1 orange rind, grated	½ orange rind, grated
1 lemon rind, grated	½ lemon rind, grated
1 tsp. cinnamon	½ tsp. cinnamon
1 tsp. cloves	½ tsp. cloves
1 tsp. allspice	½ tsp. allspice
1 tsp. mace	½ tsp. mace
1 quart wine	1 pint wine

Method

Soak gelatine in water for one hour. Add the lemon juice and the rinds, spices, and sugar. Boil mixture for ten minutes and strain. When cool, add wine.

Note: Jellies which are to be served in glasses may contain less gelatine than those which have to be cut, used as glaze, or as shells for puddings.

Fruit Charlottes

(Use raspberries, peaches, apricots, almond paste, or strawberries.)

1 quart ripe berries, mashed	2 cups ripe berries, mashed
1 lb. powdered sugar	1½ cups powdered sugar (generous)
2 ozs. gelatine	1 tbsp. gelatine
1½ pints whipped cream	1½ cups whipped cream

Method

Line sides and bottom of a round cake tin with sponge cake. Soak gelatine in a little cold water and bring to a boil slowly. Add gelatine mixture and sugar to the fruit. When mixture has cooled, but is still liquid, fold in whipped cream and pour into prepared tin. Refrigerate for several hours. Turn out from tin and decorate.

Chocolate Charlotte Tosca

1 quart milk	2 cups milk
1 quart whipped cream	2 cups whipped cream
1¼ ozs. gelatine	1½ tbsp. gelatine
18 egg yolks	9 egg yolks
14 ozs. sugar	1 cup sugar
5 ozs chocolate	2½ squares chocolate
vanilla	vanilla

Method

Soak gelatine in a little cold water. Over medium heat stir together the milk, yolks, sugar, and flavoring. Continue stirring until the mixture has thickened. Melt chocolate and add to above. Let cool. Blend in whipped cream. Pour mixture into oiled and sugared pudding form. Chill in refrigerator for several hours. Turn out on platter and decorate with whipped cream and lady fingers.

Alaska Flammé Pudding

Line a flat serving dish with a thin layer of sponge cake. Set brick of ice cream on end and cut in half from upper left corner to lower right corner. Set two pieces of ice cream in form of a pyramid on the cake. Cover with thin layer of cake. Prepare meringue and dress the pyramid with a star tube. Decorate sides with lady fingers. Place in very hot oven with plenty of over heat to brown the meringue. Decorate further with glazed fruits and angelica.

VII

YEAST DOUGH PRODUCTS

INTRODUCTION

In order to understand any problems that may arise in the making of yeast dough, it is necessary to analyze the chemical reactions of the elements involved. There are two types of yeast. The first is fresh yeast, which is a product of the beer breweries, and the second is dry yeast. The latter is basically the same but is dried under a vacuum process to stop the growth of the cells temporarily. Dry yeast must be completely dissolved in water before it can be mixed with flour. Yeast consists of millions of micro-organisms, and when these are combined with certain elements found in flour, such as calcium, phosphorous, carbon, and sugar, the basic ingredients for the fermentation process are present.

What Actually Happens?

At first the living yeast cells split the starch cells which are found in flour and free the sugar content. A small part of this sugar will start its own chain reaction, stimulating the growth of yeast cells, while the larger part of it will divide into carbonic acid and alcohol. This carbonic acid, under the influence of warm temperatures, will expand and grow—in other words, the dough will rise.

This short explanation should indicate the importance of a proper start. The cells may not develop because of too low a temperature, or, just as harmful, too high a temperature. The result in the first case would be an under-developed dough, while in the second case the expanding power of the yeast may be completely destroyed. The average temperature of the liquid used to dissolve the yeast should be 85° F. In areas of extremely cold temperatures, a little bit of sugar will help the fermenting power of yeast during the sponge process.

What Is Yeast Sponge?

Yeast sponge is a mixture of all the required yeast for one formula plus a small part of the flour blended together with either milk or water. (The liquid should be at 85° F.) This sponge, when put in a warm place, will start the above-mentioned chemical reaction. Since all the yeast,

but only part of the flour is used, the yeast cells will have no difficulty in tripling the bulk of the yeast sponge. It is wrong to believe that yeast doughs which are mixed together without starting a sponge first are as good as doughs using the sponge process. In the former case, the yeast has to work harder in order to lift the weight of the mass of flour, and thereby loses some of its power.

When mixing the yeast sponge with the remaining ingredients, always add the eggs and sugar before the fat. Yeast cells, as well as all other living cells, need oxygen. If the yeast cells were surrounded by insulating fat particles, their ability to develop and multiply would be restricted.

How To Mix Yeast Dough

The yeast sponge should be of the same consistency as the final dough. Properly prepared sponge will rise within a short period of time, indicating its readiness by sending gas bubbles to the surface. The remaining ingredients should then be added, making sure that the fat is added last. When the ingredients are well blended, the actual kneading process begins. The dough must be kneaded until it takes on a silky appearance and no longer sticks to the hands. If the dough is mixed by machine, the danger of over-beating is ever present. This machine-killed dough can be found in many stores. The pastries look as if they were made of clay rather than flour, and have no flexibility or spring. As the flavor-making carbonic acid cannot develop, over-beating also results in a loss of the characteristic flavor of yeast dough.

When the dough has been kneaded it is put in a warm place to rise. Then it is pushed back to its former size and the desired goods are shaped and placed on the baking sheets. When the goods have risen again they are ready to be baked. To give the final product a finer texture, the dough may be allowed to rise three times instead of the above-mentioned twice-risen method. This method, although it eliminates large holes in the baked goods, will result in a less flexible product.

How To Bake Yeast Dough

Before baking, the goods must be put in a warm place, from 75° F. to 80° F., to allow them to rise for the last time. The rising must be checked at frequent intervals. Pastries which have risen too much will collapse when exposed to high temperatures, while those with too little fermentation will stay small, bake hard, and lose flavor. It is difficult to be specific as to the amount each item should rise, as it will vary with the material and temperature. However, small pieces such as buns or rolls should gain about one-third of their original size, and larger pieces such as coffee cakes or breads baked in tins should just about double in size.

To obtain a golden brown color, the goods should be egg washed immediately after shaping. After the goods have risen, a touch of the pastry brush may cause them to collapse slightly.

Baking temperatures are given with each formula. Small pastry pieces should be baked swiftly in a hot oven to prevent their drying out. After baking, any items which are to be glazed or iced should be done while still hot to assure a shiny finish.

BASIC YEAST DOUGHS AND THEIR PRODUCTS

Basic Yeast Dough 1

4 lbs. bread flour	$6\frac{3}{4}$ cups bread flour
$4\frac{3}{4}$ ozs. yeast	$4\frac{1}{2}$ cakes yeast
5 eggs	$2\frac{1}{2}$ eggs
$6\frac{1}{2}$ ozs. sugar	scant $\frac{1}{2}$ cup sugar
8 ozs. butter	$\frac{1}{2}$ cup butter
warm milk	warm milk
$1\frac{1}{4}$ ozs. salt	dash salt
vanilla	vanilla
1 orange and lemon rind, grated	$\frac{1}{2}$ orange and lemon rind, grated

Method

Dissolve the yeast in a little warm milk. Add about one-third of the flour. Blend well to form yeast sponge. Let sponge rise well. Blend in remaining ingredients, adding the butter last. Add enough warm milk to make a medium-stiff dough. Knead thoroughly. This dough may be used for a variety of buns, rolls, or coffee cakes.

Basic Yeast Dough 2

4 lbs. bread flour	$3\frac{1}{2}$ cups bread flour
1 lb. 8 ozs. butter	$\frac{3}{4}$ cup butter
20 egg yolks	5 egg yolks
3 ozs. yeast	$1\frac{1}{2}$ cakes yeast
7 ozs. sugar	$\frac{1}{4}$ cup sugar
$1\frac{1}{4}$ ozs. salt	dash salt
1 quart milk	1 cup milk
vanilla	vanilla
1 orange and lemon rind, grated	$\frac{1}{4}$ orange and lemon rind, grated

Method

Proceed as directed in "Basic Yeast Dough 1." This dough is richer and more tender than the first one. It can be made one day ahead, placed in a stainless steel bowl, and refrigerated.

FANCY SWEET BREADS OF YEAST DOUGH

Fruit Spirals

Roll a piece of yeast dough into a rectangular shape. Brush lightly with melted butter and apply any of the following fillings. Roll dough tightly in the fashion of a jelly roll. Cut pieces $\frac{1}{2}''$ wide. Set on baking sheet and egg wash. Let rise. Bake at 375° F. to 400° F.

Fillings:

(1) raisins, cinnamon sugar, grated lemon rinds
(2) mixed fruits, grated orange, and lemon rind
(3) slivered or chopped almonds, cinnamon sugar
(4) shredded cocoanut, sugar, grated orange rind, rum
(5) chopped walnuts, cinnamon, nutmeg, sugar

Vanilla Rolls

Roll a piece of "Basic Yeast Dough 2" into rectangular shapes. Brush lightly with melted butter. Dust freely with vanilla-flavored powdered sugar. Cut wide strips lengthwise. Cut each strip into triangles. Roll each triangle from its widest side to the point. Egg wash and let rise. Bake at 400° F.

Honey Cream Slices

Prepare filling first. Roll a piece of "Basic Yeast Dough 2" to a thickness of $\frac{1}{2}''$ to cover the pan completely. Spread filling on top. Let rise. Bake at 375° F.

Preparing vanilla rolls.

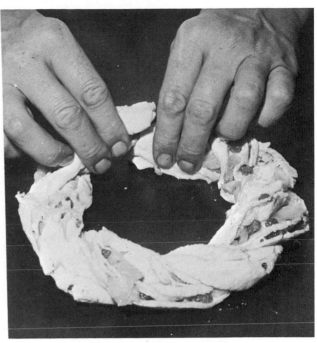

Braiding a fruit wreath.

Preparing brioche.

Vienna brioche.

Brioche fruit loaf.

Soaking rum babas in sugar and rum solution

Filling

3 ozs. butter	⅜ cup butter
1½ ozs. almonds	⅜ cup almonds
1 tbsp. honey	1 tbsp. honey
5 ozs. sugar	¾ cup sugar
approx. 5 tbsp. milk	approx. 5 tbsp. milk
cinnamon	cinnamon
1 lemon rind, grated	1 lemon rind, grated

Method

Mix ingredients together and cook, stirring constantly until mixture binds well. Spread on rolled dough. This will cover a piece of dough about 6″ x 12″. After baking, cool and split in half horizontally. Fill with custard cream and slice.

Apricot Slices

Roll a piece of dough, ¼″ thick and the full length and width of a baking sheet. Cover top with cake or cracker crumbs. Set apricot halves very close together on dough. Sprinkle with cinnamon sugar and grated lemon peel. Let rise. Bake at 350° F. After baking, glaze with hot apricot jam or sugar syrup. Cut in slices or squares.

Note: Other fruits such as peaches, cherries, apples, plums, pineapple, and so on may be used. If canned fruit is used, care must be taken that it is well drained, as the dough will otherwise become too soggy.

Fruit Wreath of Yeast Dough

Roll a sheet of "Basic Dough 2" to a rectangle 10″ x 18″. Brush with melted butter. Sprinkle with mixed fruits, raisins, grated lemon and orange rinds. Roll in the fashion of a jelly roll. Split open lengthwise and twine the two strips together. Form a ring and set on baking pan. Egg wash. Let rise. Bake at 375° F. Ice with water icing after baking.

Cinnamon Wreath

Proceed as directed under "Fruit wreath of yeast dough." Use a filling of sliced almonds, sugar, cinnamon, and grated lemon rind.

Brioche

4 lbs. bread flour	3½ cups bread flour
2 ozs. yeast	1 cake yeast
18 eggs	4 eggs
½ pint milk	¼ cup milk
1 lb. butter	½ cup butter
6 ozs. sugar	¼ cup sugar
2 ozs. salt	dash salt
vanilla	vanilla

Method

Dissolve yeast in warm milk and add enough of the flour to form yeast sponge. Let rise. Add rest of ingredients. Knead well. Let rise and push back. Divide the dough into two parts, the larger piece two-thirds of the whole quantity. Cut the larger section into pieces about three-quarters of an ounce each. Cut the smaller piece into enough sections so that there is one for each of the three-quarter ounce pieces. Roll the larger pieces into balls and place in tart forms, well greased. Roll the smaller pieces into balls, indent the large balls and place the little ones in each of the holes. Let rise. Apply strong egg wash. Make three cuts with scissors into the edge of lower piece in each tart form. Bake at 400° F.

Brioche Fruit Loaf

Roll the desired amount of brioche dough and add one and one-half to two ounces of mixed fruits for each pound of dough. Form a smooth roll large enough to half-fill a loaf tin. Egg wash and let rise. Slit loaf down the middle lengthwise with a sharp knife. Sprinkle with sliced almonds and powdered sugar. Bake at 325° F. to 350° F. Remove from the tin at once. Cool on a wire screen. Serve in toasted and buttered slices

Vienna Brioche

Roll the desired amount of brioche dough into a rectangular shape. Spread with a filling of walnuts or poppy seed *(see Index)*. Roll dough from one side to center and from remaining side to center. Place upside down into a greased loaf tin. Egg wash and let rise. Bake at 300° F. When cold, sprinkle with vanilla-flavored powdered sugar.

Croissants

9 lbs. bread flour	7 cups bread flour
8 ozs. butter	$\frac{1}{4}$ cup butter
7 ozs. sugar	$\frac{1}{4}$ cup sugar
$1\frac{1}{2}$ ozs. salt	dash salt
4 quarts milk	1 quart milk
$4\frac{1}{2}$ ozs. yeast	$2\frac{1}{4}$ cakes yeast
2 portions butter of 1 lb. 4 ozs. each	2 portions butter of $\frac{1}{2}$ cup each

Method

Dissolve yeast in a little warm milk. Add about one-eighth of the flour to form a hard dough (sponge). Put dough into a container of warm water. When sponge has risen enough it will float on the top. Remove from water and mix with remaining ingredients except butter. Set dough on table, cover with cloth, and allow to rest for thirty minutes. Then roll dough into a rectangular shape. Cover two-thirds of it with one portion of butter. Fold butterless part over next third and fold remaining third on top, so that the original butterless third is now between two layers of butter. Let rest in refrigerator for fifteen minutes. Roll dough to original rectangular shape and repeat procedure with remaining portion of butter. Let rest again for fifteen minutes. Roll and fold two more times in the same fashion without butter. Let dough rest several hours, preferably overnight. *Croissants* are made up like vanilla rolls (*see Index*) for illustration).

Roll dough $\frac{1}{4}$" thick and cut into long strips approximately $3\frac{1}{2}$" wide. Cut strips into triangles and let rest again in refrigerator. Place triangle on table and roll towards you with small rolling pin, thus getting a shape about 3" wide 5" long. Roll dough up from base to point, form crescents and place on lightly greased baking sheet. Egg wash and let rise. Bake at 400° F.

Note: Croissants may be served plain, or split open, buttered and toasted and filled with various meats.

RUM BABAS

$\frac{1}{2}$ cup milk	$\frac{1}{2}$ cup milk
$1\frac{1}{2}$ ozs. sugar	$\frac{1}{4}$ cup sugar
8 eggs	8 eggs
1 lb. bread flour	$3\frac{1}{2}$ cups bread flour
$1\frac{1}{2}$ ozs. yeast	3 cakes yeast
5 ozs. butter	$\frac{5}{8}$ cup butter
salt	salt
vanilla	vanilla
2 ozs. raisins	scant $\frac{1}{2}$ cup raisins

Method

Dissolve yeast in warm milk and add enough of the flour to form a thin yeast sponge. Let rise well. Add rest of ingredients and beat dough by hand or with a spatula until silky soft. Cover with towel. Let rise again. Using a pastry bag with large, round tube, or a spoon, fill greased, small tart forms three-quarters full with dough. Let rise. Bake at 350° F.

Boil sugar syrup (1 lb. sugar, 1 pint water), with one-half lemon, orange, a dash of cloves, and few bay leaves. Put babas upside down into the solution and let them soak until they have gained one-third of their original size. Remove from syrup and set on screen to drain. The rum may be sprinkled on at this stage, or it can be mixed with the sugar syrup before the babas are put in to soak. Glaze babas with hot apricot jam. Decorate with whipped cream and cherries. Serve with rum-flavored apricot sauce.

Savarin

7 ozs. bread flour	$\frac{3}{4}$ cup bread flour
$\frac{1}{2}$ pint milk	$\frac{1}{2}$ cup milk
$1\frac{3}{4}$ ozs. yeast	$1\frac{3}{4}$ cakes yeast
10 ozs. butter	$1\frac{1}{4}$ cups butter
$1\frac{1}{2}$ ozs. sugar	$\frac{1}{4}$ cup sugar
dash salt	dash salt
1 lb. bread flour	$1\frac{3}{4}$ cups bread flour
12 egg yolks	6 egg yolks
3 ozs. almonds, chopped	$\frac{1}{4}$ cup almonds, chopped
1 lemon rind, grated	$\frac{1}{2}$ lemon rind, grated
1 orange rind, grated	$\frac{1}{2}$ orange rind, grated
nutmeg	nutmeg

Method

Use the smaller amount of flour, warm milk, and yeast to form yeast sponge. Cream the butter, egg yolks, and sugar. Add flavoring, flour, and almonds. Slowly mix in the risen sponge. Place in greased tube pan and let rise. Bake at 325° F. After baking, remove cake from tin, fill tin one-third full of hot sugar syrup (See "Rum Babas."), and put cake back into tin. Let stand until all

Vienna marble *Gugelhopf* iced with chocolate fondant

Vienna *Buchteln* made with plum jam

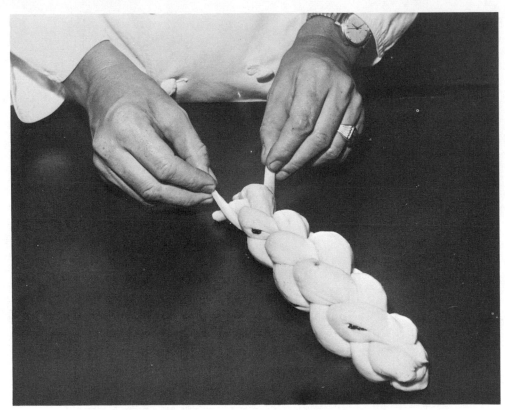

Braiding sweet Vienna bread

Cherry coffee ring decorated with glazed cherries

moisture is absorbed. Then turn cake onto wire screen, and glaze with hot apricot jam. Decorate with glazed cherries and angelica. Serve with rum or vanilla sauce.

Streusel Cake

3 ozs. flour	$\frac{3}{4}$ cup flour
2 ozs. sugar	$\frac{1}{4}$ cup sugar (generous)
1$\frac{1}{2}$ ozs. butter, melted	$\frac{1}{8}$ cup butter, melted
dash baking soda	dash baking soda
dash cinnamon	dash cinnamon
vanilla	vanilla

Method

Mix all ingredients together well. Press dough through large wire screen, or crumble between hands.

Use square or round cake tin of desired size. Fill up to one-half with basic yeast dough 1. Spread thickly with *streusel*. Let rise. Bake at 375° F. Let cool. Cut cake in half and fill with vanilla custard cream. Sprinkle powdered sugar on top.

Vienna Gugelhopf 1

13 ozs. flour (half bread, half cake)	2$\frac{3}{4}$ cups flour (half bread, half cake)
$\frac{3}{4}$ oz. yeast	1$\frac{1}{2}$ cakes yeast
4 ozs. milk	$\frac{1}{2}$ cup milk
4$\frac{1}{2}$ ozs. butter	$\frac{5}{8}$ cup butter
3 eggs	3 eggs
2 yolks	2 yolks
1$\frac{1}{2}$ ozs. sugar	scant $\frac{1}{4}$ cup sugar
dash salt	dash salt
1 lemon rind, grated	1 lemon rind, grated
vanilla	vanilla

Method

Soften the yeast in milk, add one-half of the flour to form yeast sponge. Cream together the butter, eggs, yolks, and sugar, then salt, flavoring, and flour slowly. Add risen yeast sponge. Beat with wooden spoon until dough is silky soft. Place dough into greased *gugelhopf* form (a dome-shaped, ribbed form). Let rise. Bake at 325° F. When cold, brush with hot apricot jam and glaze with vanilla-flavored fondant icing.

Viennese Marble Gugelhopf

Use above formula. When dough is beaten enough, lightly mix in the following mixture : Liquify one ounce (4$\frac{1}{2}$ tbsp.) cocoa with sugar syrup until a creamy consistency is obtained. Add a few drops of rum, grated orange rind, and a dash of baking powder. After baking, ice with chocolate fondant as shown in illustration.

Viennese Gugelhopf 2

10 ozs. butter	$\frac{5}{8}$ cup butter
3 ozs. shortening	3 tbsp. shortening
12 egg yolks	6 egg yolks
6 egg whites	3 egg whites
1 lb. 2 ozs. flour (half bread, half cake flour)	2 cups flour (half bread, half cake flour)
1$\frac{1}{4}$ ozs. yeast	1$\frac{1}{4}$ cakes yeast
1$\frac{1}{2}$ ozs. milk	2 tbsp. milk
5 ozs. sugar	$\frac{3}{8}$ cup sugar
1 lemon rind, grated	$\frac{1}{2}$ lemon rind, grated
vanilla	vanilla

Method

Cream together the butter, shortening, and sugar. Add yolks slowly. Blend in half of the flour. Dissolve yeast in warm milk and add to above. Mix in rest of flour, salt, and flavoring. Lastly, blend in the stiffly-beaten egg whites. Grease form and sprinkle with bread crumbs. Put dough in pan, let rise. Bake at 325° F. Dust with powdered sugar.

Note: Do not make usual yeast sponge.

Sweet Vienna Bread

2 lbs. bread flour	3$\frac{1}{2}$ cups bread flour
1 oz. yeast	1 cake yeast
9 eggs	4 eggs
$\frac{1}{4}$ pint milk	$\frac{1}{4}$ cup milk
8 ozs. butter	$\frac{1}{2}$ cup butter
3 ozs. sugar	$\frac{1}{4}$ cup sugar
1 oz. salt	dash salt
4 ozs. raisins	$\frac{1}{8}$ cup raisins
vanilla	vanilla
1 lemon rind, grated	$\frac{1}{2}$ lemon rind, grated
rum flavoring	rum flavoring

Method

Dissolve yeast in warm milk. Add one-third of flour to form yeast sponge. Cream butter and sugar, adding eggs slowly. Mix with the risen sponge. Add rest of ingredients and knead well. Form three or four strips of dough of equal size and braid them together. Egg wash and let rise. Bake at 350° F. Glaze with hot rum-flavored sugar syrup.

Filbert Coffee Ring

Use approximately one pound of either of the basic yeast doughs. Roll the dough into an oblong and spread with the following filling :

3½ ozs. butter	⅜ cup butter
3½ ozs. sugar	½ cup sugar
1½ ozs. flour	⅜ cup flour
4 egg yolks	4 egg yolks
5 ozs. ground filberts, toasted	2 cups ground filberts, toasted
dash cinnamon	dash cinnamon

Method

Mix all ingredients well and spread over dough. Roll the dough as a jelly roll, join the two ends, and place in a tube pan. Let rise. Bake at 350° F. Ice with vanilla fondant and decorate with whole filberts.

Cherry Almond Ring

4 ozs. marzipan	4 ozs. marzipan
3 ozs. sugar	scant ½ cup sugar
1 egg	1 egg

Method

Mix all ingredients until smooth. Roll an oblong piece of dough using basic formula 1. Spread above mixture on dough. Cover generously with fresh or drained canned cherries. Sprinkle with grated lemon rind. Roll. Grease a tube pan and line the bottom with almond halves. Place roll on top, joining ends to form a ring. Let rise. Bake at 325 to 350° F. When cold, glaze with cherry-flavored water icing.

Note: If marzipan is not available, use grated almonds instead.

Walnut Cake

5 ozs. butter	½ cup butter (generous)
5 ozs. sugar	¾ cup sugar
4 eggs	4 eggs
7 ozs. custard cream	1 cup custard cream
walnuts	walnuts

Method

Cream butter with sugar, add eggs. Blend in custard. Roll about one and one-half pounds of basic yeast dough into an oblong and spread with above mixture. Cover generously with chopped walnuts. Let rise. Bake at 375° F. Sprinkle with powdered sugar.

Apple Desserts

Roll an oblong piece of basic yeast dough. Cover well with sliced apples flavored with cinnamon, grated lemon rind, raisins, and chopped almonds. Top with *streusel.* Let rise. Bake at 375° F. Sprinkle with powdered sugar.

Bugles

1 lb. 4 ozs. bread flour	4 cups bread flour
1½ ozs. sugar	¼ cup sugar
¾ oz. yeast	1½ cakes yeast
8 ozs. butter	1 cup butter
1 lemon rind, grated	1 lemon rind, grated
vanilla	vanilla
milk	milk

Method

Dissolve yeast in a little milk. Add the rest of the ingredients, then knead thoroughly with enough milk to form a smooth, stiff dough.

Note: All ingredients should be cool to keep the yeast inactive. Do not make a yeast sponge. Divide dough into pieces of one ounce each. Roll pieces smoothly into balls. Let dough loosen up for a few minutes, then press balls perfectly flat. Form small rolls of the desired filling, roll into dough. Form crescents and set on greased baking sheet. Brush with an eggwash made of one whole egg plus two egg yolks. Set pans in a cool place to allow egg wash to dry completely. Apply a second layer of egg wash and let dry again. Then squeeze each crescent gently to crack surface of glaze. Bake at 350° F. Yeast will immediately expand cracks on top, giving a unique design.

Note: This type of yeast dough is similar to shortbread dough and will keep fresh for a few days. Following are two suitable fillings.

Walnut Filling

1 lb. cake crumbs	5 cups cake crumbs
2 ozs. butter	¼ cup butter

Walnut coffee cake

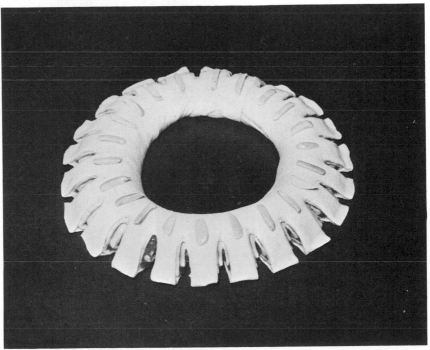

Cocoanut coffee ring decorated with almond slivers

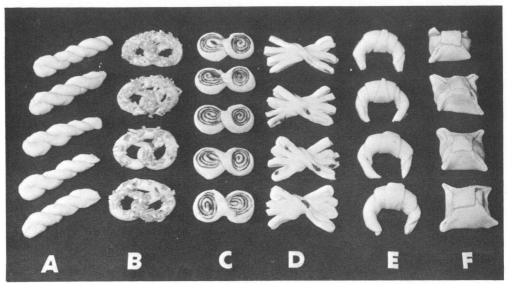

A. Twists B. Pretzels C. Twin rolls D. Cream fans E. Marzipan thorns F. Fruit pockets

A. Bear claws B. Raspberry stars C. Butterflies D. Cinnamon buns E. New York buns

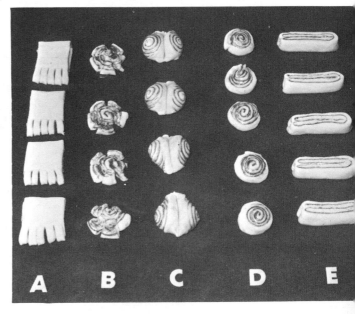

Bread basket made from brioche dough and baked over a large steel bowl. It contains various small rolls, pretzels, and French bread. Decoration is from marzipan.

10 ozs. walnuts, ground	2½ cups walnuts, ground
3 ozs. sugar	scant ½ cup sugar
1–2 ozs. rum	1–2 ozs. rum
dash cinnamon	dash cinnamon
dash nutmeg	dash nutmeg
1 lemon rind, grated	1 lemon rind, grated

Poppy Seed Filling

10 ozs. poppy seed, ground	2 cups poppy seed, ground
2 ozs. butter	¼ cup butter
5 ozs. sugar	¾ cup sugar
12 ozs. cake crumbs	1¾ cups cake crumbs
vanilla	vanilla
1 lemon rind, grated	1 lemon rind, grated
2 orange rinds, grated	2 orange rinds, grated
boiling milk	boiling milk

Note: Mix all ingredients of both formulas with enough boiling milk to get a hard dough. To make the fillings finer, replace some or all of the crumbs with either poppy seed or walnuts.

Prune Goulatches

Cut pieces of yeast dough of one and one-half ounces each. Roll smooth balls and set on greased pans. Let rise slightly. Using a cylindrical piece of wood about 1″ in diameter, press a hollow into the center of each piece of dough. Fill with prune jam. Egg wash and let rise. Bake at 375° F. Glaze with fondant.

Poppy Seed Crescent

⅜ pint milk	¾ cup milk
10 ozs. flour	2½ cups flour
1 oz. yeast	2 cakes yeast
1½ ozs. sugar	scant ¼ cup sugar
2 egg yolks	2 egg yolks
7 ozs. butter	¾ cup butter (generous)
3 ozs. flour	¾ cup flour

Method

Mix the last two ingredients together, form a block, and set aside. Mix the rest of the ingredients as described under "Basic Yeast Dough." Let rise. Roll dough flat and set block of last two items in center. Fold over ends and apply four single turns. (*See Index*, "Puff Paste.") Allow dough to rest for ten minutes between turns. Roll dough ¼″ thick and cut equal triangles. Fill with poppy seed filling. (*See Index*.) Roll triangles and form crescents. Let rise. Egg wash. Bake at 375° F.

Vienna Buchteln

2 lbs. bread flour	3½ cups bread flour
1½ ozs. yeast	1½ cakes yeast
6½ ozs. sugar	½ cup sugar
4 egg yolks	2 egg yolks
dash salt	dash salt
2 eggs	1 egg
5 ozs. butter	⅜ cup butter
milk	milk
1 grated lemon rind.	½ lemon rind, grated
vanilla	vanilla
plum jam	plum jam

Method

Form a yeast sponge, using one-quarter of the flour, and the yeast softened in milk. Cream together the butter, eggs, yolks, and sugar. Add flavoring. Combine rest of ingredients, except plum jam, with the sponge and knead to form smooth, medium-soft dough. Add more milk if necessary. Let rest for thirty minutes.

Roll out dough ¼″ thick and cut small oblongs about 2″ x 3″. Place jam on short side of oblong and roll. Dip rolls into melted butter and place close together in a cake tin. Let rise until double in size. Bake at 350° F. Take from tin while still hot. Serve with hot vanilla sauce. (*See Index,* "Vanilla Sauce.")

Cottage Cheese Pockets

1 lb. cottage cheese	2¼ cups cottage cheese
4 egg yolks	4 egg yolks
5 ozs. sugar	¾ cup sugar
1 oz. raisins	¼ cup raisins
1 lemon rind, grated	1 lemon rind, grated
vanilla	1 orange rind, grated
yeast dough as in "Vienna Buchteln"	vanilla
	yeast dough as in "Vienna Buchteln"

Method

Press cheese through a sieve and mix with rest of ingredients. Roll out dough and cut into squares. Put a spoonful of the filling in center of each square. Moisten corners with egg wash. Fold the four corners to the center and press down firmly. Place a small piece of square dough on top to prevent pockets from opening during baking. Egg wash and allow to rise. Bake at 375° F. Ice with water icing. (*See Index.*)

ZWIEBACK

The name zwieback, originally from the German language, means two (*zwie* or *zwei*) baked (*back*). The biscuit-like dough is baked twice, first in the fashion of bread, and again after it has been cooled and sliced. It is this second baking, or toasting, which gives zwieback its distinguished aroma, and allows it to be stored over a long period of time without changing its quality. Therefore it is important to bake the zwieback thoroughly. The drying process must be so complete that not a trace of moisture remains, thus preventing formation of mold. Over-baking must be avoided also as it would make the zwieback bitter. The oven temperature should be between 250° to 260° F. The zwieback slices may be baked on pans or wire screens. Screens are recommended as their use will make turning of the slices unnecessary.

As zwieback is often recommended by doctors for invalids' diets, only the best materials should be used.

Zwieback must be packed in air-tight containers or sealed in cellophane bags.

Old Country Zwieback

2½ lbs. flour	8½ cups flour
1 pint milk	2 cups milk
2½ ozs. yeast	5 cakes yeast
3 eggs	3 eggs
4 ozs. sugar	½ cup sugar
7 ozs. butter	scant 1 cup butter
dash salt	dash salt

Method

Dissolve yeast in a little milk, add about one-half of the flour to form yeast sponge. Let rise. Beat eggs, sugar, and salt in double boiler until warm. Add egg mixture and softened butter to sponge. Mix in remaining ingredients and knead

to a smooth dough. Let rise (double in size). Push down and let rest for a few minutes. Form smooth rolls and place in loaf tins. Let rise. Bake at 350° F. Cool, then slice and toast in oven, turning once if placed on pans.

Whole Wheat Zwieback

3 lbs. whole wheat flour	7 cups whole wheat flour
¼ oz. salt	dash salt
6 ozs. milk	⅜ cup milk
7 ozs. sugar	½ cup sugar
6 ozs. butter	⅜ cup butter
3¾ ozs. yeast	3½ cakes yeast

Method

Proceed as described under "Old Country Zwieback," using only one-quarter of the flour for yeast sponge.

Anis Zwieback

Use "Old Country Zwieback" recipe. Add a few drops of anis oil and one teaspoon of anis seed. Before the second baking, rub slices in cinnamon-flavored powdered sugar. Toast slowly.

Diabetic Zwieback

14 ozs. wheat germ	1 cup wheat germ
3 lbs. 5 ozs. bread flour	2¾ cups bread flour
1 quart milk	scant 1 cup milk
10 ozs. butter	5 tbsp. butter
2½ ozs. yeast	1¼ cakes yeast
8 egg yolks	2 egg yolks

Method

Proceed as described under "Old Country Zwieback."

DEEP FRYED YEAST DOUGH

Deep-fryed yeast doughs are generally known as doughnuts. As they are seldom made in hotels, and bakeries usually use prepared mixes, this branch of yeast dough will be covered only briefly. Formulas are provided from different countries to help bring new selections to the professionals and to give excellent dessert ideas to the housewife.

When using the deep-fat method of frying, a

number of rules must be followed to assure that the final product has a fine, delicate aroma and a silky smooth texture.

(1) Doughnut dough must contain a certain percentage of eggs to decrease the dough's absorbancy. Grease-heavy doughnuts are not only flavorless, but also hard to digest.
(2) Use only the best frying fats, such as vegetable shortening, butter, or oil.
(3) Clean fryer frequently. The crumbs that collect on the bottom will burn and make the fat bitter.
(4) If no automatic fryer is available, watch temperature of fat carefully.

The most economical frying temperatures are :

(1) Vegetable shortening 365°–375° F.
(2) Butter 365°–375° F.
(3) Cocoanut fat 350°–360° F.
(4) Lard 370°–380° F.
(5) Oil 375° F.

Note: If fat is too cold, the doughnut will be light in color and heavy because of fat penetration into dough cells. Hot fats will brown too fast and might leave the center unbaked. If you have no thermometer, sprinkle a few drops of water on the fat. If the water sizzles, fat is probably ready. Turn heat to medium and fry sample.

Viennese Carnival Doughnuts (Faschingskrapfen)

5 lbs. pastry flour	4¾ cups pastry flour
3⅔ ozs. yeast	1¾ cakes yeast
1 quart milk	½ cup milk
12 ozs. sugar	scant 1 cup sugar
12 ozs. butter	6 tbsp. butter
12 egg yolks	3 egg yolks
½ pint rum	3 ozs. rum
½ oz. salt	dash salt
vanilla	vanilla
2 lemon rinds, grated	½ lemon rind, grated

Method

Dissolve yeast in a little warm milk, add one-third of the flour to form yeast sponge. Let rise well. Cream sugar, butter, yolks, flavoring, and salt in top of double boiler until fluffy and luke warm. Add sponge and rest of flour plus any remaining milk. Knead well to get a soft, silky

dough. Divide dough into small pieces of one ounce each and roll into smooth balls. Cover a board with cloth, dust with flour and place balls on it. Cover with cloth and let rise in warm place until double in size. Meanwhile, heat the fat according to temperatures suggested in the chart. To make it easier to remove doughnuts after frying, a wire screen should be put on the bottom of the pan. If a screen is not available, fry only a few at a time. Lay doughnuts into the fat upside down. As soon as the lower part has browned, turn over. Properly fried doughnuts will show a white ring around the center.

To fill the doughnuts, form a tube of waxed paper. Fill with apricot jam, cut off the point with scissors. Stick tube sideways into the doughnut and squeeze. Special filling devices are on the market for use by professionals, and are certainly very practical.

Berlin Doughnuts (Berliner Pfannkuchen)

3 lbs. pastry flour	5¾ cups pastry flour
5 ozs. yeast	5 cakes yeast
6 ozs. sugar	scant ½ cup sugar
10 ozs. butter	⅝ cup butter
6 egg yolks	3 egg yolks
dash salt	dash salt
vanilla	vanilla
2 lemon rinds, grated	1 lemon rind, grated

Method

Proceed as described under "Viennese Carnival Doughnuts." After dough is kneaded, let rise twice and push back again. Divide dough into one ounce pieces and form smooth balls. Push a hole in the middle of each and fill with raspberry jam. Pull sides of dough towards inside center and squeeze tight with fingers. Let rise with squeezed side facing up. Continue as described under "Viennese Carnival Doughnuts."

Swiss Egg Fritters

1 lb. 10 ozs. pastry flour	2¾ cups pastry flour
⅓ oz. salt	dash salt
1½ ozs. kirsch liqueur	⅛ cup kirsch liqueur
⅔ oz. powdered sugar	⅛ cup powdered sugar
2 ozs. whipping cream	⅛ cup whipping cream
2 egg yolks	1 egg yolk
6 eggs	3 eggs
vanilla	vanilla

Method

Beat all ingredients except flour together until fluffy. Add flour and mix well. Let rest about twenty-five minutes. Divide dough into half-ounce pieces. Form small balls and let rest again. Roll balls out until thin. Fry swiftly in hot fat. Dust with icing sugar.

Dutch Snowballs

2 lbs. pastry flour	3¾ cups pastry flour
1 quart milk	scant 2 cups milk
6½ ozs. sugar	scant ½ cup sugar
10 ozs. butter	⅝ cup butter
25 eggs	12 eggs
¼ oz. salt	½ tsp. salt

Method

Bring to a boil the milk, butter, and sugar, then add flour. Cook like éclair formula. (*See Index.*) Let cool. Mix in salt and eggs slowly. Heat fat. Fill a spoon or small ice cream scoop with dough and drop into fat. Fry until golden brown, remove from fat, and roll in cinnamon sugar.

Tyrolian Spritz Doughnuts

8 ozs. bread flour	1¾ cups bread flour
½ pint water	1 cup water
1 oz. sugar	¼ cup sugar
4 ozs. butter	scant ½ cup butter
8 eggs	8 eggs
vanilla	vanilla
1 lemon rind, grated	1 lemon rind, grated
dash salt	dash salt

Method

Cook mixture as directed under "Dutch Snowballs." Grease a paper slightly smaller than diameter of frying pan. Using a pastry bag with star tube, press rings of dough on the paper. Turn paper upside down into hot fat. Paper will come lose immediately. Fry both sides golden brown. Sprinkle with cinnamon sugar.

Venetian Plum Balls

1 lb. bread flour	3½ cups bread flour
1¼ ozs. yeast	2½ cakes yeast
1¾ ozs. sugar	¼ cup sugar
½ pint milk	1 cup milk
3 ozs. butter	⅜ cup butter
6 egg yolks	6 egg yolks
dash salt	dash salt
¼ tsp. cinnamon	¼ tsp. cinnamon
stoned plums	stoned plums

Method

Dissolve yeast in milk, add half of flour to form yeast sponge. Let rise. Add remaining ingredients, form a smooth dough, and let rise. Push back dough and divide into one ounce pieces, roll into balls, and flatten. Replace the stones in the plums with rum-flavored marzipan. Place each plum in the middle of a piece of dough and close dough over it tightly. Let rise, then fry in hot lard. Roll in cinnamon sugar.

Bow-knots

4 ozs. butter	scant ½ cup butter
4¾ ozs. sugar	¾ cup sugar
1 lb. flour	3½ cups flour
7 egg yolks	7 egg yolks
1 lemon rind, grated	1 lemon rind, grated
4 ozs. white wine	½ cup white wine
vanilla	vanilla

Method

Cream butter and sugar, add yolks one at a time. Mix in flavoring and wine. Knead in flour. Let rest about fifteen minutes. Roll dough with rolling pin into an oblong shape. Cut strips 1″ wide and form bow-knots. Fry in hot butter or lard. Sprinkle with powdered sugar.

Danish Cheese Doughnuts

1 lb. 4 ozs. pastry flour	2¼ cups pastry flour (generous)
5 ozs. butter	5 tbsp. butter
2½ ozs. sugar	¼ cup sugar
5 egg yolks	3 egg yolks
2 eggs	2 eggs
⅔ oz. yeast	¾ cake yeast
2 ozs. rum	1 oz. rum
1 lemon rind, grated	½ lemon rind, grated
vanilla	vanilla

Filling (Blend all ingredients together thoroughly)

1 lb. cottage cheese	$\frac{1}{2}$ lb. cottage cheese
5 ozs. sugar	$\frac{3}{8}$ cup sugar
4 egg yolks	2 egg yolks
1$\frac{1}{2}$ ozs. raisins	$\frac{1}{4}$ cup raisins
1 lemon rind, grated	$\frac{1}{2}$ lemon rind, grated
1 orange rind, grated	$\frac{1}{2}$ orange rind, grated
vanilla	vanilla

Method

Proceed as directed under "Viennese Carnival Doughnuts." Let dough rest about fifteen minutes. Roll out dough to a sheet about $\frac{1}{4}''$ thick. Cut rounds 3″ in diameter. Using one-half of the rounds, brush the outside edges with egg wash. Place one spoonful of filling exactly in center. If filling is off-center, goods will bake lopsidedly. Place the other half of the rounds on the filled ones, pressing down slightly. Finally, using a cutter about $\frac{1}{4}''$ smaller than the original rounds, re-cut the filled doughnuts. This system will assure a smooth edge. Let rise on a cloth-covered board. Place upside down into hot butter or vegetable shortening. Fry both sides until golden brown. Sprinkle with sugar.

DANISH PASTRIES

Danish pastry is a well-known international delicacy. Its basic parts consist of yeast dough and butter, which, combined with fine fillings, produce an excellent pastry for the most exclusive coffee parties.

The roll-in process is similar to puff pastry. However, instead of four turns, Danish pastry will get only two as a rule. Three turns are applied only when a higher percentage of butter is desired.

The butter is mixed with part of the flour to prevent its moisture from producing steam. A thick, square block of butter is formed and placed in the center of a square sheet of yeast dough. The four sides are then alternately placed over the butter and pressed down thoroughly to prevent the butter from coming out during the roll-in process. The dough is now to be rolled carefully and evenly to an oblong shape. All excess flour must be brushed off. Fold the left side of dough over center and place right side on top of it, thus cutting the original oblong to one-third its size and showing three layers of dough. This is called one single turn. Let the dough rest in a cool place for fifteen minutes. Then apply one more single turn. The pastries are now ready to be made up. They can be made in a large variety of sizes and shapes. The individual pieces should have different fillings to distinguish them from one another. Danish pastries should be left to rise at normal room temperature, or else the butter may run out. Bake the pastries in a hot oven, from 385° to 400° F., and glaze with fondant or plain water icing while still hot.

Problems in making Danish Pastries

Problem	Cause	Solution
Layer formation not visible.	Dough may have had too many turns. Dough may not contain enough butter.	If 50% butter or less is rolled into yeast dough (50% of total dough weight), two turns should be sufficient.
Dough has no spring.	Overbeating of yeast dough. Not enough proof. Not enough yeast or too much old yeast.	Dough should never be whipped with paddle. Use dough hook. Add sugar to yeast sponge to increase rising power.
Pastries are dry and tough.	Butter has run out during baking or proofing process. Butter was rolled in too fast without resting between turns.	Yeast will develop best at temperatures from 70°–80° F. Do not overheat proofer. Butter will also run out when baked at too low a temperature. Oven should be at 380°–400° F.
Pastries look flat after baking.	Too much steam formation due to butter with high percentage of moisture. Baked in a steamy oven.	If butter is too moist, add part of flour to it before rolling into dough. During baking keep damper all the way or partly open.

Problems in making Danish Pastries

Problem	Cause	Solution
Pastries have large pores.	Yeast sponge is too large compared to total amount of dough. Pastries have proofed too much.	When yeast sponge is made, one-quarter of the flour is sufficient. When dough has accidentally overproofed, increase baking temperature by a few degrees.
Pastries break easily and are hard to handle.	Too much butter or not enough turns.	If amount of butter exceeds 50% of total dough weight, apply third turn.
Pastries appear rough.	Dusting flour during roll-in process has not been removed properly. This flour will not bind with the dough.	Before folding the dough remove all flour carefully with pastry brush. Brush frequently while making up as well.
One batch of dough contains differently browned pieces	Use of different egg washes.	Egg wash should always be prepared in the same way. Make a formula and abide by it.
Pastries contain coarse flecks.	Butter unevenly distributed. Dough formed crust during storing time.	Butter must be distributed evenly between all the dough layers. If dough is made one day ahead, it should be covered with a wet cloth to prevent formation of crust.
Pastries shrink and stay small.	Rolled in and made up too fast. Dough did not rest enough between turns. Flour too strong.	Let dough rest between 15 and 20 minutes in refrigerator during roll in process. When making up pastries, use only as much dough as needed for one batch of pastries. If flour is too strong, add 10% of cake flour.

Danish Yeast Dough

4 ozs. yeast	2 cakes yeast
3½ lbs. bread flour	3 cups bread flour
6 ozs. butter	3 tbsp. butter
1 oz. salt	dash salt
1 quart milk	1 cup milk
4 eggs	1 egg
2 egg yolks	1 egg yolk
dash cardamon	dash cardamon
3½ lbs. roll-in butter	1¾ cups roll-in butter

Method

With the exception of the roll-in butter, form a yeast dough with all ingredients as described under general rules for yeast doughs. Use approximately one-sixth of the flour for yeast sponge. Put aside about four ounces flour (¼ cup for home recipe) to mix with roll-in butter. Let completed dough rest for fifteen minutes, and proceed as directed in the introduction to Danish pastries. This dough is very rich and requires three turns.

Copenhagen Yeast Dough

2 lbs. flour	3½ cups flour
3 ozs. yeast	3 cakes yeast
1 pint milk	scant 1 cup milk
½ oz. salt	dash salt
2 eggs	1 egg
4 egg yolks	2 egg yolks
2½ ozs. sugar	¼ cup sugar
1½ ozs. butter	3 tbsp. butter
cardamon	cardamon
1½ lbs. roll-in butter	1⅓ cups roll-in butter

Method

Do not form yeast sponge for this formula. Add all liquids cool. Mix all ingredients except four ounces flour (¼ cup for home recipe). Mix the small amount of flour with the roll-in butter. Follow general directions for mixing yeast dough.

Roll in butter in two turns. This formula may be made more economical by reducing the roll-in butter to thirteen ounces ($\frac{3}{4}$ cup for home recipe).

Danish Pastries Universal

2 lbs. bread flour	7 cups bread flour
$\frac{3}{4}$ quart milk	3 cups milk
$2\frac{1}{2}$ ozs. yeast	5 cakes yeast
$3\frac{1}{2}$ ozs. butter	scant $\frac{1}{2}$ cup butter
$\frac{2}{3}$ oz. salt	4 tsp. salt
3 ozs. sugar	scant $\frac{1}{2}$ cup sugar
3 ozs. cornstarch	$\frac{3}{8}$ cup cornstarch
2 egg yolks	2 egg yolks
1 lemon rind, grated	1 lemon rind, grated
1 lb. 10 ozs. roll-in butter	1 lb. 10 ozs. roll-in butter
13 ozs. puff pastry	13 ozs. puff pastry

Method

Use half of the flour, the yeast, and a little water for the yeast sponge. Let rise well. Form firm dough by adding all but last two ingredients to the yeast sponge. Wrap dough evenly around block of butter. Roll to a square about 2″ thick. Roll the puff paste (see Index) to twice the size of the first dough. Place first dough in center of puff paste and fold each side to center of dough. Continue rolling in three single turns, allowing dough to rest between turns for at least twenty-five minutes.

Note: Puff paste must have the same degree of softness as the yeast dough to insure perfect binding. This dough is excellent for pastries with heavy fillings, small individual rolls, crescents, et cetera. If sugar is left out and yeast content increased by ten percent, this dough may be used as a base for hors d'oeuvres, sausage rolls, meat rolls, and similar items.

Cherry Coffee Ring

Roll a thin piece of Danish dough to a rectangle 18″ x 8″. Cover the dough with chopped, sweet cherries and sprinkle with cinnamon sugar. Grate one-half of a lemon rind over the filling and roll up the dough. Egg wash the extreme bottom edge and seal roll firmly. Bring the ends together to form a ring and seal. Set the ring on a baking sheet and make cuts two-thirds of the way into the roll at $\frac{1}{2}$″ intervals. Turn loose sections so that the filling faces up as indicated in illustration. Let rise. Bake at 375° F. Glaze with hot fondant while cake is still warm and decorate with glazed cherries.

Almond Coffee Ring

Roll Danish dough as described in "Cherry Coffee Ring." Spread with the following filling, roll, and seal. Form ring. Place cake on baking sheet and cut top at $\frac{1}{2}$″ intervals with scissors. Bake at 375° F.

Almond Cream Filling

8 ozs. almonds, toasted, ground	3 cups almonds, toasted, ground
$2\frac{1}{2}$ ozs. sugar	$\frac{3}{8}$ cup sugar
$1\frac{1}{2}$ ozs. bread crumbs	$\frac{1}{2}$ cup bread crumbs
$1\frac{3}{4}$ ozs. milk	3 tbsp. milk
dash cinnamon	dash cinnamon
vanilla	vanilla

Method

Mix all ingredients together. Cake crumbs may be used instead of bread crumbs. If mixture is too stiff, add enough milk to give it a creamy consistency.

Walnut Coffee Cake

Filling

$6\frac{1}{2}$ ozs. walnuts, chopped	$1\frac{1}{2}$ cups walnuts, chopped
3 ozs. crumbs	$\frac{3}{4}$ cup crumbs
1 oz. butter	$\frac{1}{8}$ cup butter
$1\frac{1}{2}$ ozs. sugar	scant $\frac{1}{4}$ cup sugar
1 oz. raisins	$\frac{1}{4}$ cup raisins
1 egg	1 egg
dash cinnamon	dash cinnamon
1 lemon rind, grated	1 lemon rind, grated

Method

Mix all ingredients together and spread on Danish dough as described under "Cherry Coffee Ring." Form roll, seal, and set straight on a baking sheet. With scissors or knife make cuts two-thirds of the way into the loaf at $\frac{1}{2}$″ intervals. Fold loose pieces alternately to left and right. Egg wash and let rise. Bake at 375° F. Glaze. Decorate with walnut halves.

Cocoanut Coffee Ring

5 ozs shredded cocoanut	2 cups shredded cocoanut
5 ozs. sugar or fondant	$\frac{3}{4}$ cup sugar or fondant
milk to bind	milk to bind
2 ozs. cake crumbs	$\frac{1}{2}$ cup cake crumbs
$\frac{1}{2}$ lemon rind, grated	$\frac{1}{2}$ lemon rind, grated
$\frac{1}{2}$ orange rind, grated	$\frac{1}{2}$ orange rind, grated
2 tbsp. rum	2 tbsp. rum
few drops red coloring	few drops red coloring

Method

Mix all ingredients and spread on Danish dough as described under "Cherry Coffee Ring." Roll and seal. Form ring and set on baking sheet. Make cuts with scissors at 1″ intervals on the outer edge of ring. Egg wash and decorate with almond slivers. Bake at 375° F. Ice with water icing.

Cottage Cheese Ring

Filling

8 ozs. strained cottage cheese	1 cup strained cottage cheese
2$\frac{1}{2}$ ozs. sugar	$\frac{3}{8}$ cup sugar
2 egg yolks	2 egg yolks
$\frac{3}{4}$ oz. currants or raisins	3 tbsp. currants or raisins
1 lemon rind, grated	1 lemon rind, grated
vanilla	vanilla

Method

Mix all ingredients and spread on Danish dough as directed under "Cherry Coffee Ring." Roll, seal, form ring, and set on baking sheet. Make cuts with scissors in center of dough all around the ring. Bake at 375° F. Decorate with cherries and glazed fruit cubes.

Danish Peach Cake

Roll out a round of Danish dough, 8″ diameter. Sprinkle with cake crumbs. Cover surface with halved or quartered peaches and sprinkle with cinnamon-flavored granulated sugar. Cut narrow strips of same dough and form lattice on top. Place one strip around the outer edge of cake to keep lattice in place. Let rise and bake at 325° F. Glaze with hot apricot jam.

Note: Different kinds of fruit may be used, such as cherries, apricots, plums, papaya, apples, and so forth.

Danish Vanilla Cake

Line bottom of an 8″ cake tin with **Danish** dough. Egg wash and sprinkle with sliced almonds. Let rise. Bake at 350° F. When cold, split in half. Spread a thin layer of apricot jam on the bottom half, and top with a few scoops of vanilla custard cream. Replace top half. Place a 3″ round of cardboard in center of cake, sprinkle with powdered sugar. Remove cardboard. Serve with whipped cream.

Pineapple Cake

Roll out Danish dough $\frac{1}{4}$″ thick and 8″ diameter. Sprinkle with cake crumbs. Arrange whole, sliced pineapple on top. Put strip of dough around outer edge. Decorate with cherries. Let rise, then bake at 325° F.

Individual Pieces of Danish Pastries

A. Twists

Roll a sheet of Danish dough $\frac{1}{4}$″ thick. Spread a thin layer of almond cream filling over one-half of the dough. (For filling, see Index under "Almond Coffee Ring.") Fold plain half over filling and cut strips $\frac{1}{2}$″ wide. Hold the individual strips at both ends and twist in opposite directions to form a spiral. If desired some of these pieces may be decorated with cherries or filled with jam. Let rise. Bake at 375° F. to 400° F. Ice with fondant icing.

B. Pretzels

Roll Danish dough and cut strips $\frac{1}{2}$″ wide. Form pretzels. Egg wash and turn upside down into sliced or chopped almonds. Set on slightly greased baking sheet and let rise. Bake at 400° F. Ice with vanilla-flavored water icing.

C. Twin Rolls

Roll a piece of Danish dough $\frac{1}{8}''$ thick. Sprinkle shredded, toasted filberts on top. Sprinkle with cinnamon-flavored granulated sugar. Roll dough as in jelly roll, then cut pieces 1″ wide. Cut each piece just about to the bottom, set on greased pan, and spread open to show double roll. Egg wash and let rise. Bake at 400° F. Ice with vanilla-flavored water icing.

D. Cream Fans

Roll Danish dough 1″ thick and 9″ wide. Spread top with custard cream. Sprinkle with mixed fruit cubes. Fold twice to reduce width 3″. Cut pieces 2″ wide. Make three small cuts on the long side of each piece. Egg wash and let rise. Bake at 400° F. Ice with fondant.

E. Marzipan Thorns

Roll a strip of Danish dough $\frac{1}{8}''$ thick and 4″ wide. Cut triangles. Place a piece of marzipan on one side of each triangle and roll in. Set on greased baking sheet in crescents. Egg wash and let rise. Bake at 375° F. Sprinkle with icing sugar.

F. Fruit Pockets

Roll Danish dough $\frac{1}{8}''$ thick. Cut squares about 4″ x 4″. Put some cake crumbs in center to absorb juice. Add desired fruit, fresh or canned, and fold as illustrated. Ends may be secured in center with toothpick. Egg wash and let rise. Bake at 400° F.

A. Bear Claws

Roll Danish dough $\frac{1}{8}''$ thick. Cut long strips $3\frac{1}{4}''$ wide. Spread the strips with walnut filling (See Index). Fold strips three times lengthwise. Cut pieces 4″. Make a few small cuts along one side of each piece, running from the center to the outer edge. Egg wash and let rise. Bake at 375° to 400° F.

B. Raspberry Stars

Roll Danish dough $\frac{1}{8}''$ thick and 12″ wide. Spread with raspberry jam. If fresh raspberries are used, sprinkle with granulated sugar. Form a roll. Cut pieces $\frac{3}{4}''$ wide and set cut-side on a greased pan. With scissors make six cuts in each piece, running from the center to the outer edge. Egg wash and let rise. Bake at 400° F.

C. Butterflies

Roll Danish dough $\frac{1}{4}''$ thick. Spread with apricot jam and sprinkle with grated lemon rind and lemon juice. Form a roll. Cut pieces 1″ wide. Using a thin piece of wood, press down in center of each piece. Spread open to form butterfly. Set on greased pans. Egg wash and let rise. Bake at 400° F.

D. Cinnamon Buns

Roll Danish dough $\frac{1}{4}''$ thick. Sprinkle with sliced almonds, raisins, and cinnamon sugar. Form a roll. Cut pieces $\frac{3}{4}''$ wide and set on greased baking sheet. Egg wash and let rise. Bake at 350° F. Glaze with fondant or water icing.

E. New York Buns

Roll a length of Danish dough, 12″ wide. Spread with jam of your choice. Fold both ends toward center. Spread this surface with jam. Fold in half as a book. Cut pieces about $1\frac{1}{2}''$ wide. Set close together on a greased baking sheet, cut-side facing up. Sprinkle with streusel. (See Index.) Let rise. Bake at 350° F.

Apple Strudel

Roll Danish dough $\frac{1}{4}''$ thick. Cut strips 6″ wide and the length of a pan. Sprinkle cake crumbs generously down the center of each strip. Top with sliced, sweetened apples. Sprinkle with cinnamon-flavored granulated sugar and grated lemon rind. Fold one side of dough over apples and brush with egg wash. Fold over second side of dough. Egg wash. Put a narrow zigzag strip of dough down the center. Let rise. Bake at 350° F. Glaze with water icing.

Cherry Strudel

Follow same procedure as under "Apple Strudel." Substitute cherries for apples and omit the lemon rind. When the dough has been folded over, make cuts along the sides of the strudel with scissors. Egg wash and let rise. Bake at 350° F.

Note: Different fruits may be used if so desired.

Pineapple Strudel

Roll Danish dough ¼″ thick and cut strips 5″ wide the length of the pan. Place drained pineapple rings along center of strip. Place a half cherry in each pineapple hole. Fold dough on both sides partly over fruit. Secure during baking with toothpicks. Egg wash the dough and let rise. Bake at 350° F.

Poppy Seed Strudel

Roll Danish dough ⅛″ thick. Spread with poppy seed filling. *(See Index.)* Form a roll. Place in loaf tin and let rise. Bake at 325° F.

Note: Strudels may be filled with different fillings such as walnut, cottage cheese, almond, et cetera. Formulas are given under "Fillings for Yeast Dough." *(See Index.)*

FILLINGS FOR YEAST DOUGHS AND PUFF PASTRIES

Mix ingredients together well, adding enough liquid to obtain good spreading consistency. All fillings containing milk must be heated to the boiling point to prevent spoilage. In addition to the formulas given here, all kinds of canned or fresh fruits may be used. Soft fruits do not require cooking. Others such as apples or pears should be half-cooked before using.

There are also a number of dry fillings used, made of different shredded nuts, mixed with granulated sugar and flavoring. The dry fillings are sprinkled onto or between the layers of dough. No specific formulas are necessary because the final combination depends entirely upon the cost of materials. To economize, cake crumbs may be substituted for part of the nuts. However, a corresponding loss of flavor and quality must be expected.

Walnut Filling

1 lb. cake crumbs	5 cups cake crumbs
2 ozs. butter	(generous)
10 ozs. walnuts, ground	¼ cup butter
3 ozs. sugar	2½ cups walnuts, ground
2 ozs. rum	½ cup sugar
dash cinnamon	2 ozs. rum
dash nutmeg	dash cinnamon
1 lemon rind, grated	dash nutmeg
1 pint milk	1 lemon rind, grated
	2 cups milk

Poppy Seed Filling

10 ozs. poppy seed, ground	5 cups poppy seed, ground
2 ozs. butter	¼ cup butter
5 ozs. sugar	¾ cup sugar
12 ozs. cake crumbs	1¾ cups cake crumbs
vanilla	(generous)
1 lemon rind, grated	vanilla
2 orange rinds, grated	1 lemon rind, grated
1 pint milk	2 orange rinds, grated
	2 cups milk

Cottage Cheese Filling

1 lb. strained cottage cheese	2¼ cups strained cottage cheese
4 egg yolks	4 egg yolks
5 ozs. sugar	¾ cup sugar
1 oz. raisins	¼ cup raisins
1 lemon rind, grated	1 lemon rind, grated
1 orange rind, grated	1 orange rind, grated
vanilla	vanilla

Almond Cream Filling

1 lb. ground almonds, toasted	6 cups ground almonds, toasted
5 ozs. sugar	¾ cup sugar
3 ozs. cake crumbs	1 cup cake crumbs
3½–4 ozs. milk	⅜ cup milk
vanilla	vanilla
dash cinnamon	dash cinnamon

Cocoanut Filling

1 lb. dessicated cocoanut	4½ cups dessicated cocoanut
12 ozs. powdered sugar	2½ cups powdered sugar
4 ozs. glucose	⅓ cup glucose
3 egg whites	3 egg whites
2 tbsp. rum	2 tbsp. rum
2 orange rinds, grated	2 orange rinds, grated

Method

Whip egg whites with powdered sugar until stiff. Blend in remaining ingredients.

Marzipan Filling

Soften almond paste with sugar syrup until creamy. Add two egg yolks for every one-half pound of paste.

Butterscotch Filling

Part 1	Part 1
5 ozs. brown sugar	1 cup brown sugar
4 ozs. granulated sugar	½ cup granulated sugar
8 ozs. water	1 cup water
2 ozs. glucose	⅙ cup glucose

Part 2	Part 2
3 ozs. water	⅜ cup water
2 ozs. cornstarch	¼ cup cornstarch

Part 3	Part 3
1 oz. butter	⅛ cup butter
1 tbsp. maple flavoring	1 tbsp. maple flavoring
vanilla	vanilla

Method

Bring to a boil Part *1*. Add Part *2* and cook until clear. Remove from heat. Stir in Part *3*. Let cool before using.

BREADS

There is a considerable difference in the various brands of flour. This is the reason that flour quantities are to be taken as approximations. It is up to the baker to determine the final consistency of the dough by adding more or less flour.

Whenever a formula calls for fat, it should be added shortly before the mixing process is completed. Otherwise, the fat particles would clog the yeast cells and prevent the proper growth of the micro-organisms.

Most bakers will add a chemical preservative to prevent the formation of mold. Follow the manufacturer's recipes.

Do not wrap bread in cellophane while still warm.

White Bread 1

50 lbs. bread flour	9½ cups bread flour
3¾ gallons water	3 cups water (generous)
12 ozs. yeast	1½ cakes yeast
8 ozs. malt	1 tbsp. malt
10 ozs. granulated sugar	¾ tbsp. granulated sugar
12 ozs. salt	4 tsp. salt
10 ozs. shortening	1½ tbsp. shortening

Method

Dissolve the yeast in part of the water. Mix the remaining ingredients, except fat, at low speed until loosely bound and then add the yeast solution. Mix a little longer and add shortening. Continue mixing at low speed for about fifteen to twenty minutes. Let rise at 75° to 80° F. Punch down after one and one-half hours. Let rise again and punch down after one hour. Make up loaves, place in greased tins, and let rise until just about doubled in size. Bake at 400° F.

White Bread 2

50 lbs. bread flour	9½ cups bread flour
1 lb. 4 ozs. powdered milk	scant ¼ cup powdered milk
1 lb. 4 ozs. yeast	1½ cakes yeast
1 lb. 8 ozs. lard	1¾ tbsp. lard
1 lb. salt	4 tsp. salt
1 lb. sugar	½ tbsp. sugar
3½ gallons water	3 cups water (generous)

Method

Dissolve yeast in one-quarter of the water. Add enough flour to make stiff dough. Put yeast sponge in container and cover with warm water. When sponge floats, remove from water and mix with remaining ingredients to smooth dough. Add fat a few minutes before mixing process is completed. Let dough rest for one hour and then push back. Let rest one more hour and make up loaves. Let double in size and bake at 400° F. to 425° F.

French Bread

3 quarts water	1½ cups water
3 ozs. yeast	1 cake yeast
3 ozs. salt	1 pinch salt
9 lbs. bread flour	3½ cups bread flour
4 ozs. shortening	1 tbsp. shortening

131

Method

Mix as described under "White Bread *1*." Allow to rise twice, pushing back after one hour each time. Make up loaves of desired size. Set on greased pans. Let rise. Mark a few deep cuts with a razor blade. Bake at 400° F.

Dinner Rolls

1 quart water or skim milk	2 cups water or skim milk
1 oz. salt	1 tbsp. salt
2 ozs. lard	1 tbsp. lard
2 ozs. sugar	scant ¼ cup sugar
2 ozs. egg whites	1 egg white
2 ozs. yeast	2 cakes yeast
3½–4 lbs. flour	6 cups flour

Method

Dissolve yeast in liquid. Add remaining ingredients, making sure that the fat goes in last. Knead until smooth. Let rise. Push back after one hour. Let rise again for one hour. Make up smooth rolls and set on greased pans. Make cut on top of each with a razor blade. Let rise. Bake at 390° to 400° F. in steam filled oven. Formula yields approximately six-and-a-half dozen rolls for each quart of liquid.

Whole Wheat Bread

50 lbs. whole wheat flour	14 cups whole wheat flour
4 gallons water	4 cups water
1¾ lbs. shortening	4 tbsp. shortening
1 lb. salt	1 tbsp. salt
5 ozs. malt	1 tsp. malt
8 ozs. sugar	1 tbsp. sugar
1 lb. yeast	2 cakes yeast

Method

Process as described under "White Bread *1*."

Vienna Bread

Part 1

12 lbs. bread flour	2¼ cups bread flour
3 ozs. malt	1 tsp. malt
8 ozs. yeast	1 cake yeast
1¼ gallons water	1¼ cups water

Part 2

1¼ gallons milk	1¼ cups milk
4 ozs. sugar	¼ tbsp. sugar
20–22 lbs. bread flour	4½–5 cups bread flour
10 ozs. salt	dash salt

Method

Mix Part *1* to form yeast sponge. Let rise. Combine with remaining ingredients. Knead well. Let rise once, push back, and make up loaves, set on greased pans. Let rise again. Make cuts with a razor blade. Wash with thin egg wash. Sprinkle with poppy or sesame seeds. Let rise until about doubled in size. Bake at 450° F. in well-steamed oven.

Pumpernickel Bread

4½ lbs bread flour
4½ lbs. graham flour
10½ lbs. rye flour
6 quarts water
6 ozs. sugar
6 ozs. salt
9 ozs. yeast

Method

Dissolve yeast in one-half of water. Place remaining ingredients in mixer, add yeast solution and knead well. Let rise slightly, push back and make up. Let rise and bake at 400° F. Brush with water before baking.

THE FREEZING OF BAKED GOODS

Since the beginning of commercial baking, the left-over articles have been a problem. Naturally, baked goods taste best shortly after they have cooled. Some articles show signs of staleness only a few hours after baking. Others last a whole day or longer without a loss in quality. Obviously all items cannot be fresh at the same time, especially when business is spread over a period of eight or ten hours.

Some stores began to wrap their goods in cellophane, but the loss of time and cost of wrappers just about equaled the loss through staleness. Besides, some articles with yeast leavening were subject to mold formation when wrapped while still slightly warm.

The freezing of raw dough was not the answer

either, although time was saved because large quantities could be made up at one time. However, an experienced baker had to be present to bake what was needed when supplies ran low. Freezing dough also altered the baking ability of a number of doughs. Although raw dough was frozen in almost every shop, experiments were being conducted extensively on the freezing of baked goods.

Many professionals are now of the opinion that freshness and quality can be preserved by freezing the baked articles. The goods should be satisfactory even if they have been frozen for several days or even weeks. The sooner the baked items are frozen, the better they will be. However, the freezing should be performed step by step in order to preserve the best of the flavors.

Small articles will cool to the required 7°C. within one hour, while larger items such as cakes will take two or three hours to cool right through. During the cooling process the moisture within the porous structure will be stabilized and the evaporation cut to eight per cent on the average. The cooled articles are then exposed to 18°C. of frost and kept at that temperature. Experiments have proven that a warmer temperature is not satisfactory and a lower temperature dam-

aging. It is not advisable to ice pastries with sugar icings before freezing, as the condensation of water caused by thawing would dissolve the sugar. This does not apply to fat icings.

Economically, this method has a great advantage over the freezing of raw dough, as even inexperienced staff members should be able to thaw the pastries and prepare them for the evening rush hours. Frozen goods should thaw at room temperature, the length of time varying with the thickness of the various items. If pastries must be ready in a hurry, they may be placed in a steamed oven for two to five minutes. This will thaw them quickly. However, pastries thawed in this way are liable to have a thick crust and get stale faster. The thawing time at room temperature is about the same as the time required to cool the goods to 7°C.

With the freezing of baked goods, the number of stale or left-over pastries is kept to a comfortable minimum. If only a few pieces of a certain article are needed each day, it is possible to make up a week's supply ahead of time. The pastries will retain their freshness, spring, and flavor. Not only is material saved, but also the time required for preparation.

VIII

PUFF PASTRIES

Some of the most delicious pastries, as well as hot meat dishes can be made of puff paste.

Puff paste, which in other languages is often referred to as leaf dough, is exactly that. Between every layer of dough is one layer of butter or fat of equal thickness. An average rolled puff paste formula of fifty percent flour and fifty percent butter should have two single and two double turns, giving a total of 288 layers. It is this tender dough formation which gives puff paste its distinctive texture. Since there is no chemical leavening added, the butter or fat must not only separate the layers of dough, but also perform the "lifting." It is therefore safe to say that the failure or success depends to a large degree upon the butter used. Sweet butter with very little moisture fulfills all the necessary requirements. Salted butter is usually tougher. When salted butter is used a little sugar should be added to neutralize the salt and boost the butter's lifting power. Special roll-in fats consisting of vegetable shortenings or margarine are offered by food manufacturers. These are highly demoisturized with the lifting power artificially created. However, these fats are tasteless and some of them leave a greasy film and taste in the mouth.

The roll-in dough consists of bread flour, water, salt, butter and rum or vinegar. The dough must be kneaded well to allow all ingredients to blend into the flour cells perfectly. Vinegar or rum will not only improve the flavor, but also add lift to the heavy layers of dough. Most professionals use water as binder, but milk will definitely increase the pastries' tenderness.

The roll-in butter is mixed smooth (but not creamed) with a small part of the flour. Butter and dough must have the same softness, as it is impossible to roll soft butter into a hard dough or vice versa. Once the dough is made it is very easy to soften the butter until it is of the same consistency. The greatest emphasis must be put on the correct rolling procedure. Puff paste which is rolled to a large sheet will not bake properly as the butter layers will be too thin. On the other hand, if it is rolled too small and the butter layers thus become too thick, the butter will inevitably run out during the baking process, leaving only a frame of straw-like dough. The rolled, oblong

area of four or five pounds of puff dough should measure approximately 14" x 24". Between the individual turns the dough should rest for at least twenty-five minutes.

The best results have been obtained with puff paste which has been mixed and made up the same day. Many professionals have a certain amount of raw dough handy at all times. The older the dough gets, the poorer its lifting quality and flavor will become.

Various fillings for puff pastries will be found under "Yeast Dough Products."

Basic Puff Paste Formula

Dough Mixture

5 lbs. bread flour	8¾ cups bread flour
5 ozs. butter	5 tbsp. butter
1 oz. salt	½ tbsp. salt
½ cup vinegar or rum	¼ cup vinegar or rum
3 lbs. water or skim milk	3 cups water or skim milk

Roll-in Fat

4½ lbs. butter	4½ cups butter
1 lb. bread flour	1¾ cups bread flour

Method for Dough Mixture

Mix all ingredients together until dough loses its toughness and becomes smooth. Form a round ball and set on floured table. With a knife, make a deep cross-cut on top. This will speed the loosening process. Cover dough with a damp cloth to prevent formation of crust. Allow to rest for fifteen or twenty minutes.

Method for Roll-in Fat

Mix butter with flour until smooth and of the same softness as the dough. Form a thick square block as shown in the illustration. Set aside until dough is ready to be rolled.

How To Roll in Butter

Roll out dough in the shape of a cross, leaving the center approximately twice as thick as the cross ends. Place block of butter in center and fold the dough ends over it, thus wrapping the butter

137

completely inside the dough. Using the hands or a rolling pin, press down on the block gently and evenly until the shape of the original block has doubled in size. Continue rolling to desired size with rolling pin. Brush off flour and apply one single turn.

What Is a Single Turn?

Visualize three equal areas on the sheet of dough. Fold left third over center and place right third on top. This gives three layers. Cover dough with damp cloth and let rest for twenty-five minutes in refrigerator. After that, roll out dough to its original size and apply one double turn.

What Is a Double Turn?

Visualize the exact center of the sheet of dough. Fold both ends to the center line. Fold dough at center in book fashion. This gives four layers. Cover with damp cloth and let rest for twenty-five minutes in refrigerator.

Roll dough to its original size and apply single and one more double turn as described above. Let dough rest again between turns. The finished rolled puff paste has now two single and two double turns. Allow dough to rest for forty minutes, after which the puff paste is ready to be made up.

Problems in Preparation of Puff Pastries

Problem	Cause	Solution
Pastries bake wild.	Dough had not enough turns or was rolled too thick, therefore the butter layers give too much lift, causing the dough layers to slide off in all directions.	Two single and two double turns are sufficient as a rule. If more butter is used than shown in basic formula, apply one more single turn. Increase flour content in roll-in butter.
The dough shrinks during baking.	Dough mixture too hard and butter too soft or vice versa. Not enough rest between turns. Pastries did not rest enough before baking.	Dough and butter must be equally soft. Resting period increases with amount of dough. If pastries are needed in a hurry, dampen baking sheets to prevent shrinkage.
Dough bakes unevenly.	Dough was not folded evenly during rolling process.	When applying the turns, dough must be folded exactly to distribute dough and fat layers evenly.
Dough has no spring.	Too many turns made, compared to percentage of butter.	Fat layers become too thin and weak, cannot provide necessary lift. When rolling dough, note number of turns applied.
Rough and straw-like pastries.	Too much flour dusted under dough during rolling. This flour cannot bind with dough and will bake separately.	Use little flour and brush thoroughly before folding dough.
Fat runs out of dough during baking.	Oven too cool or not enough flour mixed into roll-in butter.	Small pastries should be baked around 400° F., larger pieces around 350° F. For every one pound of flour add butter the size of a walnut and the same amount of flour to the butter.
Pastries show good lift during early stage of baking and drop flat towards the end.	Oven too hot. Baked with too much steam.	Steam will cause the dough to rise fast and keep the inside layers from baking. Therefore, the layer formation has not enough body. Keep damper or door partly open.

Dough and butter before roll-in process

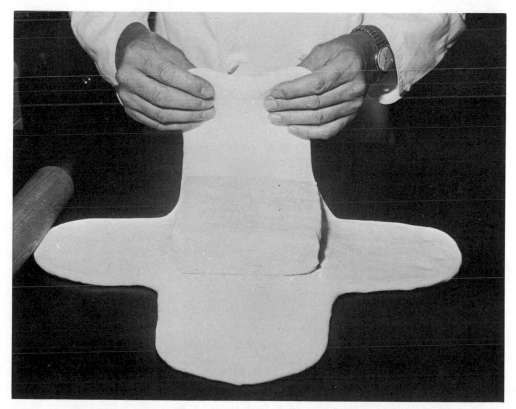

Initial stages of the roll-in process

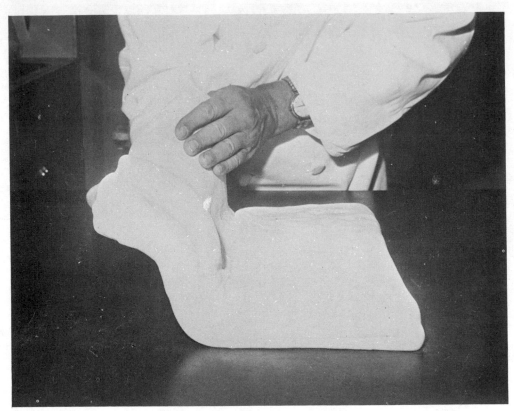

Folding the dough a single turn

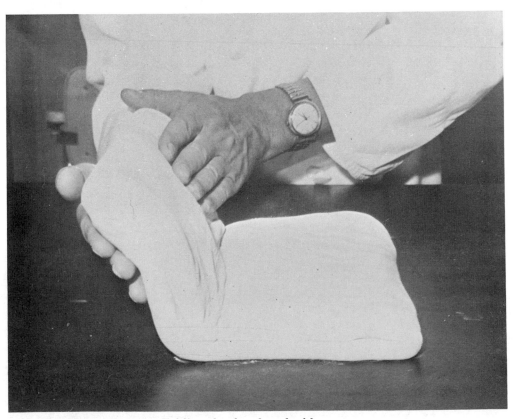

Folding the dough a double turn

French Puff Paste

In basic puff paste, the butter is rolled into the dough. The French style is exactly reversed. The butter is mixed with part of the flour and formed into a square not less than ¾" thick. Place dough in center of butter, fold into butter and roll as described under "Basic Puff Paste."

The advantage in this method is that the dough may be rolled in two single and two double turns without resting periods. The prepared pastries, however, must rest for at least five minutes before baking. If puff pastries are needed in a hurry, this method will have them ready for the oven within one hour. There is no difference between the two systems as far as quality or economy is concerned.

Note: In order to keep the butter from becoming too soft, this dough should be rolled in a cool place. If a marble slab is available it should be cooled with trays of chopped ice set on top of it shortly before starting to roll.

Apple Turnovers

Roll a piece of dough ⅛" thick and cut squares 4" x 4". Put cake crumbs in center and apples on top of each square. Sprinkle with cinnamon-flavored sugar. Egg wash extreme edges of dough and fold upper left corner toward lower right corner. Press edges lightly to seal. Make three small cuts with scissors. Let rest. Egg wash and bake at 400° F. Ice with sugar icing immediately after baking if desired.

Note: Pre-cook apples (1 lb. apples, 4 ozs. sugar, 1 oz. raisins, 1 lemon rind, grated, and 2 ozs. butter). Apple turnovers may be baked without apples to allow dough to rise better and then filled after baking.

Apple Strudel

Roll dough ¼" thick. Cut strips 4" wide and the full length of the pan. Put cake crumbs or strip of sponge cake down center of strip. Cover with thin slices of partially cooked apples or larger, cooked pieces, leaving a ¾" strip along each side plain. Sprinkle apples with cinnamon sugar and grated lemon rind. Roll more dough as long as the baking pan and cut strips ¾" wide. Cut small strips for the lattice top. Criss-cross the short strips over the apples and egg wash the sides of the dough. Place the long strips along the sides. Egg wash thoroughly. Bake at 375° F. Glaze with hot apricot jam.

Nougat Cherry Strudel

Roll dough ⅛" thick. Cut strips 8" wide and the full length of the pans. Place nougat-flavored custard cream in pastry bag. Press two strips of cream 1½" from the edge along the sides of each dough strip. Fold sides of dough over cream towards center and secure with egg wash. Place sweet, stoned cherries along center. Decorate with dough strips and sliced almonds. Bake at 375° F. Glaze with rum-flavored fondant.

Apple Macaroon Strudel

8 ozs. almond paste	8 ozs. almond paste
2 ozs. sugar	¼ cup sugar
egg yolks	egg yolks
1 lemon rind, grated	1 lemon rind, grated

Method

Mix sugar and rind into almond paste. Slowly add enough yolks to make mixture creamy. Roll dough as in "Apple Strudel." Put cooked, sweetened apples down center and sprinkle with rum and chopped almonds. Put creamed mixture in pastry bag and form lattice strips over apples. Bake at 375° F.

Peach Strudel

Roll dough as in "Apple Strudel." Place crumbs or cake strips down center of dough. Set peach halves on top. Sprinkle fruit with sugar, lemon rind, and a few drops of lemon juice. Decorate edges with dough strips. Bake at 375° F. Glaze with hot apricot jam. Serve with whipped cream

Ham Crescents

Roll dough ¼" thick. Cut into triangles. Take thinly sliced ham and form rolls with chopped pickles in center. Roll into the dough triangles and form crescents. Egg wash and bake at 400° F. Heat crescents in hot oven before serving.

Sausage Rolls

Roll a thin sheet of dough. Egg wash. Using a pastry bag with large, round tube, dress a strip of meat filling along extreme upper edge of dough. Roll meat into dough, allowing to overlap $\frac{1}{2}''$. Cut off meat roll from rest of dough and proceed to dress another strip of filling. Continue until desired amount of filling is used up. Set the rolls close together on board and cut pieces 2" to 3" long. Egg wash and set on slightly greased pan. Bake at 400° F.

Meat Filling

>   1 lb. ground beef
>   8 ozs. ground pork
>   2 bread rolls, softened in water
>   2 eggs
>   dash salt, pepper, cayenne
>   6 strips of bacon, diced
>   1 medium sized onion, chopped
>   1 tsp. marjoram

Method

Mix all ingredients together thoroughly. Mixture must be soft enough to squeeze through a tube. To soften, use more eggs or sour cream.

Note: Pork or cocktail sausages may be used instead of ground meat. Place rolls in hot oven ten minutes before serving.

Patty Shells

Roll puff paste $\frac{1}{2}''$ thick. For large shells use cooky cutter 3" in diameter. Cut shells at least 1" from edge of rolled dough to make sure layers are even. Set dough disks on greased, dampened baking pans. Use a 2" cutter dipped into hot butter and cut each patty shell to a depth of one-third, making certain that the cutter is properly centered. Egg wash. Let rest for twenty minutes in cool place. Bake at 400° F.

Note: When brushing with egg wash, care must be taken that the liquid does not run down the sides. The eggs would bake and keep the layers from rising evenly. After baking, remove the smaller center piece carefully and take out the soft part from the inside. Put shells, without tops, back into the oven for a few minutes to allow inside walls to dry. Patty shells may be filled with meat pie fillings, oysters, chicken, or fruit fillings.

Patty Shells 2

Instead of cutting the patties in one piece as described above, the number 2 shells are cut in three parts and put together.

Part 1
Roll thin sheet of puff dough. Cut disks with 3" cooky cutter and set on greased, dampened pan. Moisten extreme edges with water.
Part 2
Roll another sheet of dough $\frac{1}{4}''$ thick and cut disks the same size as above. Using a 2" cutter, make inside cuts to separate rings from tops.
Part 3
Set ring on first part, egg wash, and let rest before baking. Set the remaining 2" disks on another pan, egg wash and let rest. After baking, the latter are used as lids. Bake at 400° F.

Fancy Patties Vol-au-Vent

These patties are somewhat complex to make, but very attractive and always something special on a buffet table.

Make a ball a little smaller than the size of the desired patties, using paper strips wrapped in white paper (usually the size of a small soup bowl). Roll thin layer of puff dough, cut a round slightly bigger than the ball, and set on dampened baking pan. Egg wash out-side rim. Place paper ball in center. Cut another round of dough large enough to cover the ball. With egg wash, mold this piece perfectly smooth and secure to bottom layer. Trim off excess dough around bottom layer and crimp dough to get decorative design. Decorate sides with dough strips or animals and flowers cut from puff paste. Cut a lid-sized, round piece and set on egg washed top of ball. Prick patty with fork and egg wash. Let rest for twenty minutes in a cool place. Bake at 350° F.

After baking, cut off lid. Cut open paper with scissors and remove all paper from the patty. Return patty to medium hot oven to allow inside to dry.

Suitable Fillings are fowl ragout, creamed meat, or vegetable mixtures, salads, meats in aspic, whipped cream and fruit mixtures, and ice creams. Decorate with fruit or vegetable flowers to match filling.

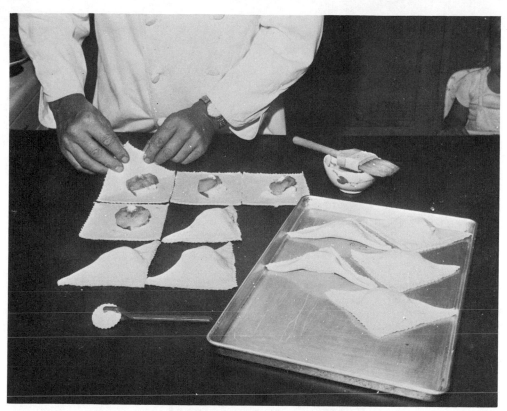

Apple turnovers before baking

Apple turnovers after baking

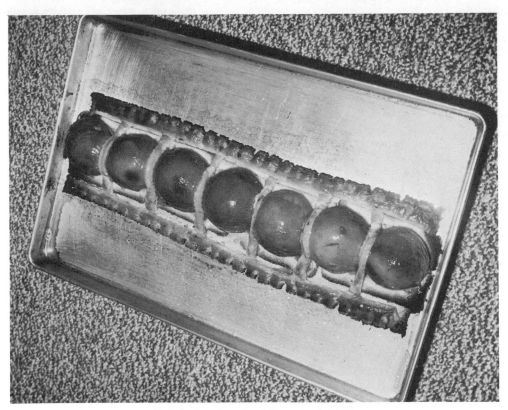

Peach strudel glazed with apricot jam

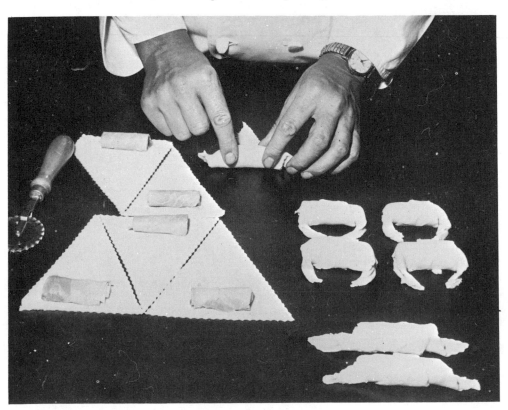

Preparing ham crescents

Patty shells made in three parts

Preparing sausage rolls

Puff paste patty before baking

Puff paste patty after baking

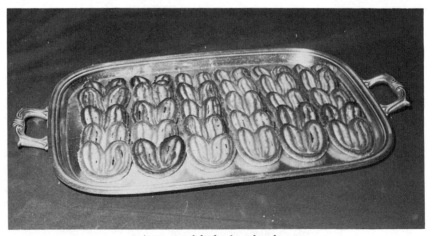

A tray of baked palm leaves

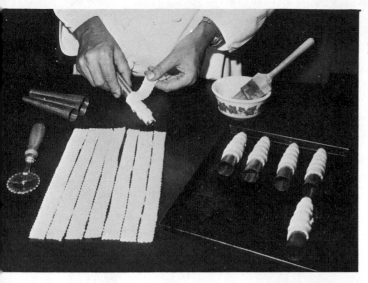

Preparing cream horns

French peach cake

Pineapple cake

Pear cake

Strawberry Patties

Palm Leaves

Roll sheet of puff paste 18″ x 24″ and ⅛″ thick. Use granulated sugar for rolling instead of flour. Fold dough 3″ toward center from both ends of 18″ width. Fold each end another 3″ and fold remaining dough to get one thick strip. Cut pieces ⅜″ wide. Dip cut side in granulated sugar and set on greased pan cut-side up. Let rest ten minutes. Bake at 400° F. When bottom gets brown turn leaves over. Sugar will turn to caramel. After baking, remove from pan and set leaves on cold, greased pan. If leaves are made several days in advance, store in warm place to retain crispness.

Note: As indicated above, palm leaves are rolled in sugar. Contrary to flour, the sugar should not be brushed off before folding. This aids the opening and spreading of the layers during baking.

Shoe Soles

Roll puff dough ¼″ thick, using sugar instead of flour. Cut round disks with a 3″ cooky cutter. Use small rolling pin and give disks an oval shape, making sure that the ends are slightly thicker than the center. Bake on greased pan at 400° F. When cold, split open and fill with raspberry jam.

Eccles Cakes

Roll puff paste ⅛″ thick, using sugar instead of flour. Cover one-half of the dough with currants and sprinkle with cinnamon sugar. Fold remaining half of dough over currants. Press down lightly with rolling pin to make currants show through dough. Cut 2″ x 2″ squares. Bake at 400° F. When bottom has browned, turn cakes over to brown other side.

Caramel Pretzels

Roll puff paste ⅛″ thick, using sugar instead of flour. Cut strips 12″ and ⅜″ wide. Twist the strips and then form pretzels. Dip in sugar, set on greased pan with sugar side down and bake at 400° F. Turn pretzels over after bottom has browned.

Cream Horns

Using flour on the board, roll a sheet of puff paste ⅛″ thick. Brush off excess flour. Cut strips 12″ long and ¾″ wide. Egg wash. Take a metal tube or wooden stick in right hand, place the end of strip on extreme end of the tube, and wind the dough around the tube in spiral fashion, making certain that the dough edges overlap at least $\frac{1}{16}$″. If desired, dip rolls in coarse granulated sugar. Set on lightly greased pan. Let rest. Bake at 375° F. While still hot, pull out stick or tube.

Note: Wooden sticks must be greased before using. Wind strips around without stretching the dough. Stretched dough will break open during baking. Fill rolls with custard or whipped cream. Dust with powdered sugar or ice with chocolate fondant.

Napoleons

Roll sheet of puff paste ⅛″ thick. Cover the desired size of wet pan with dough. Prick holes with a fork. Let rest. Bake at 400° F. When cold, cut strips 3″ wide. Join three strips with a mixture of custard and whipped cream. Spread apricot jam on top. Glaze with rum-flavored pink fondant. Cut slices 1½″ wide.

Cake Bases of Puff Paste

Roll dough ⅛″ thick. Cut 8″ or 9″ rounds. Prick thoroughly with fork. Adjust rims as illustrated. Egg wash. Bake at 375° F.

Pear Cake

Spread vanilla custard on puff paste. Top with thin layer of sponge cake. Moisten with jam. Arrange fruit as illustrated. Glaze with hot apricot jam.

Strawberry Patties

Fill puff paste patties with whipped cream mixed with chopped strawberries. Decorate top with fresh berries and angelica. Glaze with jelly.

IX

CHEESE AND SALT GOODS

Cheese is used shredded, chopped, sliced, or creamed for making pastries, *hors d'oeuvres*, canapés, and snacks. Many pastry shops carry a variety of cheese goods which delight the customers and attract new business. For the housewife or hotel chef, cheese goods enrich every menu.

Puff paste with shredded parmesan cheese rolled between the layers is a basic medium for a large number of items which may be made a long time in advance and stored in air-tight containers. These goods are usually warmed before serving.

A special cheese short dough serves as a liner for tarts. These tarts may be filled with creamed cheese, salt biscuits, et cetera and decorated with the same materials used in garnishing sandwiches or *hors d'oeuvres*.

Cheese *petits fours* are very decorative and a challenge to the individual's artistic imagination.

Cheese Puff Paste 1

8 ozs. butter	scant $\frac{1}{2}$ cup butter
8 ozs. grated parmesan cheese	3$\frac{3}{4}$ cups grated parmesan cheese
$\frac{1}{2}$ pint cream	$\frac{1}{2}$ cup cream
13 ozs. flour	1$\frac{3}{8}$ cups flour
dash salt	dash salt
1 tsp. paprika	$\frac{1}{2}$ tsp. paprika
1 lb. 14 ozs. puff paste	15 ozs. puff paste

Method

Mix all ingredients well to get a smooth, medium-soft dough. Let rest in cool place for thirty minutes. Roll the puff paste to an oblong shape $\frac{3}{8}''$ thick. Roll the cheese dough to the same size and place on top of puff paste, making certain that the puff paste is well covered. Apply one double turn (*see Index*, "Puff Paste") and let rest. Apply another double turn, let rest, and make up dough.

Cheese Puff Paste 2

This is the fastest method of making cheese puff paste. Use a regular puff paste formula. (*See Index*.) Sprinkle grated parmesan cheese between every layer during the roll-in process.

The cheese may also be used on the board instead of flour during the rolling of the dough.

Cheese Puffs

Part 1

$\frac{1}{2}$ pint milk	scant 1 cup milk
2$\frac{1}{2}$ ozs. butter	5 tbsp. butter
4 ozs. flour	$\frac{7}{8}$ cup flour
4 egg yolks	4 egg yolks
4 whole eggs	4 whole eggs
dash salt	dash salt

Part 2 (filling)

5 ozs. butter	$\frac{5}{8}$ cup butter
3 egg yolks	3 egg yolks
3$\frac{1}{2}$ ozs. cottage cheese	$\frac{1}{2}$ cup cottage cheese
3$\frac{1}{2}$ ozs. grated parmesan cheese	1 cup grated parmesan cheese
$\frac{1}{2}$ pint whipping cream	1 cup whipping cream
dash salt, pepper, and paprika	dash salt, pepper, and paprika

Method

Process Part *1* like éclair dough. (*See Index*.) Using a star tube, dress small mounds on greased pan. Bake at 375° F. to 400° F. (As cheese puffs cannot be iced or sugared, the mounds must be egg washed before baking.)

Part 2 Cream together the strained cottage cheese, parmesan cheese, and butter, adding the egg yolks slowly. Blend in spices. Whip the cream and combine with cheese mixture. When the baked puffs have cooled, poke holes in the bottom, and fill, using a pastry bag and tube.

Cheese Short Dough

4 ozs. Swiss cheese, shredded	1$\frac{1}{4}$ cups Swiss cheese, shredded
4 ozs. flour	scant $\frac{3}{4}$ cup flour
4 ozs. butter	scant $\frac{1}{2}$ cup butter
2 egg yolks	2 egg yolks
pinch nutmeg	pinch nutmeg
dash salt, pepper, paprika	dash salt, pepper, paprika

Method

Cream butter, cheese, and spices. Add egg yolks. Mix in flour. Knead well to get smooth dough. Let rest for twenty minutes. Roll dough

$\frac{1}{4}''$ thick. Cut with small, differently shaped cooky cutters. Egg wash. Sprinkle individual pieces with poppy seed, parmesan cheese, caraway seed, chopped almonds, peanuts, et cetera. Bake at 350° F.

Tart Dough

10 ozs. flour	scant 2½ cups flour
5 ozs. butter	⅝ cup butter
3 egg yolks	3 egg yolks
dash salt	dash salt

Method

Knead all ingredients together to get smooth dough. Add a little milk, or increase yolks if dough is too stiff. Excellent for lining tart forms.

Cheese Tarts

4 ozs. parmesan cheese, grated	1 cup parmesan cheese, grated
4 egg yolks	4 egg yolks
1½ ozs. flour	3 tbsp. flour
¼ pint milk	½ cup milk

Method

Blend all ingredients together well and fill into tart forms lined with cheese puff paste or tart dough. Sprinkle top with grated parmesan. Bake at 375° F.

Salt Biscuit

5 egg whites	5 egg whites
5 egg yolks	5 egg yolks
5 ozs. flour	scant ¾ cup flour
1 tbsp. parsley, chopped	1 tbsp. parsley, chopped
dash salt	dash salt

Method

Mix salt, yolks, parsley, and one-third of the flour until smooth. Beat whites until stiff. Combine with yolk mixture and blend in rest of flour. Spread batter $\frac{1}{4}''$ thick on waxed paper. Bake at 375° F. When cold, cut biscuits into small squares. Use salt biscuits on bottom of tarts, before filling in cheese cream.

Cheese Butter Cream

6½ ozs. butter	¾ cup butter
5 egg yolks	5 egg yolks
3½ ozs. cottage cheese, strained	½ cup cottage cheese, strained
¼ pint whipping cream	½ cup whipping cream
3½ ozs. parmesan cheese, grated	1 cup parmesan cheese, grated
1½ ozs. Edam cheese	1 cup Edam cheese
1½ ozs. Roquefort cheese	1 cup Roquefort cheese
1 tbsp. cognac	1 tbsp. cognac
dash salt, pepper, paprika	dash salt, pepper, paprika
1 tsp. parsley, chopped	1 tsp. parsley, chopped

Method

Cream butter, adding yolks slowly. Blend in cheeses and spice. Add whipped cream. This cream is excellent for filling cold tarts, puff rolls, cheese puffs, et cetera.

Liptauer Cheese Cream

3½ ozs. cottage cheese, strained	½ cup cottage cheese, strained
6½ ozs. butter	¾ cup butter (generous)
2½ ozs. onions, chopped	scant ½ cup onions, chopped
1 tsp. parsley	1 tsp. parsley
¼ tsp. caraway seed	¼ tsp. caraway seed
dash salt, paprika	dash salt, paprika
6 tbsp. red wine or beer	6 tbsp. red wine or beer

Method

Cream butter with cottage cheese. Blend in remaining ingredients. Mix smooth. Excellent for fillings, sandwich spread, et cetera.

Boiled Cheese Cream 1

3½ ozs. butter	scant ½ cup butter
1 pint milk	2 cups milk
4 egg yolks	4 egg yolks
1¼ ozs. cornstarch	⅛ cup cornstarch
1½ ozs. parmesan cheese, grated	scant ½ cup parmesan cheese, grated
dash salt, paprika	dash salt, paprika

Method

Put all ingredients except butter into sauce pan. Bring to a boil, stirring constantly. As soon as cream thickens, pour mixture onto marble slab or pan and allow to cool. Mix in soft butter.

Preparing cheese straws and pretzels

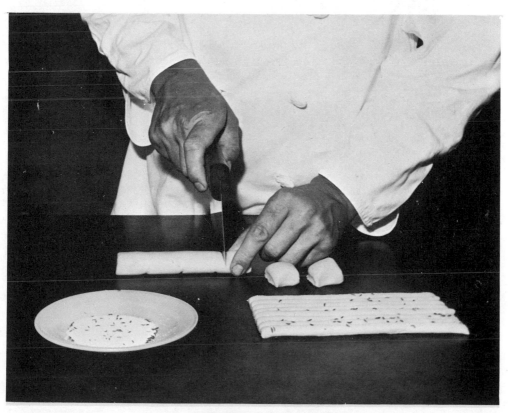

Preparing salt sticks

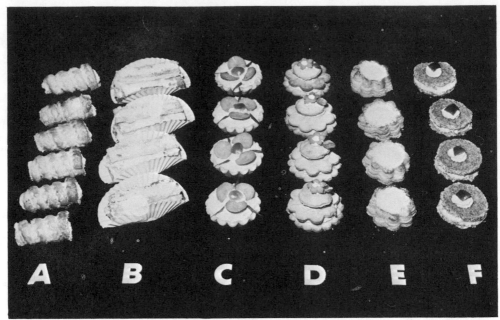

A. Cheese rolls B. Cream cheese slices C. Cheese tartlettes D. Cheese pyramids
E. Cheese patties F. Cheese snaps

Preparation of Vienna salt rolls

Boiled Cheese Cream 2

2 ozs. Roquefort cheese	1⅓ cups Roquefort cheese
2 ozs. butter	¼ cup butter
4 egg yolks	4 egg yolks
¼ pint milk	½ cup milk
⅜ ozs. cornstarch	1 tbsp. cornstarch
3 egg whites	3 egg whites
dash salt, paprika	dash salt, paprika

Method

Put all ingredients except egg whites in sauce pan and bring to a boil, stirring constantly. As soon as cream thickens, blend in stiffly-beaten whites.

Cheese Straws and Pretzels

Use cheese puff paste formula *1* or *2*. Roll dough ¼″ thick. Do not underdust with flour during rolling, but use grated parmesan cheese instead.

For cheese straws, cut strips 6″ to 7″ long and ¼″ wide. Put twist on strips and set on greased pans.

For pretzels, cut strips approximately 5″ long, form pretzels and set on greased pans. Bake both items at 300° F. Goods should be golden-brown and must be crispy. When storing away for any length of time, use a tin can with tight-fitting lid. Warm before serving.

Salt Sticks

6½ ozs. flour	scant 1½ cups flour
4 ozs. butter, melted	scant ½ cup butter, melted
2 egg yolks	2 egg yolks
1 oz. yeast	2 cakes yeast
milk	milk
dash salt	dash salt

Method

Dissolve yeast in a little milk. Add remaining ingredients and knead until smooth, firm dough is obtained, adding more milk if necessary. Form sticks the thickness of a pencil and 4″ to 5″ in length. Egg wash and roll in coarse salt. Caraway seed may be added to salt, if so desired. Let rise a little before baking. Bake at 300° F.

Note: Same dough may also be used for making pretzels. When used commercially, sticks should be packed in cellophane bags.

A. Cheese Rolls

Form small rolls of puff paste, 2″ in length, as described under "Cream Horns." (*See Index.*) When cold, fill horns with cheese butter cream. Dip both ends into grated parmesan cheese.

B. Cream Cheese Slices

Cover greased baking sheet with cheese puff paste ⅛″ thick. Bake at 400° F. Let cool. Cut three strips of equal size approximately 3″ wide. Fill with boiled cheese cream number 2. Sprinkle top with grated parmesan cheese. Cut slices 1″ to 1½″ wide. Slices may be served hot or cold.

C. Cheese Tartlettes

Line small forms with cheese short dough. Place paper cup filled with dried beans inside tart form to secure dough during baking. Bake at 350° F. Let cool. Put salt biscuit on bottom, or pumpernickel bread if so desired. Fill tarts with *liptauer* cheese cream. (*See Index.*) Decorate as illustrated.

D. Cheese Pyramids

Roll cheese short dough ⅛″ thick. Cut three different sizes of cookies, (1″, 2″, and 3″ in diameter). Bake at 357° F. When cold, set cookies together with cheese cream. Decorate tops with onions and olives.

E. Cheese Patties

Use regular small patty shells. (*See Index.*) Fill with cheese cream. Decorate with unsweetened whipped cream.

F. Cheese Snaps

Cut round pieces of pumpernickel bread, using a cooky cutter 1½″ in diameter. Form circle with cheese butter cream. Place piece of pickle in center. Cover with second bread disk. Roll sides into grated cheese.

Vienna Salt Rolls

1 lb. flour	3½ cups flour
½ pint milk	1 cup milk
⅔ ozs. yeast	1¼ cakes yeast
2½ ozs. lard	5 tbsp. lard
dash salt	dash salt

Method

Soften yeast in a little of the milk. Add rest of ingredients. Knead until dough becomes smooth and firm. Wrap into cloth and let rest over night. Divide dough into thirty to thirty-five equal pieces.

Form round balls and let rest ten minutes. Roll out balls to ovals 5″ in length. Brush with melted butter. Form rolls, tapered on both ends. Set on greased pans. Let rise approximately one-half hour. Egg wash. Sprinkle with salt and caraway seed. Bake at 375° F. When cold, split open and fill with *liptauer* cheese cream. (*See Index.*)

Hungarian Crackling Puffs

8 ozs. flour	1¾ cups flour
1 oz. yeast	2 cakes yeast
2 tbsp. white wine	2 tbsp. white wine
milk	milk
dash salt	dash salt
8 ozs. crackling (pork)	1–1½ cups crackling (pork)

Method

Dissolve yeast in a little of the milk. Add rest of ingredients, except crackling, and knead to smooth dough. Let rise. Knead in finely chopped pork crackling. Give dough two single turns, as described under "Puff Paste." (*See Index.*) Let rest. Roll dough ½″ thick. Cut pieces 1½″ in diameter. Set on greased pans. Egg wash. Let rise. Make criss-cross cuts with sharp knife. Bake at 400° F. Serve with cheese cream.

Note: To make crackling, cut strips of pork fat into small cubes. Fry until light brown in color and very crisp. Squeeze excess lard from crackling.

Caraway Pretzels

1 lb. flour	4 cups flour
5 ozs. butter	½ cup butter (generous)
1½ ozs. sugar	scant ¼ cup sugar
dash salt	dash salt
1 oz. yeast	2 cakes yeast
½ pint milk	1 cup milk
caraway seed	caraway seed

Method

Form yeast sponge with one-half of the milk. (See "Yeast Dough.") Let rise. Add remaining ingredients and knead to a smooth dough. Divide dough into small, equal pieces. Roll each piece about 5″ long and the thickness of a pencil. Form pretzels. Cover with cloth and let rise. Egg wash and sprinkle with caraway seed and salt. Bake at 425° F.

Munich Beer Pretzels

1 oz. yeast	2 cakes yeast
⅓ oz. sugar	1 tsp. sugar
milk	milk
2 lbs. flour	7 cups flour
1½ ozs. lard	3 tbsp. lard
dash salt	dash salt

Method

Dissolve yeast and sugar in a little milk. Knead with rest of ingredients to make a firm, smooth dough. Form pretzels as above. Let rise slightly and then put them into a large pan filled with hot alkali solution (make solution of two quarts water and one-third ounce alkali). Cook over medium heat until pretzels float on top. Drain pretzels, sprinkle with coarse salt and place on greased baking pan. Bake at 375° F. until crisp and dark brown.

Croutons

Cut slices of bread 1½″ x 2½″ and fry in hot butter. Put slices of Swiss cheese cut to same size between two croutons. Place in hot oven until cheese has melted. Serve with baked parsnip.

Sour Cream Pattiès

1 pint sour cream	2 cups sour cream
1 tbsp. parmesan cheese, grated	1 tbsp. parmesan cheese, grated
flour	flour
dash salt	dash salt

Method

Mix as much flour into cream as necessary to get medium batter. Add the cheese and salt. Using a tablespoon, form small round disks on greased pan. Sprinkle with caraway seed. Bake at 375° F. When cold, join in pairs with cheese filling or cream.

X

THE PRESERVATION OF FRUITS

Preserving Fruit - Gelees

Methods of preserving food are as old as mankind. Man has always looked for ways of preventing food spoilage to assure nourishment during the cold season when fresh foods were not available. Methods of preservation range from drying and freezing, to boiling and sealing. The most practical methods for the preservation of fruits are given here.

Fruits in Sugar Syrup

The most common way of preserving fruits is referred to as the thick-sugar method. This method can be used for cherries, peaches, apricots, pears, oranges, plums, pineapple, lemon and orange rind, and black walnuts. The sugar syrup is prepared the same way for all fruits. As the sugar is the preservative, it is important to have the fruit thoroughly soaked in the syrup. To obtain maximum assimilation, the fruits must undergo a softening process first. This is the most critical stage of the thick-sugar process, and determines whether or not the final product will be a beautifully preserved fruit with natural form, color, and aroma. If the fruit is too hard, resulting in poor assimilation of the syrup, it will inevitably spoil. Fruit that is too soft will lose its color and become mushy.

The type of fruit must be considered when deciding upon the cooking method. Some fruit require only blanching in boiling water. To retain the natural fruit color, a little salt or lemon juice should be added to the water. When the fruit has reached the proper stage of softness it should be carefully removed from the hot water and placed in clear, cold water. Change the water several times. The fruit must be thoroughly drained before being covered with the sugar syrup.

The first sugar-water solution should have twenty percent sugar. The following example shows the formula for one gallon of water.

1 gallon water = 8 pounds = 128 ounces

20% sugar = 1 pound, $9\frac{1}{2}$ ounces = 25.6 ounces

Boil the sugar water solution until it has cleared, remove from heat, and let it become cold. Place fruit in a clean bowl or crock and cover completely with the syrup. To prevent dust from settling on the fruit, cut a piece of waxed paper to fit bowl opening exactly.

After twenty-four hours, drain the syrup from the fruit into a pan and increase the sugar content to twenty-four percent. According to the example given, about five more ounces of sugar would be added. Boil the syrup until clear, removing all foam with great care and thoroughness. Pour syrup over fruit when it has become luke warm, replace paper cover and let stand twenty-four hours.

The third day, the sugar content must total twenty-eight percent. Thus another five ounces of sugar is added to the syrup, and it is then boiled as above. At this stage twenty percent of the total amount of sugar is now calculated, and that measure of glucose is boiled with the syrup until clear. (25.6 ozs. sugar + 10 ozs. sugar = 35.6 ozs.) sugar. Since 20% of 35.6 is 7.1, the amount of glucose added would be 7 ozs.) Glucose must be added to prevent the crystallization of the sugar. The syrup is poured over the fruit while still hot. Let stand twenty-four hours.

The fourth day the sugar content is increased to thirty-two percent by adding five ounces of sugar. This time the syrup and fruit are brought to a boil together. Carefully skim off foam as it forms. When syrup is clear, remove from heat, and let stand for twenty-four hours.

On the fifth and final day the sugar content is raised to thirty-six percent with the addition of five ounces of sugar. The syrup is boiled until clear. Place the fruit in sterilized jars and cover with the hot syrup. Seal the jars and store in a cool place.

If colors are desired, they must be added to the first, light sugar solution. Differently colored cherries may be made for decorating purposes. The natural fruit color can be neutralized by soaking the cherries in a solution of water and twenty-five percent vinegar. When the color has been removed the fruit must be rinsed thoroughly to avoid leaving any trace of vinegar. The cherries can then be processed with the thick-sugar method. These cherries are an excellent decorating medium for cakes, pastries, desserts, and cocktails.

Apricots and Peaches

Fruits that are not fully ripened are cut open, stoned, and placed in gently boiling water. Cook until the fruit slides easily off a fork which has been stuck into it. Drain well and proceed as described in thick-sugar method.

Oranges

Small, whole oranges are used. Poke several holes in each with a fork. Prepare a twenty percent sugar-water solution and thicken it by boiling it little thicker every day over a period of five days. Boil the solution with the oranges in it gently for a few minutes each day. On the final day, remove fruit, bring sugar solution up to 234° F. (soft ball stage). Place fruit in sterilized jars and pour thick sugar over it. Seal containers and store in a cool place.

Pears

Use hard pears, peel, and cut in half. Remove pits. Poke holes in each with a fork. Boil in water gently until tender. Proceed as directed in thick-sugar method. If colored fruit is desired, add colors to first sugar solution.

Plums

Process as described under "Apricots and Peaches." Plums are sufficiently tenderized by simply soaking them in boiling-hot water for fifteen minutes.

Black Walnuts

Green, whole walnuts are used. Poke nuts thoroughly with fork from all sides and soak in cold water for approximately eight days. During this time the water must be changed daily. Allow nuts to boil until they slide easily off of a fork which has been stuck into them. Remove from heat and rinse well in cold water. Process according to thick-sugar method. Add a few cloves and cinnamon stick to final solution. Black nuts are very flavorful and make an excellent decorating medium.

Preserved Compote Fruits

All fruit must be sterilized. This is done by placing it in hot water (180° F.) and keeping it at that temperature for forty minutes. Large pieces need more, smaller pieces, less time. The jars are kept in boiling water and the rubber rings in hot water. The fruit is piled into the jars while still hot, covered with the sugar solution, sealed and left to cool slowly. This method requires absolute cleanliness in order to prevent fermentation. Different antibiotics are offered for sale, which will guarantee success even to the most inexperienced operator. As these chemicals differ from one another considerably, the manufacturer's formulas must be used in order to get the proper fruit-sugar-preservative combination.

How to steam the fruits

The fruit may be placed in jars, bottles, or cans. The containers must be sealed. When using glass containers, insulating materials such as towels, straw, or wood shavings must be put between and underneath the glasses to prevent cracking. In order to prevent overheating from the bottom, jars should be placed on a wooden rack. Tin cans may be piled into the steamer as close together as possible and covered with a rag. The steamer is filled with enough water to cover two-thirds of the containers. The water is heated slowly until the boiling point is reached. The boiling time depends upon the type of fruit used. When the boiling period is completed remove container from heat and allow goods to cool slowly before taking the jars from the steamer. Bottles with fruit juices or puree may be dipped in liquid wax to seal opening completely or stored upside down.

Cherry Compote

Remove pits and stems from cherries, and sterilize. Pack cherries solidly into jars or cans. Cover with sugar syrup. Seal containers and steam about ten minutes.

Apricot Compote

Ripened apricots are preferred to those used for decorating in the thick-sugar method. Remove stones, sterilize, and drain well. Place in a bowl, cover with sugar syrup, and let soak for twenty-four hours. Place fruit and syrup in jars adding a few cloves to each. Seal jars and steam for fifteen to twenty minutes.

Pineapple Compote

Method 1

Cut pineapples into cubes. Roll in powdered sugar, making sure that every piece is well covered. Place fruit in jars and cover with tight-fitting lids. Keep containers in warm place. Shake well occasionally until all the sugar has melted.

Method 2

Boil pineapple cubes in light sugar syrup until tender. Remove fruit and boil sugar to 234° F. (soft ball stage). Strain through a cloth. Place pineapple in jars and cover with syrup. Seal and steam for ten minutes.

Plum Compote

Sterilize stoned, ripe plums. Pack tightly into container, adding cinnamon sticks and cloves for flavoring. Cover with sugar syrup and seal. Steam for fifteen to twenty-five minutes, depending upon the size of fruit used.

Pear Compote

Peeled, cored pears (whole or halves) are tenderized in boiling water to which a little salt has been added. Rinse well in cold water and pack into jars. Cover with syrup. Seal and steam for twenty to twenty-five minutes.

Red Currant Compote

Place cleaned berries in jar. Sprinkle granulated sugar on top, using three tablespoons for every one pint of berries. Seal and steam for ten minutes. The berries should not be too ripe or they will become mushy.

Apple Compote

Use hard apples only. Peel, core, and slice each apple into six or eight pieces. Place immediately into water containing a little lemon juice to prevent the apples from turning brown. Boil apples in fifteen percent sugar syrup (one pint water to 2½ ozs. sugar) until soft. Place into containers and cover with the syrup. A preservative chemical may be added to the syrup, making steaming unnecessary. Otherwise the apples are

sealed and steamed for fifteen minutes. To improve the flavor add cloves and a cinnamon stick to each jar before steaming.

Raspberry Compote

Use dry, hard berries. Place in bowl and cover with red-colored sugar syrup (twenty-five percent sugar, one pint water and four ounces sugar). Cover bowl with towels and let stand for twenty-four hours. Heat the fruit mixture to 212° F. Let cool. Add a chemical preservative and place fruit in jars. Seal.

Strawberry Compote

Five pounds of sugar and one and one-half pints of water are heated to 238° F. (soft ball stage). Remove from heat and add red food coloring. Add ten pounds of slightly ripened strawberries. Stir carefully and cover with waxed paper. After twenty-four hours drain off the juice and bring it to a boil. Let cool and add a preservative. Pour juice over fruit and let stand another twenty-four hours. Fill jars with fruit mixture and seal.

Peach Compote

Peel peaches, blanching if necessary to remove skin. Cut in half and take out stones. Boil in sugar syrup until tender. Add preservative and place mixture into jars. Seal tightly.

Rum Fruit Compote

Prepare the desired ripe fruits, wash them, and peel if possible. Pack fruits into sterilized glass jars. Prepare syrup as follows: Dissolve one pound of sugar in five ounces of hot water. Let cool and add five ounces of Jamaica rum. Pour syrup over fruit and seal. Store in cool place.

GELÉES

Gelées are fruit juices thickened with sugar until they become firm and easy to cut. Some fruits have enough pectin to create a strong *gelée*, while others have none at all. To the latter gelatine must be added. To obtain the best possible results only fresh-picked fruits should be used. Neutral *gelée,* such as apple, may be colored and used for decorating purposes.

How to cook Gelées

All *gelées* must be cooked quickly or they will lose some of their jellying power. *Gelée* which has been cooked too long will become tough and if not cooked enough will stay liquid. Following are three simple methods of testing *gelée.*

(1) Fill a large glass with ice cold water. Let a drop of hot *gelée* fall into it. If the *gelée* reaches the bottom of the glass without dissolving, the proper degree is obtained.

(2) Place a dab of *gelée* on a plate and set in refrigerator. Hardness of *gelée* will indicate present degree of solution.

(3) If *gelée* slides off the spatula in large pieces instead of drops, *gelée* is cooked enough.

Remove from heat immediately and pour into molds. *Gelée* does not have to be stirred during the cooking process.

Red Currant Gelée

Press ripe berries through a fine sieve or through a piece of cheese cloth to separate juice from fruit pulp. Add sugar to equal weight of juice. Cook as described above.

Note: Ten pound fruit juice and ten pounds of sugar will cook approximately eight minutes.

Apple Gelée

Cut apples into small pieces. Cook until very soft. Press through a sieve and boil the juice with the same weight of sugar as directed. The juice and rinds of oranges and lemons will add a delicate flavor. The apple pulp may be used for marmalade. Add three-quarters of a pound of sugar to every pound of pulp and cook as directed under "*Gelées.*"

Boysenberry Gelée

Cook berries in water until soft. Separate juice from pulp and proceed as described under "Red Currant Gelée."

Marmalades or Jams

Marmalades can be made of all types of fruits. While *gelée* is not to be stirred during the cooking process, marmalade must be stirred constantly to prevent burning. To test the proper cooking degree, follow the methods suggested under "*Gelées.*"

How to Cook Marmalade

The most common fruits for marmalades are oranges, apples, apricots, raspberries, peaches, red currants, strawberries, and plums. The fruit must be tenderized and then pressed through a sieve. Sugar is then added in ratio of three-quarters of a pound sugar to every one pound of fruit. Berries which are naturally soft may be used as they are. Add an antibiotic, a few drops of suitable coloring and cook, stirring constantly. Marmalades are stored in glass jars. Seal the jars with paraffin. Melt wax slowly, let cool, and pour onto cooled marmalades.

XI

ART IN THE PROFESSION

Sugar Art Work - Boiled Sugar and Its Uses - Marzipan - How to Make Flowers from Marzipan - Ice Sculpturing

Artistic center pieces for banquets, parties, and show windows will always attract the public's attention. As in other art mediums, the possibilities are limited only by the worker's creative ability and imagination. Food materials lend themselves to a great many artistic forms and enable the artist to copy nature, to create motion, and even convey feeling in his work. To understand food painting, sculpturing, and carving is as important for the pastry chef as it is for a painter to know his oils. As soon as the behavior of foodstuffs is understood, success will depend only upon practice.

Many people are afraid to attempt artistic works such as the fashioning of a marzipan or sugar rose. If they will but try, fears will disappear as their interest in the job increases. That the first attempt looks more like a cabbage is only natural—the second will undoubtedly look better. With a little practice the creation of marzipan roses will become easy and pleasant. Although the rose is not difficult, the novice might find a flower such as the daisy easier to begin with. Take a real flower apart and observe how the petals are joined to the stem, their shape and direction of growth. The success of the reproduction depends upon the artist's ability to observe accurately.

Although nature is a marvelous painter, care must be taken in coloring foods, as our creations are not always for display alone. Extremely bright or strong colors have their place in displays, but are less than attractive when they have to be eaten. The three basic coloring mediums are transparent liquids, solid fat colors, and powdered makeup paints. Most of these colors are mixed into the materials. Transparent colors are also used to touch up flower centers. Makeup paints are especially useful in coloring marzipan fruit.

For sculpture work, a set of modelling tools and chisels is essential. While the modelling can be performed to a certain extent by hand without special tools, the carving as such requires a set of chisels. The chisels come in many different sizes and shapes. For the beginner, a set of six chisels ranging in size from $\frac{1}{4}''$ to $1\frac{1}{2}''$ should be sufficient. These should include flat, curved, and triangular instruments. Miniature chisels for very fine carving and other suitable tools are available in any hobby shop.

A small set of modelling tools made of either hard wood, plastic or, ivory will certainly be very useful also.

For the cake decorator a good set of different flower, round, and star tubes is a necessity. They should be made of non-corroding materials, preferably stainless steel, for greater durability.

A small atomizer for spraying paints and glazes, a set of various cooky cutters, plus a good mercury sugar thermometer should be enough equipment to allow the average professional to tackle most problems.

The Boiling of Sugar

Few things require as much attention as the boiling of sugar. A little slip or carelessness is sure to show its effect on the final product. Never be in a hurry while attempting to boil sugar. The result may be a total failure, and cost double the time having to do it over again.

Before boiling the sugar one must know in advance how to dissolve it. Sugar which is to be boiled to a high degree needs less water than that which is boiled to a lower stage. As a general rule one should keep in mind the basic formula: sugar, plus half its weight in water; *for example,* ten pounds sugar plus five pounds water. Sugar which has been boiled in too much water will turn yellow. If too little water is used, not all of the crystals will dissolve and total crystallization will be most likely. Only highly refined sugar should be used, such as cube or granulated sugar.

Sugar should be dissolved slowly over low heat. As soon as the boiling point is reached, increase the heat and continue boiling to the desired degree. During the boiling process, the boiler wall must be washed down frequently with a bristle brush until no more crystals are visible. Cheaper grades of sugar will foam in the early stage and care must be taken to prevent the brew from boiling over. As soon as the sugar starts to rise, remove from heat and let stand for a few minutes. The sugar will settle again, leaving a layer of foam on top which can now be removed with a spoon. The process of boiling may then be continued. If the formula calls for glucose, it should be mixed into the sugar at the beginning. Color or cream of tartar should be added a few minutes before the final degree is reached.

Note: Under no circumstances should the spoon or spatula be left in the syrup during the boiling process, nor should the sugar be stirred after it has completely dissolved.

The different stages of boiling sugar are determined by thermometer or the finger test. Thermometers, of course, are much more accurate and are certainly a wise investment. However, as there are different kinds of thermometers, a few words should be said about them. Instruments with mercury scales should be given preference over those with alcohol scales. Besides the commonly used Fahrenheit thermometer, we know of instruments with Reaumur and Centigrade readings. The readings differ from one another considerably. A conversion table has been added to this book to convert the different degrees to Fahrenheit at a glance. (*See Index.*)

Cooking Temperatures for Various Stages

Crystal	220° F.
Soft ball	238° F.
Medium ball	240° F.
Stiff ball	244° F.
Hard ball	250° F.
Light crack	264° F.
Medium crack	272° F.
Hard crack	290° F.
Extra Hard Crack	330° F.
Caramel	360° F.

The finger test is made as follows : Have a pan of cold water ready. Put a few drops of the boiling sugar into it. Hardness of ball formed between fingers indicates degree of sugar.

BOILED SUGAR AND ITS USES

Sugar Syrup

This is the first stage. Remove the sugar from heat as soon as it has reached the boiling point of 212° F. Clean off the accumulated foam and pour syrup into a clean container. Cover and store. Sugar syrup is used for different purposes, such as the thinning of fondant, moistening of cakes and pastries, various sauces, thickening and flavoring, et cetera.

Crystallized Sugar

Sugar is boiled to 220° F. At this point the sugar will develop crystals when left to cool. The crystals will form not only on the container's wall, but upon everything put into the solution. The goods placed in it are referred to as being candied. Crystallized sugar is used for candying orange and lemon peel, various candies and liquid liqueur pralines.

Sugar Casting

Granulated sugar dissolved in a little water and swiftly boiled to **244° F. For every two** pounds of sugar one tablespoon of white fondant is added as soon as the solution reaches the proper degree. The sugar is then stirred constantly until it becomes milky-white, at which point it is poured into the desired plaster-of-paris molds (The molds have to be soaked in cold water overnight to prepare them for the sugar.) The moment the hot sugar comes in contact with the chilled mold, it will begin to harden from the outside. If the crust formed is between $\frac{1}{8}''$ and $\frac{1}{4}''$ thick, depending upon the size of the object, the mold must be turned upside down onto a wire screen to allow the liquid sugar center to drain out. After a few minutes the mold may be opened and the cast object removed carefully. This requires a little practise for the unskilled. However, small things such as rabbits, chicks, eggs, et cetera, will as a rule slide easily from the mold, providing the molds have been soaked long enough in cold water. The moment the boiling hot sugar comes in contact with the wet plaster some of the moisture will evaporate, leaving a thin layer of steam between the mold and the sugar object. This will prevent the binding of the sugar with the porous plaster-of-paris wall. In continuous operation the warming of the molds is inevitable. It is therefore necessary to return the molds to cold water after each casting.

The sugar animals usually show rough edges on the bottom left by the outflowing sugar. Smooth them immediately after the objects have been taken from the molds, as cold casting sugar is very brittle.

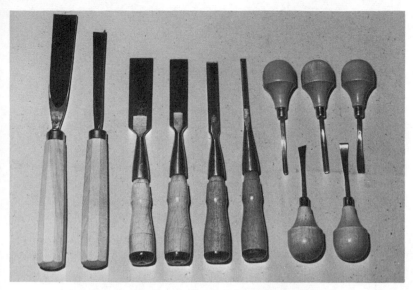

A set of chisels is essential for sculpture work

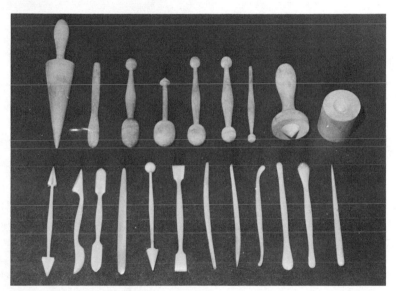

A set of modelling tools made from wood *(above)* and plastic *(below)*

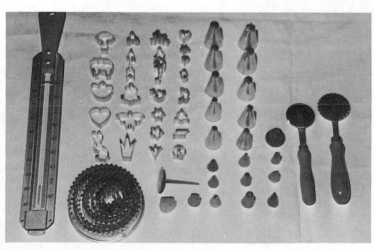

Miscellaneous tools helpful for sculpture work

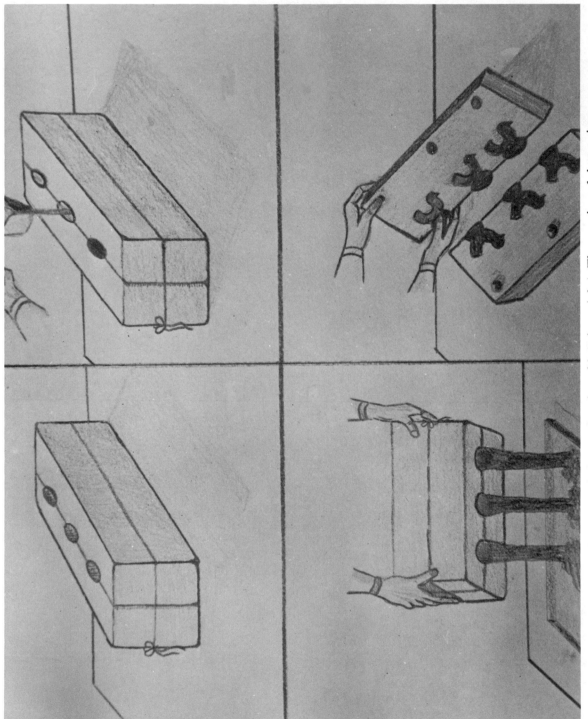

The prepared plaster-of-paris mold (*left to right*). The pouring of the casting sugar. The draining out of the excess sugar. Removing the objects from the molds.

The casted sugar articles should be kept in a warm, moisture-free place and allowed to dry completely before application of the final decorations. If colored objects are desired, the colors may be boiled with the sugar or applied with a bristle brush after drying.

Sheep, little dogs, rabbits, or bears may be dipped in dessicated cocoanut, giving the animals a unique appearance. For this purpose the bodies are to be placed on a wire screen, held over steam for a few seconds and are then dipped into the cocoanut. Eyes, mouth, claws, et cetera should be indicated very generally with royal chocolate icing. Do not attempt to copy an eye exactly. The special characteristics of an individual animal may be slightly exaggerated, adding a touch of humor.

Casted sugar objects may be made up far in advance of a season, such as Easter, since they will keep almost indefinitely.

What To Do With Left-Over Sugar

In continuous operation, left-over sugar may be added in not more than ten percent proportions to the new sugar solution. Too much left-over sugar will weaken the crystallizing power and also discolor. This left-over sugar is, however, excellent for making up mint patties, sugar *couleur,* or sugar syrup.

How to Make Plaster-of-Paris Molds

Before starting to make a mold, we must have a model. It should be simple in form and may be of any kind of solid material, such as glass, porcelain, clay, metal, or wood. There are three kinds of plaster-of-paris molds : single molds, double molds, and molds in multiple cuts.

Single Molds

All models which are flat on one side may be used for single molds. Since the objects are usually small, as many as four or six may be put into one mold. This is a must in large scale operations. Of course that makes it necessary to have more than one model available. The models must be thoroughly greased, as well as the table top, wooden frame, and anything else the plaster

is not to adhere to. Oil or glycerin is most suitable for greasing.

The models are then layed on a perfectly flat base, such as a marble slab, thick glass or a metal plate. The models should be at least $\frac{3}{4}''$ apart. A wooden frame is then placed around them. It is usually of rectangular shape and must be greased very well. The frame must be big enough to allow approximately $1''$ of plaster-of-paris to flow all around and above the models. The frame can be secured against sliding simply by putting a few heavy objects around it. The frame is now ready for the plaster.

How to Mix Plaster of Paris

To obtain a perfectly smooth, hard mold, the best plaster available must be used. The best choice is alabaster, used in dental laboratories.

Starting out to mix, we have to begin with the water first. The plaster is then added slowly, a spoonful at a time. Sprinkle it over the water until all the liquid is absorbed. The mixture is stirred a few times and poured over the models. During the pouring process the frame should be tapped a few times to get rid of possible air bubbles. Properly mixed plaster will bind quickly and warm considerably. At this point, the frame is to be removed carefully and the models taken from the molds. This usually is easy to accomplish providing they have been greased well. Before the plaster hardens completely, the edges should be trimmed neatly with a small, sharp knife. The molds should then be left to dry for a couple of days.

Note: When mixing plaster do not attempt to pour water into the dry powder as this will undoubtedly fail to mix properly.

Double Molds

All models which are irregularly shaped, or are larger than $2''$ or $3''$ in width or height must be processed in two parts. Since both parts must fit perfectly, the greatest emphasis should be placed on accuracy.

First an evenly rolled strip of modelling clay is needed. If clay is not available, use marzipan or sugar plastic. The greased models are pressed exactly half way into the clay, approximately

¾" apart. The bottoms of the models must be in a perfectly straight line at one edge of the clay. This can be done by placing the lower piece of the frame wood snugly against the model bottoms. Place the rest of the frame around the clay as described under "Single Molds." Again, the frame must be deep enough to allow the upper half of the molds to be covered with at least 1" of plaster. Make several dents in the surface of the clay with a rounded stick. These will eventually be the locks to prevent the molds from sliding open. Grease the whole cast—frame, clay, and models—once more with a brush. Proceed with the plaster -pouring as in single molds. The first half of the double molds is now finished.

When the plaster has hardened, remove the frame and turn the cast upside down. Remove the clay carefully and thoroughly. Make certain the models stay in place. Replace the frame and grease the models, frame, and plaster surface thoroughly. Fill frame with plaster. When this second half has hardened the molds should come apart easily. If necessary a small knife can be inserted between the two halves. Remove the models and clean away the excess plaster.

Note: When pouring sugar into double molds, the two halves are secured with a string around them lengthwise, or strong rubber bands around each end.

Molds with Multiple Cuts

Multiple-cut molds are used on objects which are too large or too irregularly shaped for the ordinary double mold. Each section of the model to be molded is outlined in red. The section is greased and then covered with thick plaster of paris. When the plaster has hardened, the edges are trimmed carefully to match the red line. The larger the object being molded, the thicker the plaster must be. Remove the hardened section, then replace it carefully and grease the exposed, trimmed edges with hot shortening or wax. Proceed to grease the adjacent section to be molded. Apply the plaster and allow it to harden. Trim off excess plaster at edge of red outline. Proceed section by section until entire object is covered. The fat between the sections will prevent them from sticking to each other. Remove all the hardened plaster sections and rebuild the object with them, securing the sections with string or metal clamps. This hollow plaster object must dry at least three days. It is then soaked in cold water for twenty-four hours. Fill with casting sugar and allow a thick wall of sugar to form—the thickness depends upon the size of the object. Large objects should have sugar walls at least 1" thick. Pour or scoop out the liquid center and carefully trim excess sugar from bottom. Let sugar harden. Gently remove the plaster, section by section. Decorate or color object as desired.

The multiple cut molds, although more complex than the others, enables the professional to make spectacular show pieces of sugar.

Sulphur Molds

Sulphur molds, because they have hard, glassy surfaces, are excellent for casting very fine or delicate objects. Much of the intricate sculpture work on the model of St. Charles Cathedral *(see Index)* was cast in sulphur molds.

The models must be of heat-resistant material, as molten sulphur is very hot. The system of casting is almost the same as that of plaster molds. Place the models flat-side down on aluminum foil. Instead of a wooden frame, a wide strip of modelling clay is put around the objects. Model and foil base must fit perfectly close, as sulphur is much more liquid than plaster.

How to Melt Sulphur

Place the sulphur in an iron pot (Don't use copper.) and allow it to melt slowly, stirring constantly. The sulphur will begin to brown almost immediately and become very liquid. Continue stirring over heat until the mixture becomes syrup-thick. Remove from heat at once. Let cool slightly. In a few minutes the element will return to its original liquid form. Dip a piece of wood into it and let a few drops fall onto a marble slab or on a baking sheet. If the drops stay glassy, it indicates that the element is still too hot. If the drops harden with a dull and brittle effect, the sulphur must be poured quickly into the prepared cast. The cooled mold is then to be cleaned thoroughly of all clay and oil. Sulphur molds at this stage will break easily. It is there-

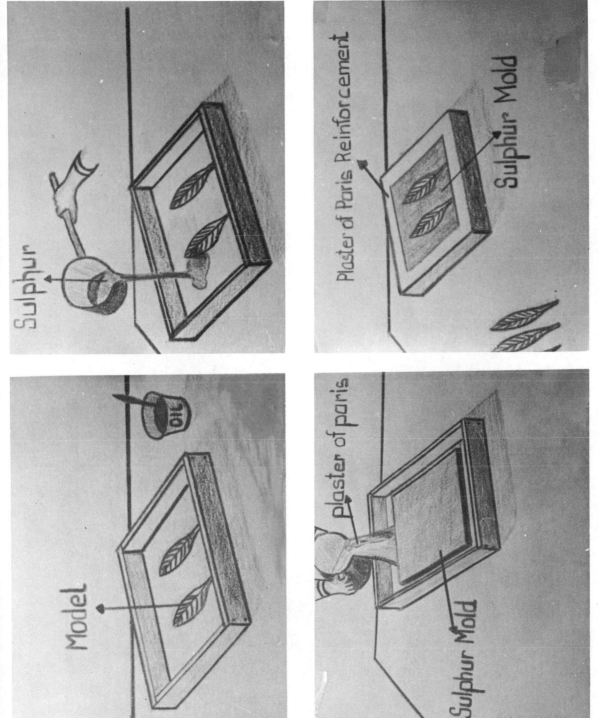

The prepared frame and model. The pouring of the liquid sulphur. The plaster-of-paris covering. The finished mold with ready-made marzipan objects (*left to right*).

Preparation of spun sugar

fore necessary to put a protective plaster-of-paris cover around the molds. This is accomplished as follows: Form a wooden frame approximately $\frac{1}{2}''$ larger than the mold. Pour plaster into the frame and set sulphur mold into soft plaster, model-side facing up. When the plaster has hardened, sulphur molds will be very durable.

Note: Casting sugar cannot be used in sulphur molds. Use marzipan or sugar plastic instead. Before using molds, dust freely with powdered sugar or talcum powder.

Rock Sugar

Rock sugar is an excellent decorating medium for show pieces, advertising objects, or wherever rocks are needed. A few rocks placed between floral arrangements, or used to build grottos will always look original. Rock sugar may be colored to harmonize with the general appearance of the display, or for special effects. Unlike any other sugar objects, rock sugar will last a long time when wrapped in a box and stored in a warm place.

How to Cook the Sugar

Dissolve the desired amount of granulated sugar in water and boil swiftly to 290° F. without tartar or glucose. Quickly stir into the hot solution one tablespoon of royal icing for every one pound of sugar. The sugar will immediately rise considerably and drop back after a few seconds. Continue stirring. This will cause the sugar to rise again. Pour it quickly into a prepared, oiled metal dish. Place cover on top and keep dish for a few seconds inside of hot oven. Additional heat will swiftly stabilize the porous foam-sugar formation. To obtain perfectly white rocks add a few drops of blue coloring. Break sugar to desired sizes.

Spun Sugar

Spun sugar is one of the most versatile and attractive of decorating mediums, but also the most susceptible to changes in climate. The fine, delicate threads will collapse quickly when left exposed to high humidity. Desserts such as cocktails, ice *bombes,* et cetera are therefore decorated

shortly before they are served. Spun sugar should not be made in large quantities a long time in advance. To keep the sugar for a while it should be placed in a tightly-closed container, preferably with a double bottom. If quick lime is put into the bottom compartment, spun sugar will keep for a few weeks. The chemical will absorb all moisture and thus keep the sugar dry and shiny. If no such container is available, keep sugar wrapped inside a moisture-proof box, stored in freezer.

Dissolve the desired amount of sugar in water and boil swiftly to 300° F. In climates with low humidity add eight percent glucose. Observe all rules governing the boiling of sugar carefully to avoid formation of sugar crystals. When 300° F. is reached, place pot in chipped ice or cold water to prevent after-burning and to cool the sugar as quickly as possible. Chip a little paraffin on top and let melt. Do not stir. Sugar must cool a little before being spun.

How to Spin Sugar

Put several lightly oiled metal rods or wooden sticks on a table, allowing two-thirds to stick out in front. Secure remaining thirds with heavy objects. With a wire whisk or cut-off beater, dip into sugar and swing freely and frequently back and forth over the rods. The sugar will fall off the beater in long silvery threads and harden immediately upon landing on the rods. Place a large sheet of paper underneath the rods to collect excess sugar. If the sugar threads break or hang in single rods to the floor, it indicates that the sugar had not cooled enough.

Note: Do not pile sugar too thickly on rods as it might get sticky. Spin only a little, remove, store, and continue until sugar is used up.

Krokant

1 lb. granulated sugar	2¼ cups granulated sugar
1 tbsp. glucose	1 tsp. glucose
7 ozs. blanched, sliced almonds	1½ cups blanched, sliced almonds

Method 1

Melt sugar and glucose, stirring constantly. Add almonds. Blend well. Pour onto oiled marble slab or baking sheet.

Method 2

Add a little water to sugar and glucose and bring to a boil. Continue boiling until sugar has reached the desired color. Add almonds and proceed as directed.

Krokant and Its Different Uses

(1) To make a center piece, or show piece, begin by cutting the object out of hard cardboard. Roll the hot krokant on a greased table with an oiled rolling pin to the desired thickness. Place cardboard form on top and cut quickly with a sharp knife. If sugar hardens before final cuts are made, place krokant in a hot oven for a few minutes, and continue cutting. Join pieces together with melted sugar.

(2) Let *krokant* cool completely. Grind up with rolling pin until crumbly. The crumbs may be used as a decorating medium for French pastries, cakes, chiffon pies, and others.

(3) Cold *krokant* is ground several times through a meat grinder until a creamy texture is obtained. This is an excellent flavoring medium for fine butter creams and ice cream dishes.

(4) *Krokant* is often used in candy or chocolate manufacturing. *(See Index.)*

Sugar Couleur

When boiling sugar has reached the caramel degree and the boiling is still continued, the solution will become brown first and eventually turn to deepest black. In order to be able to use this sugar as a coloring medium, it must be diluted with hot water as soon as the desired mahogany-like color is obtained. The hot sugar will lump when brought in contact with water and the cooking must therefore be continued until all lumps are dissolved. The sugar solution should be kept at the light thread stage. Sugar *coleur* is excellent for intensifying coffee aromas and colors.

Sugar Plastic

One of the best modelling materials in the food industry is known as sugar plastic. This plastic material is clay-like in texture, will keep its form immediately and dry very hard when exposed to air long enough. As it is spotlessly white in its original form, it may be colored in any shade.

The processing is very simple. One-half pint of egg white is mixed with approximately three pounds of powdered sugar just long enough to bind the two ingredients. Add five to six ounces of glucose and between one and two ounces of glycerin. Mix all ingredients for a few minutes and dump mixture onto a table. Knead sifted corn or wheat starch into the mixture until a firm, clay-like texture is obtained. (Do not attempt to mix with potato starch.) Keep the sugar plastic wrapped in a wet towel to prevent it from drying out.

A simplified way of making sugar plastic is as follows : Boil a gelatine-water solution (water, plus 25% of its weight in gelatine), and add as much sifted, powdered sugar and cornstarch as necessary to get the above-mentioned texture.

Sugar plastics are excellent building materials for all kinds of show pieces. The St. Charles cathedral *(see Index)* is made almost entirely of sugar plastic.

Polish pieces twice with shellac after they have dried.

Chocolate Plastic

Show pieces created from chocolate plastic, such as the treasure chest ("Candies and Chocolate") are very elegant in appearance. Contrary to sugar plastic, chocolate plastic is not very hard and can only be used for flowers, animals, and other small pieces.

1 lb. semi-sweet chocolate	16 squares semi-sweet chocolate
6 ozs. glucose	$\frac{1}{2}$ cup glucose

Method

Melt chocolate completely. Let cool. Stir in glucose. Chocolate will harden immediately. To soften plastic, knead well by hand. Body temperature will soften plastic to desired texture. When rolling the chocolate plastic, underdust with sifted powdered sugar. Before cutting the desired pieces, brush off excess sugar, and rub surface with palm. Plastic will begin to shine. Let dry for a couple of days exposed to the air. When joining individual pieces together, use melted chocolate.

Note: Chocolates differ from one another considerably. If mixture does not bind well, add few drops of water-gelatine solution.

Pulled Sugar Work

Pulled sugar is mainly used for making flowers, baskets, and ribbons. Its shiny silk-like appearance adds a fascinating touch of beauty to any banquet table. Unfortunately pulled sugar articles don't last long unless they are displayed inside of a glass case with a special quick lime compartment. The lime absorbs the moisture and thus keeps the air dry. Pulled sugar articles should be made in very pale colors.

How to Boil the Sugar

To keep sugar workable for any length of time thirty percent of glucose must be added. Use only highly refined granulated or cube sugar. Add glucose to sugar, dissolve in cold water, and boil swiftly to 286° F. If only one color is desired, add coloring shortly before the sugar reaches the correct degree. If more colors are wanted, divide sugar into smaller utensils after cooking and add a few drops of desired coloring to each. Spin pot slightly to blend the colors. Do not stir with spoon. Pour sugar onto oiled marble slab and let cool. The individual pieces of clear colored caramel may be stored in a tightly covered container for further uses.

Note: Cook sugar exactly as directed under "The Boiling of Sugar."

How to Pull Sugar

Use only as much as you are able to handle at one time. Place on batch-warmer and allow to soften slowly. Rub hands with talcum powder to stop perspiration. Take sugar in your hands, pull apart, and fold together. Repeat procedure until sugar shows high lustre. (If sugar articles are pulled while the sugar is still too hot, heat will absorb all shine. Wait with molding until sugar has cooled, but is still soft enough to handle.) When pulling sugar petals, leaves, ribbons, et cetera, keep sugar rolled in warm place in order to retain its softness.

When softening the original caramel pieces, do not apply great or direct heat. Sugar might crystallize. If batch-warmer is not available, place sugar on a sieve inside medium-hot oven.

How to Make a Pulled Sugar Basket

The basket board should be approximately 2″ thick. The basic basket shape—round, oval, square, or oblong, is drawn on top. Holes must be drilled into the wood at even intervals, not more than $1\frac{1}{2}″$ apart, around the basic outline. These will hold the metal or wooden sticks. In order to get even weaving, an odd number of sticks must be used. The sticks should pull out easily, without straining, but at the same time must be firm enough to hold the shape correctly. To weave a basket, two persons are needed. The first one pulls the strings in an even flow from the sugar batch, while the second one weaves them around the stick. As soon as the desired height is obtained, set a twisted sugar ring on top of weaving. Allow the delicate sugar structure to harden completely. Lift carefully off the frame and set upside down onto an oiled marble slab. Pull wooden sticks from the basket and replace with sticks pulled from sugar. Form one more twisted ring and set around bottom of basket. If closed bottom is desired, set woven framework on oiled marble slab and fill in bottom $\frac{1}{4}″$ thick with plain caramel. Cut frequently under basket to prevent from sticking. Form desired size and shape of handle from wire, wrap with a sugar strip, and secure bottom ends with melted caramel inside of basket. The handle might be decorated with flowers or ribbons from pulled sugar. As soon as the basket is completed, wrap a piece of quick lime in tissue paper and place it inside of basket.

Baskets are usually filled with chocolates, marzipan fruit, or *petits fours*.

Note: Baskets may be woven in multiple colors if so desired.

Pulled Sugar Roses

Before attempting to form any kind of flower, its color, structure, and number of petals should be studied on a real plant. The inexperienced are advised to begin with a simple rose first. Pull a leaf-shaped piece of sugar, mold it paper-thin on the upper end and roll it up. Bend the thin end outward slightly. Here is the rosebud. Mold three petals according to the model in mind, soften the bottom end over a flame, and stick onto bud. The second petal overlaps the first a little and so on. When making larger roses, make every row of petals gradually larger. Place the last petals around very loosely. This will give the impression of a full-bloomed flower. Close bottom with five dark, green leaves. To imitate the leaf veins, use a small hot knife.

Roses in Multiple Shades

If a flower in shades of red is desired, we must have three or four sugar batches in the different red shades. The centers are always darker, so we start out with the darkest shade, and gradually work toward the lighter. The outside petals should be very pale. In this way, wonderful effects can be obtained.

Ribbons of Pulled Sugar

Sugar ribbons are used in decorating sugar baskets, cakes, or chocolate candy boxes. In order to obtain silk-like ribbons, only pale colors should be used. Very attractive are the ribbons in two, three, or more colors. For this purpose, two differently colored pieces of sugar are stuck together and pulled out until very thin. To get evenly pulled ribbons two persons are needed. To make a ribbon bow, pull five or six strips of sugar, cut with scissors, form loops and stick the ends together well, using melted caramel. Use slightly smaller loops in center, increasing the size gradually until desired size is reached.

Flowers Made of Clear Caramel

The sugar is to be cooked as described under "Pulled Sugar Work." In climates with high humidity, raise boiling temperature by two or three degrees. Warm only as much sugar as needed for one particular object. The sugar might be softened in the batch-warmer or over a small gas flame. Small blossoms such as apple, or cherry blossoms, poppies, and daisies, are easy to make, providing the real plants have been studied carefully enough.

Bowls and Baskets from Clear Caramel

Mix together the sugar and fifteen to twenty percent of the sugar's weight in glucose. Boil with enough water to dissolve the mixture to 290° F. If objects are to be colored, add coloring shortly before correct degree is reached. Bowls can be made in a large variety of shapes. Pour sugar into an oiled metal ring 15″ to 20″ in diameter. As soon as the sugar has cooled slightly, lay it on the bottom of a tin can, bowl, or similar object and pull ends down to desired shape. The edges might be pinched between the fingers to give a unique appearance. The handle is also formed of clear caramel. The ends are carefully softened and attached to the main body. If objects in oval shapes are desired, pour sugar into an oval ring. Caramel show pieces may be held over steam for a few seconds and dipped into granulated sugar. Marvellous effects can be obtained with this method. The handles might be decorated with caramel flowers. These objects are often used for serving ice *bombes,* ice cream desserts, *petits fours* or marzipan fruit.

MARZIPAN

Marzipan is known the world over for its excellent modelling and molding qualities. It is also used as a flavoring material for delicate creams, sauces, cakes, fillings, and chocolates.

How to Make Marzipan

The raw material of marzipan is almond paste, which consists of two parts almonds and one part sugar. As special machines are necessary to make the paste, it has become economically impossible to compete with the manufacturers. Almond paste can be purchased in vacuum packed cans.

For those professionals who have machines, the manufacture of almond paste is explained here. The almonds are blanched, peeled, and then soaked in cold water until they are ready to be used. The cold water prevents the oil from separating. The almonds are chopped and mixed with part of the sugar. This mixture is ground through a special cylinder-roller machine. The creamy mash is boiled with the remaining sugar to dissolve the sugar crystals. At the same time the excess liquid will be evaporated and sugar and almonds will bind together to form a solid paste. The cooking also sterilizes the almond paste. If part of the paste is used, the rest should be kept in the refrigerator.

The prepared basket board with wooden sticks. The weaving of the basket. Adjusting the twisted ring on top. The handle is secured with melted caramel inside of basket. The finished basket, decorated with pulled sugar flowers and filled with almond *petits fours*

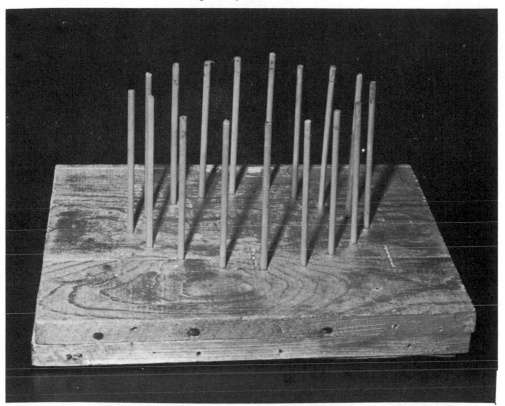

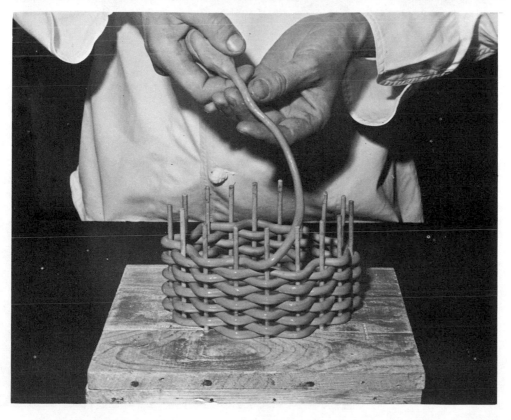

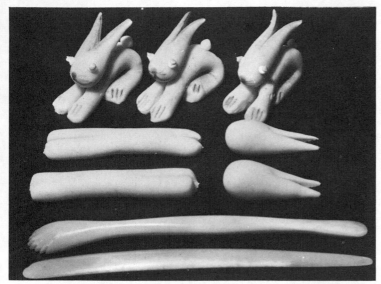

Figure made in two separate parts. Head and body are molded and stuck together
with melted cocoa butter or sugar syrup. The body is lightly touched up with brown
coloring. Eyes and feet are indicated with chocolate royal icing.

Rabbit modelled in two separate parts. Legs are marked with a modelling tool.
The figure is slightly colored and eyes indicated with chocolate icing. The pussy
willow is made of caramel sugar.

Head and body are modelled separately. Eyes are made of white royal icing. Legs
are almond slivers.

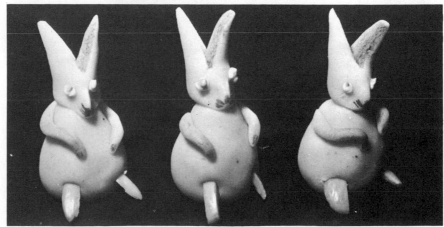

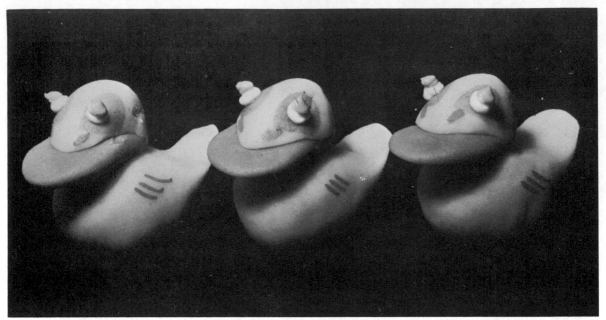

Ducks modelled in three operations. The bill is attached to the head, and the completed head to the body. Eyes are royal icing and figure is sprayed with light yellow coloring.

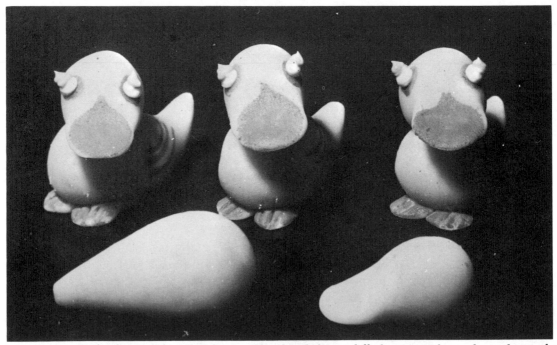

Body formed in egg shape. The head is modelled separately and stuck to the main body with melted cocoa butter or warm fondant icing. Eyes are made of royal icing.

Two balls are formed for these chicks. The larger one, slightly pointed toward the end, is for the body, and the smaller for the head. The bill is indicated with almond slivers. Comb is marzipan, wings are painted, and eyes are of royal icing. The figure is stained with pale yellow coloring.

The body is formed in egg shape. The head is modelled separately. The figure is partly placed inside an egg shell.

For these figures a sulphur mold was made, slightly dusted with talcum powder and pressed out with molding marzipan. Comb, beak, and wings are indicated with royal icing. The figure is slightly colored with pale food colors. The nest is made of pie dough, iced with sweet chocolate and sprinkled with cocoanut.

Pigs are modelled in one piece from pink colored marzipan. Ears and feet are indicated with almond halves. Eyes of royal chocolate icing.

Head and body are modelled individually and stuck together with icing or cocoa butter. These figures look very attractive when held over a steaming water kettle and rolled into white or pale blue colored granulated sugar. Eyes, mouth and claws are made of royal icing.

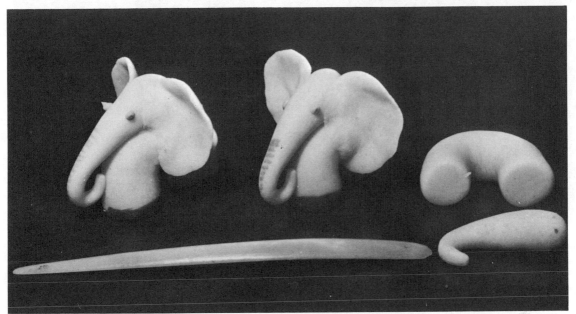

These figures are modelled in three different parts—body, head with trunk, and ears. The parts are stuck together with melted cocoa butter or sugar syrup. Lower part of legs is dipped into melted chocolate.

Swans modelled from one piece. Wings formed from marzipan and beaks colored with yellow food coloring.

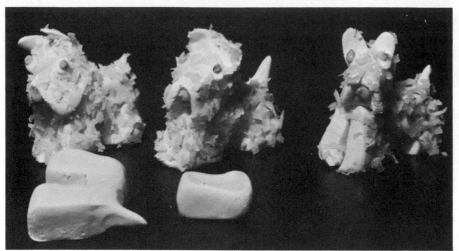

Dogs modelled in two parts and assembled with cocoa butter. The whole body is brushed with cocoa butter and thoroughly sprinkled with shredded cocoanut. Eyes and mouth are indicated with chocolate icing.

Dogs modelled in two parts and assembled with cocoa butter. Chocolate *streusel* is used instead of cocoanut.

The modelling process is the same as for other dog figures. Body is slightly touched up with pale brown coloring. Eyes and mouth are of chocolate icing.

Bodies are modelled from plain white marzipan, wings and head from chocolate marzipan. Eyes are made of royal icing.

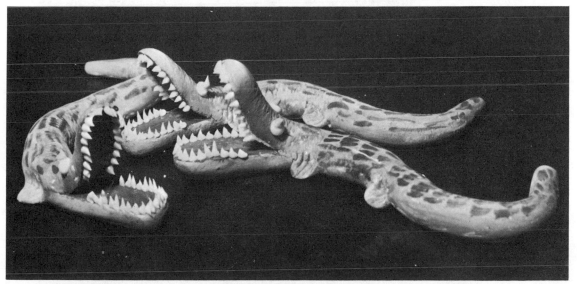

Bodies modelled from pale green marzipan in one operation. The mouth is cut open with a sharp knife, supported with a piece of cardboard and left to dry. Inside of mouth is colored red, eyes and teeth are indicated with white royal icing.

Most of these items are modelled in one operation and lightly colored. They show the great possibilities of marzipan modelling.

A selection of marzipan articles

The raw almond paste must now be mixed with powdered sugar to get the final product— marzipan. In some parts of the world, notably Europe, laws control the percentage of sugar in marzipan. There are no laws of this kind in America. However, to keep marzipan edible, not more than one pound of sugar should be mixed into each pound of almond paste. When flavoring creams, straight almond paste may be used. Following are two formulas for mixing almond paste into marzipan.

French Marzipan

8 lbs. 8 ozs. almond paste	2 lbs. 2 ozs. almond paste
2 lbs. powdered sugar	1½ cups powdered sugar
4 lbs 8 ozs. granulated	(generous)
sugar	2¼ cups granulated sugar
1 lb. glucose	⅓ cup glucose
1 pint water	½ cup water
1 cup glycerin	¼ cup glycerin
vanilla	vanilla

Method

Mix together the granulated sugar, glucose, and water. Bring to a boil. Skim surface and continue boiling to 244° F. Pour solution into mixing bowl, add rest of ingredients, and mix at low speed until all parts have bound well and paste has cooled slightly. Store marzipan in tin can with tight-fitting lid.

Molding and Modelling Marzipan

1 lb. almond paste	1 lb. almond paste
1 lb. powdered sugar	3 cups powdered sugar
¼ tsp. benzoic acid	¼ tsp. benzoic acid

Method

Knead powdered sugar into almond paste by hand. Add benzoic acid as an antiseptical preservative.

Note: For dusting table top or hands use powdered sugar or talcum powder. Do not use flour.

Marzipan Fruits

When making marzipan fruit, most realistic effects can be obtained by using real fruit for models. Most fruits have their basic colors mixed into the marzipan and only need to be touched up to indicate the fruit's highlights. Powdered colors should be mixed with a little water first and then diluted to the desired consistency with pure alcohol. Water or fat colors should not be used as they have a tendency to smear. A few drops of coloring are rubbed over the surface of a plate, leaving merely a film. This will keep the brush fairly dry and allow a very thin application. Bristle brushes are preferred to soft-hair brushes. When changing colors, the brushes should be thoroughly cleaned with a rag. Do not wash the brushes when they are still to be used. The finished, colored fruits may be polished with tragant solution or brush with hot cocoa butter. The latter method is preferable because it also prevents the marzipan from drying out. Stems and leaves may be modelled of marzipan or purchased in paper form. The fruit models should be very small (1-½ ozs), as marzipan fruits come under the classification of confections.

Marzipan fruits displayed properly on either sugar plastic plates or sugar baskets will always attract the attention of guests or customers.

Marzipan Fruits with Cake Centers

When life-sized fruits are desired, the basic shapes are made of othello mixture. (*See Index.*) The baked halves are slightly hollowed out, filled with cream, and joined together in pairs. The creams are flavored according to the kind of fruit represented. These othellos are then wrapped in thin marzipan and colored as described above.

Apples
Apples may be made in many shapes and colors. The illustrated apples have a light green-yellow background with light brown and red highlights.

Apricots
Apricots are made from apricot-flavored marzipan with a pale coral background and pale pink highlights. Dent in fruit has been made with modelling tool.

Bananas
Made from pale yellow, banana-flavored marzipan rolled to a stick, flattened with a knife, and curved slightly. Colored light green, edges touched up lightly with cocoa.

Lemons

Made from pale yellow, lemon-flavored marzipan with light green highlights. Porous skin is obtained by rolling the pieces over a lemon grater.

Oranges

Made from orange colored and flavored marzipan and processed like lemons.

Plums

Formed from vanilla-flavored marzipan and rolled into blue-colored, sweetened cornstarch.

Pears

Pears may be flavored with pear extract or cognac. Highlights are in pale red and dark yellow.

Strawberries

Made from strawberry-flavored pink marzipan and dipped into liquid red colors and rolled over a lemon grater. Stems and leaves are artificial.

Note: All fruits are polished with a tragant solution.

HOW TO MAKE FLOWERS FROM MARZIPAN

Roses

Rosebuds are made of one piece or formed of three small, curved petals stuck close together. The third petal is bent slightly outward. In making a rose, each petal is formed individually in the palm of the hand, using a modelling tool or the back of a teaspoon to give the pats a thin edge. The upper edge of each petal is bent slightly outward. Stick the petals around the basic rose bud, using sugar syrup to hold them in place. Each succeeding row of petals must be made a little larger than the rows closer to the center. The last few petals should be attached a little farther away from the rest of the flower to give a natural, full-bloomed appearance. For variation in color, start the rosebud in a darker shade than the petals.

Tulips

First form an elongated egg-shaped bud and fix it on the end of a wooden stem covered with green marzipan. Tulips have six petals. The first three are placed around the bud, overlapping each other slightly. The second three petals are made a little larger. Bend the upper edges slightly outward and attach with sugar syrup.

Carnations

Carnations are often made in many different colors. Combinations of white and pale pink or yellow and white are very attractive. Roll a narrow strip of marzipan (1¼″), making the upper edge very thin. Gather the strip together with the thicker edges at the base of the flowers. Attach to marzipan-covered wooden stem. Carnation petals may be modelled individually if desired, and joined together closely.

Flowers in Modern Style

A number of different cooky cutters are needed to make modern-looking flowers. Decorations can be of white and chocolate royal icings, glazed fruits, or nuts. These flowers are not bound to any specific pattern but subject only to the imagination.

St. Charles Cathedral of Vienna

This showpiece was made by the author and received the first prize and the Unique Display Award at the Culinary Arts Exhibition in Honolulu in 1961.

The basic structure of the cathedral was built from sugar plastic. The small figurines on the columns and above the entrance were first modelled in plasticine from which the sulphur molds were cast. The final figures were pressed from the sulphur molds with sugar plastic. The fourteen tall figures were freely modelled from the same material. The dome was first formed from papier-maché, covered with aluminum foil and then used as the model for the ¼″ thick sugar-plastic dome. The stained glass windows are of colored gelatine leaves. The flowers in the foreground were made of royal icing.

ICE SCULPTURING

Ice sockets are pieces of ice sculpture designed to hold a particular dish. Sockets carved from ice are frequently used in kitchen as well as pastry

Roses made from marzipan

Tulips made from marzipan

Carnations made from marzipan

Marzipan flowers in a modern style

St. Charles's cathedral as seen from different angles

This replica of the submarine "Pickerel" was made for the Submariners' 61st anniversary at the Royal Hawaiian Hotel in Honolulu. It is made entirely of sugar plastic. The base was covered with blue royal icing. The author received a

Vegetable color paint on a white sugar plastic background. The frame is made of the same material colored light brown.

Painting was used as a center-piece on a cold buffet. Made from sugar plastic. The base is of rock sugar.

These floral designs are combinations of colored royal icings, candied peels, and cherries. Most of the peels are carved with a sharp knife. These designs used on cakes make little or no further decoration necessary.

These ice sockets suggest some of the possibilities of ice sculpture.

Ice piece carved from a whole block (300 lbs.). The food served was put in a carved pineapple shell and placed in the center. Real flowers complete the centerpiece.

shop operations. They are not only very decorative, but also serve a useful purpose. Their coolness will maintain the flavors of such delicate dishes as ice cream *bombes,* creams, mousses, puddings, as well as caviar, and aspics, for the cold buffet.

Crystal-clear ice must definitely be considered an excellent decorative subject on any buffet table, especially when the sculptures are carved with skill and imagination. Great effects can be obtained when the ice sculptures are lit from within with small battery-powered lights. These light bulbs may be colored or wrapped in colored cellophane paper.

In ice carving as well as in other fields where artistic talents are needed, specialists have developed the skill of carving to perfection, but this article on ice carving is not written for specialists, nor has the author intended to show how to create artistically perfect sculptures. His purpose is merely to create interest in the cool art and to show how, with the littlest of knowledge or training, effective and useful ice pieces can be carved.

One of the hardest undertakings is to carve either the human body or the body of an animal. After all, a pastry chef or cook is not a sculptor. However, much can be done with practise and imagination. When carving animals, the beginner is advised to concentrate on motion or movement rather than trying to copy the animal in its exact form. Only a very few are gifted enough to copy life accurately. The jumping rabbit with its oversized ears which is shown in the accompanying drawing effects a humor which will never fail to attract attention.

Ice sockets are most commonly used and besides these, a set of four or five ice chisels and a rough saw is very helpful. It will not only save time, but also help the beginner to get straight cuts from the very first try. While ice showpieces may be made in any size, the sockets which are used for serving food should be small and light in weight.

A piece of ice is first cut from the block with the saw and given the approximate shape of the sculpture. If the socket is supposed to be lit, the opening must be cut into the bottom first to hold the battery and light bulb. Next comes the opening on top to hold the dish in which the food shall be served. This dish or container is best filled with hot water, set on top and allowed to melt into the block. If the dish is very shallow, the opening is cut with a chisel. A folded napkin is placed between the container and the ice in order to prevent its sliding. Now follows the actual carving of the block as directed in following illustrations. When serving the food, place two or three napkins on a silver platter first, put the light source in the center, and set the socket over it.

Another method of creating ice sockets is to pour boiled, colored water into wooden or metal forms and leave them in the freezer until frozen solid. This method can be very interesting as there is no limit to the variety of forms used. If natural flowers or leaves are frozen into the sockets, their beautiful colors surrounded by crystal clear ice will certainly create a picture of magical beauty.

XII

SEASONAL PRODUCTS

Christmas Season – Easter Season

Lebkuchen

Lebkuchen is a spicy delicacy which may be sweetened with either sugar or honey, while honey cakes use only honey as sweetener. In order to make good and lasting *lebkuchen* or honey cakes, study the basic rules carefully.

In the olden days, when artificial leavenings were unknown, part of the dough consisting mainly of honey and flour was mixed several months in advance and left to ferment. This dough not only had excellent lifting power, but also developed that certain flavor for which *lebkuchen* is famous the world over. Science has given us chemicals such as ammonium carbonate, potassium carbonate, and sodium pyrophosphate that make a long fermentation process unnecessary. However, what we gain in convenience, we lose in flavor. For those professionals or housewives who are willing to sacrifice a little time for a good cause, the fermentation method is given here.

Put pure, natural honey into a stainless-steel pan and heat from 180° F. to 190° F. Do not boil, as overheating destroys aromas. Let cool and pour into wooden barrel or other wooden container. Stir in sifted wheat flour to get a medium-soft dough. Place lid on container and store in a cool place. Allow to ferment without disturbing for a period of two or three months. The following formulas are worked out with artificial leavening only. If natural fermented dough is used, cut the amount of leavening in half and add approximately twenty to twenty-five percent of fermented dough. For example : The total weight of the formula is two pounds. Twenty-five percent of two pounds equals eight ounces, so eight ounces of fermented dough are used.

It is difficult to give an exact weight for the fermented dough since the power of the fermented leavening depends upon such things as the sugar content of the honey, the type of flour, the amount of flour, and fermentation time. All *lebkuchen* or honey cakes must therefore be tested as soon as the mixing process is completed. This is done by putting a few pieces on a pan and baking them before making up the whole formula. If the goods are solid, small and hard, add more

leavening. (Dissolve artificial leavening in a little water and mix thoroughly into dough.) If the goods puff up and crack open or show big pores, add more flour.

Lebkuchen can be made months in advance, as the older it gets, the better it is. Here again a few rules must be observed.

1 Do not wrap goods in cellophane while still warm.

2 Seal wrapper carefully.

3 Store in a cool place.

4 When baking do not grease pans with ordinary fats. This is important, as fats or oil will spoil in a short time and make *Lebkuchen* unfit to eat. Grease pans as follows : Cover entire surface of pans with beeswax. Dust lightly with flour and heat pans in hot oven. Allow wax to burn off completely, leaving only an insulating film on the metal. Let cool and start baking. Pans that have been treated in this way may be used over and over again.

Lebkuchen Glazes

After baking, brush excess flour from goods and glaze with one of the suggested methods.

1 Add a little sugar to egg yolks. Color light brown with sugar *couleur*. Brush cold goods lightly with mixture. Let dry.

2 Dissolve gum arabic in cold water (1 tablespoon to $\frac{3}{4}$ cup water). Bring to a boil. Brush hot glaze thinly onto warm cookies. Let dry.

3 Toast cornstarch until light brown. Dissolve in water. Boil mixture until a thin skin forms on a drop set on a table. Brush goods with hot mixture. Let dry by holding inside a hot oven for a few minutes.

4 Dip in melted, cooled semi-sweet or milk chocolate.

5 For quick sale or use, ice with colored fondant.

6 White *lebkuchen* icing. Beat six egg whites and mix in one pound of powdered sugar. Mix well. Add one-quarter teaspoon cream of tartar. Blend in three and one-half ounces cornstarch. Dilute with milk to form a heavy flowing paste. Brush on cookies thinly.

171

Basic Lebkuchen

1½ lbs. bread flour	6 cups bread flour
⅓ oz. ammonium	4 tsp. ammonium
1 lb. honey	1⅓ cups honey
6 ozs. sugar	¾ cup sugar
2 eggs	2 eggs
1½ ozs. cinnamon	6 tbsp. cinnamon
¼ oz. cloves	3 tsp. cloves
1½ ozs. chopped, candied orange peel	¼ cup chopped, candied orange peel
1½ ozs. chopped, candied lemon peel	¼ cup chopped, candied lemon peel

Method

Warm honey, add sugar and eggs. Cream well. Add flavors and peels. Knead in flour and leavening. Roll dough ¼" thick. Bake sample. Cut differently shaped cookies. Bake at 375° F. Glaze.

Nurmberg Lebkuchen

6 ozs. egg whites	6 egg whites
13 ozs. sugar	1½ cups sugar (generous)
13 ozs. ground almonds	3¼ cups ground almonds
1½ ozs. honey	⅛ cup honey
4¼ ozs. flour	1 cup flour (generous)
3½ ozs. candied orange peel	½ cup candied orange peel
⅛ oz. ammonium	1¼ tsp. ammonium

Method

Cream whites, sugar, honey, and ammonium. Mix in chopped orange peel, flour and almonds. Spread mixture on rice paper approximately ¼" thick. Cut to desired sizes. Allow to dry for two hours. Bake at 350° F. When cold, glaze with colored icing. Wrap in cellophane.

Nurmberg Filbert Lebkuchen

8 ozs. filberts, ground	2 cups filberts, ground
5 ozs. orange peel, chopped	¾ cup orange peel, chopped
5 ozs. lemon peel, chopped	¾ cup lemon peel, chopped
5 ozs. bread flour	1¼ cups bread flour
1¼ ozs. allspice	4 tbsp. allspice
1/5 oz. ammonium	2 tsp. ammonium
13 ozs. sugar	1½ cups sugar (generous)
5 egg whites	5 egg whites

Method

Place egg whites, sugar, and toasted filberts in double boiler and heat, stirring constantly. Add remaining ingredients. Spread on rice paper. Let dry. Cut to desired sizes. Bake at 375° F. After baking, turn upside down immediately to get smooth surfaces. Glaze.

White Lebkuchen

12 eggs	6 eggs
2 lbs. sugar	2 cups sugar
2 lbs. bread flour	4 cups bread flour
¼ oz. ammonium	1¼ tsp. ammonium
1 lb. almonds, toasted sliced	2 cups almonds, toasted sliced
13 ozs. citron peel, chopped	1 cup citron peel, chopped
13 ozs. orange peel, chopped	1 cup orange peel, chopped
¼ oz. cloves	1½ tsp. cloves
½ oz. cinnamon	3 tsp. cinnamon
½ oz. allspice	3 tsp. allspice
¼ oz. ginger	1½ tsp. ginger
1½ ozs. honey	1 tbsp. honey

Method

Mix sugar, ammonium, and eggs for three minutes. Add honey. Blend well. Add rest of ingredients. Roll dough ¼" thick. Bake sample. Cut pieces two or three ounces in weight. Let dry. Bake at 375° F. Glaze. Wrap in cellophane.

Tyrolian Lebkuchen

7 egg whites	7 egg whites
1 lb. 4 ozs. sugar	2½ cups sugar
⅛ oz. ammonium	¾ tsp. ammonium
5 ozs. bread flour	1¼ cups bread flour
6½ ozs. almonds, ground	1½ cups almonds, ground
6½ ozs. filberts, ground	1½ cups filberts, ground (generous)
1½ ozs. candied orange peel	¼ cup candied orange peel
1½ ozs. citron peel	¼ cup citron peel
⅓ oz. cinnamon	4 tsp. cinnamon
¼ tsp. cloves	¼ tsp. cloves
2 lemon rinds, grated	2 lemon rinds, grated

Method

Cream whites, sugar, and ammonium. Add rest of ingredients. Blend well. Spread mixture onto rice paper. Cut to desired sizes. Let dry for two hours. Bake sample at 350° F. Glaze with white, vanilla-flavored icing, or dip in chocolate. Wrap in cellophane. Store in tin can.

Almond Macaroon Lebkuchen

6 ozs. almonds, ground, toasted	1½ cups almonds, ground, toasted
10 ozs. almonds, sliced	2½ cups almonds, sliced
14 egg whites	14 egg whites
1½ ozs. baking powder	3 tbsp. baking powder
1½ ozs. sugar	3 tbsp. sugar
1 oz. cornstarch	⅛ cup cornstarch
vanilla	vanilla
1 lemon rind, grated	1 lemon rind, grated

Method

Place whites, ground almonds, rinds, baking powder, sugar, and starch in double boiler. Heat until almost boiling hot. Blend in sliced almonds. Spread quickly onto rice paper or wafers. Let cool. Cut to desired sizes. Bake at 325° F.

Chocolate Lebkuchen

4 eggs	4 eggs
8 ozs. brown sugar	1½ cups brown sugar
8 ozs. honey	¼ cup honey
12 ozs. rye flour	3 cups rye flour
4 ozs. cocoa	1⅛ cups cocoa
½ oz. baking soda	3 tsp. baking soda
½ oz. cinnamon	3 tsp. cinnamon
⅛ oz. cloves	¾ tsp. cloves
¼ oz. allspice	1½ tsp. allspice

Method

Knead all ingredients together to make smooth dough. Let rest for one day. Roll dough ¼″ thick. Cut with cooky cutters. Bake sample. Bake at 375° F. Glaze or dip in chocolate. Decorate with almonds.

Honey Cakes

1 lb. 8 ozs. honey	1 cup honey
¾ pint milk	1½ cups milk
5 eggs	3 eggs
12 ozs. brown sugar	1 cup brown sugar (generous)
1 lb. 9 ozs. bread flour	1 lb. 9 ozs. bread flour
1 lb. 8 ozs. whole wheat flour	3½ cups whole wheat flour
¼ oz. ammonium	¾ tsp. ammonium
6 ozs. granulated sugar	⅜ cup granulated sugar
10 ozs. almonds, chopped	1 cup almonds, chopped
1 oz. allspice	3 tsp. allspice
¼ oz. cardamon	¾ tsp. cardamon
¼ oz. cloves	¾ tsp. cloves
1¼ ozs. baking soda	4 tsp. baking soda

Method

Warm honey slightly. Blend in brown sugar and milk. Add remaining ingredients. Pour mixture into large, deep pan lined with paper. Egg wash. Bake at 325° F. to 350° F. Approximate baking time is threequarters of an hour. When cold, cut pieces and wrap in cellophane.

Note: Cakes may be baked in aluminum foil containers.

Honey Christmas Cookies

6 egg yolks	6 egg yolks
12 ozs. granulated sugar	1½ cups granulated sugar
1 lb. 8 ozs. honey	2 cups honey
1 lb. 8 ozs. rye flour	6 cups rye flour
1 lb. 8 ozs. bread flour	6 cups bread flour
⅔ oz. ammonium	8 tsp ammonium
1 oz. mixed spices	3 tsp. mixed spices

Method

Heat honey to 200° F. and stir in rye flour. Set aside and let cool. Cream yolks, sugar, ammonium, and spices. Blend in bread flour. Combine both mixtures well. Roll dough ⅛″ thick. Cut different suitable figures with cooky cutters. Bake sample. Bake at 375° F. Let cool. Roll a thin sheet of marzipan and cut figures with same cooky cutters. Place marzipan on top of cookies, using honey as binder. Marzipan may be colored. Dip bottoms in chocolate.

Basler Honey Cakes

1 lb. 8 ozs. honey	1 cup honey
6 ozs. granulated sugar	⅜ cup granulated sugar
3 egg yolks	2 egg yolks
7½ ozs. almonds, chopped	1 cup almonds, chopped
3 ozs. citron peel	¼ cup citron peel
4½ ozs. candied orange peel	⅜ cup candied orange peel
1 lemon rind, grated	½ lemon rind, grated
	4 cups flour

2 lbs. flour	2 tsp. ammonium
1/3 oz. ammonium	3/4 tsp. cloves
1/8 oz. cloves	3/4 tsp. nutmeg
1/8 oz. nutmeg	4 1/2 tsp. cinnamon
3/4 oz. cinnamon	1/8 cup rum
1/8 pint rum	

Method

Heat honey and sugar well. Let cool completely. Add rest of ingredients and knead to smooth dough. Cover surface of baking sheet with dough not more than 1/3″ thick. Bake at 375° F. Ice cakes while still hot with the following icing: Dissolve sugar in a little water. Boil to light thread stage. Add vanilla or lemon flavor. Stir until mixture becomes milky-white. Brush over cakes. Let dry and cut to desired size pieces.

Honey Spice Cake

2 eggs	2 eggs
5 ozs. sugar	1/2 cup sugar (generous)
14 ozs. honey	scant 1 1/4 cups honey
1/16 pint *couleur* (*See Index.*)	1/8 cup *couleur* (*See Index.*)
5 ozs. almonds, chopped	1 1/4 cups almonds, chopped
6 ozs. candied orange peel	1 cup candied orange peel
2 ozs. citron peel	1/3 cup citron peel
3/4 oz. cinnamon	3 tbsp. cinnamon
1/4 tsp. cloves	1/4 tsp. cloves
1/4 tsp. nutmeg	1/4 tsp. nutmeg
1/4 tsp. ginger	1/4 tsp. ginger
1 lb. 8 ozs. flour	6 cups flour
1/6 oz. ammonium	2 tsp. ammonium
1 oz. rum	1 oz. rum

Method

Heat honey, add sugar and eggs. Mix for a few minutes. Dissolve ammonium in *couleur* and add to honey. Blend in rest of ingredients. Knead to smooth dough. Proceed as directed under "Basler Honey Cakes."

Pfeffernuss

The German word *pfeffer* means "pepper." However, pepper is not used and has nothing to do with these cookies. The term "pepper" merely refers to the dough's sharp spices.

Pfeffernuss 1

6 eggs	6 eggs
1 lb. 8 ozs. granulated sugar	3 cups granulated sugar
1 lb. 12 ozs. flour	7 1/4 cups flour
3 ozs. candied orange peel	1/2 cup candied orange peel
1/4 tsp. ammonium	1/4 tsp. ammonium
1/4 tsp. cloves	1/4 tsp. cloves
1/4 tsp. nutmeg	1/4 tsp. nutmeg
1/4 tsp. ginger	1/4 tsp. ginger
1/2 tsp. cinnamon	1/2 tsp. cinnamon
1/2 lemon rind, grated	1/2 lemon rind, grated

Method

Cream eggs, sugar, and ammonium. Add fine chopped peels, flavoring, and flour. Knead to smooth dough. Roll dough 1/2″ thick and cut small cookies. Set on paper-lined pans and allow to dry over-night. Turn upside down, sprinkle with rum and bake at 350° F.

Pfeffernuss 2

6 eggs	6 eggs
1 lb. 8ozs. granulated sugar	3 cups granulated sugar
1 lb. 2 ozs. flour	4 1/2 cups flour
8 ozs. citron peel	1 1/2 cups citron peel
1/2 oz. baking powder	3 tsp. baking powder
1/2 oz. cinnamon	3 tsp. cinnamon
1/8 oz. cloves	3/4 tsp. cloves
1/8 oz. nutmeg	3/4 tsp. nutmeg
1 1/2 lemon rinds, grated	1 1/2 lemon rinds, grated

Method

Beat eggs and sugar until creamy thick. Sift together the flour, baking powder and spices. Fold into egg mixture. Add peels. Knead to smooth dough, adding more flour if necessary. Form rolls 3/4″ thick and cut 1/2″ pieces. Set on paper-lined pans. Bake at 350° F. Let cool completely, then ice as follows: Put approximately two cups of sugar into a sauce pan. Add enough water to get a thick, creamy mixture. Add a few drops of lemon extract. Bring to a boil. Wash down sides of pan frequently to dissolve sugar crystals. Boil to medium ball stage (240° F. to 242° F). Remove from heat. Stir sugar until mixture becomes milky white. Drop in cookies. Stir quickly and thoroughly to get all cookies coated

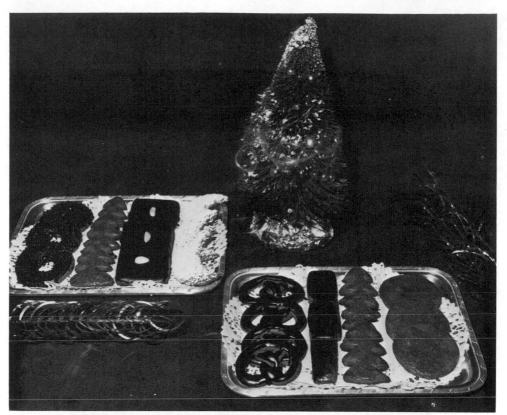

Christmas cookies

Assorted *lebkuchen* individually iced with sugar or chocolate icing

Pfeffernuesse

A gingerbread house created from *lebkuchen*

Christmas showpiece made entirely from sugar. The figures in the foreground were molded in plaster-of-paris forms. The tower was lit from within by a green light.

Stollen loaves

Figurines made from colored, baked meringue

Christmas cakes decorated with glazed fruits and wrapped in colored cellophane

Christmas cakes wrapped in colored cellophane

well. Turn onto table, separate individual pieces, and let dry. Store in cellophane bags.

Dutch Spekulatius

6 eggs	2 eggs
2 lbs. 8 ozs. sugar	1¼ cups sugar
½ pint milk	¼ cup milk
¼ oz. ammonium	¾ tsp. ammonium
1 lb. 4 ozs. lard	½ cup lard (generous)
4 lbs. flour	4 cups flour
¼ oz. nutmeg	dash nutmeg
vanilla	vanilla
½ lemon rind, grated	⅛ lemon rind, grated
½ oz. salt	¼ tsp. salt

Method

Mix sugar, eggs and milk until smooth. Add rest of ingredients. Knead to smooth, firm dough. Roll dough ¼″ thick and press into wooden molds (*spekulatius* molds). Set pieces on lightly greased pans. Let dry. Bake at 300° F.

Note: If wooden forms are not available, make design with a fork.

Springerle

1 lb. eggs (scale with shell)	5 eggs
2 lbs. granulated sugar	2 cups granulated sugar
¼ tsp. ammonium	dash ammonium
1 lemon rind, grated	½ lemon rind, grated
vanilla	vanilla
2 lbs. 4 ozs. bread flour	4¾ cups bread flour

Method

Cream sugar, rinds, and ammonium. Blend in sifted flour. Roll dough ¼″ thick and press into wooden molds. Set pieces on pans and prepare them as follows : Brush very thinly with melted butter and sprinkle with powdered anis seed. Bake at 300° F. Concentrate heat on bottom.

Note: If wooden forms are not available, make design with a fork.

Dutch Oliebollen

1 lb. flour	4 cups flour
1 pint milk	2 cups milk
3 eggs	3 eggs
6 ozs. butter	¾ cup butter

⅓ oz. baking powder	2½ tsp. baking powder
dash salt	dash salt
8 ozs. currants	1¾ cups currants
8 ozs. raisins	1¾ cups raisins
8 ozs. citron cubes	1¼ cups citron cubes
6 sweet apples, chopped	6 sweet apples, chopped

Method

Mix flour, milk, eggs, melted butter, baking powder, and salt to smooth dough. Stir in rest of ingredients. Drop dough from a small spoon into hot frying fat (360° F.). Deep fry until light brown. Set on wire screen and allow excess fat to drain off. Sprinkle with cinnamon-flavored granulated sugar.

Dutch St. Niklaas Cookies

12 ozs. butter	1½ cups butter
1 lb. brown sugar	3 cups brown sugar
2 eggs	2 eggs
4 ozs. almonds, chopped	1 cup almonds, chopped
2 tsp. baking soda	2 tsp. baking soda
4 tsp. cinnamon	4 tsp. cinnamon
4 tsp. nutmeg	4 tsp. nutmeg
2 tsp. cloves	2 tsp. cloves
1 lb. 8 ozs. pastry flour	6 cups pastry flour
½ tsp. salt	½ tsp. salt

Method:

Cream butter and sugar. Knead with remaining ingredients to smooth dough. Roll dough and cut cookies of desired shapes. Decorate with almond halves. Egg wash. Bake at 325° F.

Austrian Spice Cookies

1 lb. 13 ozs. sugar	3½ cups sugar (generous)
3 eggs	3 eggs
5 ozs. honey	¾ cup honey
2 lbs. flour	8 cups flour
7 ozs. candied orange peel	1¼ cups candied orange peel
1/5 oz. ammonium	2 tsp. ammonium
¼ oz. cloves	3 tsp. cloves
¼ oz. ginger	3 tsp. ginger
½ oz. cinnamon	2 tbsp. cinnamon
¼ oz. nutmeg	3 tsp. nutmeg
¼ oz. allspice	3 tsp. allspice
4 ozs. water	½ cup water

Method

Mix sugar, eggs, ammonium, honey, water, and spices thoroughly. Add rest of ingredients and knead to smooth, firm dough. Roll dough $\frac{1}{8}''$ thick. Cut cookies. Set on greased pans. Wash with water. Bake at 400° F.

Austrian Alpine Fruit Bread

4 lbs. dried prunes	3 cups dried prunes (generous)
4 lbs. figs	3 cups figs (generous)
2 lbs. 8 ozs. dates	2 cups dates
1 lb. 8 ozs. cherries, glazed	1 cup cherries, glazed
1 lb. mixed glazed fruits	$\frac{3}{4}$ cup mixed, glazed fruits
1 lb. 4 ozs. candied orange peel	1$\frac{1}{4}$ cups candied orange peel
1 lb. 4 ozs. citron peel	1$\frac{1}{4}$ cups citron peel
1 lb. filberts, toasted	$\frac{3}{4}$ cup filberts, toasted
1 lb. walnut halves	1 cup walnut halves
6 lbs. bread flour	6 cups bread flour
1 lb. 4 ozs. brown sugar	scant 1 cup brown sugar
14 ozs. yeast	6$\frac{1}{2}$ cakes yeast
$\frac{3}{4}$ pint rum	$\frac{3}{4}$ cup rum
2 lemon rinds, grated	$\frac{1}{2}$ lemon rind, grated
1 orange rind, grated	$\frac{1}{4}$ orange rind, grated
1$\frac{1}{4}$ ozs. anis seed	3 tsp. anis seed
$\frac{1}{4}$ oz. nutmeg	1 tsp. nutmeg
1$\frac{1}{2}$ ozs. salt	$\frac{1}{4}$ tsp. salt
1$\frac{1}{2}$ ozs. cinnamon	3 tbsp. cinnamon
$\frac{1}{3}$ oz. cloves	2 tsp. cloves
1 quart water	1 cup water

Method

Dissolve yeast in warm water. Add one-half of the flour, blend well, and let rise. Chop prunes, figs, and dates into small cubes. Put fruit on pan, sprinkle with rum, and place in luke warm oven. As soon as yeast mixture has risen, add remaining flour, sugar, and spices. Mix well. Add warmed fruits, mixing only as long as necessary to blend fruits into the yeast mixture. Let rest for several hours. Form loaves of different weights ($\frac{1}{4}$ lb., $\frac{1}{2}$ lb., 1 lb., 2 lbs.). Egg wash tops and decorate with glazed fruits and almonds. Let rise again. Bake at 450° F. Glaze loaves with gum arabic or sugar syrup while still hot. Loaves may be wrapped in cellophane when completely cold.

Salzburger Fruit Bread

1 lb. 12 ozs. walnut halves	1$\frac{1}{2}$ cups walnut halves
1 lb. 12 ozs. filberts, toasted	1$\frac{1}{2}$ cups filberts, toasted
	1 cup citron peel
1 lb. 12 ozs. citron peel	1 cup orange peel
1 lb. 12 ozs. orange peel	1$\frac{3}{4}$ cups raisins
2 lbs. raisins	1$\frac{1}{4}$ cups cherries, glazed
1 lb. 12 ozs. cherries, glazed	$\frac{1}{2}$ cup pears, candied
6 ozs. pears, candied	$\frac{1}{2}$ cup cooked prunes
10 ozs. cooked prunes	1$\frac{1}{2}$ cups cake crumbs
1 lb. 3 ozs. cake crumbs	$\frac{1}{3}$ cup rum
$\frac{3}{4}$ pint rum	$\frac{1}{2}$ lemon rind, grated
2 lemon rinds, grated	$\frac{1}{4}$ orange rind, grated
1 orange rind, grated	3 tsp. anis seed
1 oz. anis seed	4$\frac{1}{2}$ tsp. cinnamon
1$\frac{1}{2}$ ozs. cinnamon	2 tsp. cloves
$\frac{1}{4}$ oz. cloves	2 tsp. ginger
$\frac{1}{4}$ oz. ginger	

Method:

Mix chopped fruits with rum and allow to soak overnight. Add rest of ingredients and mix well. Form oblong shaped loaves of various sizes. Wrap fruit bars in thin layer of bugle dough. (*See Index.*) Egg wash. Let rest in cool place. Bake at 325° F. Wrap in cellophane when cold.

Gingerbread House

This attractive showpiece is made of *lebkuchen* dough. The individual pieces are first cut out of cardboard and then placed over the rolled dough and cut. Red cellophane was placed behind the windows and the house was lit from within. The imitation snow on the roof of the house and trees is of white royal icing. The smoke is indicated with a piece of cotton. After the showpiece was assembled it was dusted freely with powdered sugar for a unique, wintery effect.

Christmas Stollen

10 lbs. flour	8$\frac{1}{2}$ cups flour
4 lbs. butter	2 cups butter
2$\frac{1}{2}$ lbs. raisins	2$\frac{1}{4}$ cups raisins
8 ozs. almond halves	$\frac{1}{2}$ cup almond halves
1 lb. 8 ozs. sugar	scant 1 cup sugar
10 ozs. yeast	5 cakes yeast
8 ozs. citron peel	$\frac{1}{3}$ cup citron peel
20 eggs	5 eggs
1$\frac{1}{2}$ quarts milk	1$\frac{1}{4}$ cups milk
$\frac{1}{2}$ pint rum	$\frac{1}{4}$ cup rum
4 lemon rinds, grated	1 lemon rind, grated
2 orange rinds, grated	$\frac{1}{2}$ orange rind, grated
1 tsp. nutmeg	$\frac{1}{4}$ tsp. nutmeg
1 tsp. cardamon	$\frac{1}{4}$ tsp. cardamon

Method

Dissolve the yeast in one-third of the milk and add enough of the flour to form yeast sponge. Let rise. Cream the butter, eggs, and sugar. Add the flavoring and spices. Mix into yeast sponge and add the remaining flour and milk. Do not stir the raisins, citron peel, and almonds onto the dough. These should be pressed into the dough, which is done by overlapping and folding several times in order to distribute the fruits evenly. Let dough rise twice, each time for twenty minutes, and push it back twice. To make up a *stollen,* form a smooth, bread-like loaf. Let rest a few minutes. With a rolling pin, press down the center of the loaf, lengthwise, and fold dough together. Let rise about fifteen minutes. Dough will rise only a little, but loosen up considerably. Brush with thin egg wash and bake at 325° F. to 350° F. After baking, brush freely with melted butter. Sprinkle with vanilla-flavored powdered sugar.

Note: In order to obtain perfect results, all ingredients should be warm so the yeast can develop properly. The developing power of *Stollen* dough is increased when the baking process is started with the aid of steam. This will prevent formation of crust during the early stages of baking. If steam pipes are not available, pour a glass of water into the oven, and close the door quickly. *Stollen* wrapped in cellophane paper will keep fresh for several weeks.

Christmas Raisin Stollen

8 lbs. flour	3¼ cups flour
1 quart milk	scant 1 cup milk
13 ozs. yeast	6¼ cakes yeast
6 eggs	2 eggs
1 lb. 8 ozs. sugar	1 cup sugar
8 ozs. almonds, chopped	½ cup almonds, chopped
3 lbs. butter	1½ cups butter
5 lbs. raisins	4½ cups raisins
1 tsp. salt	¼ tsp. salt
1 tsp. lemon rind, grated	¼ tsp. lemon rind, grated
1 tsp. nutmeg	¼ tsp. nutmeg
vanilla	vanilla

Method

Dissolve yeast in a little of the milk, then add about two-thirds of the flour to form yeast sponge. Cream butter, sugar, and eggs. Add flavoring and spices. Mix with risen yeast sponge to form a smooth dough. Let rise for twenty minutes. Add warmed raisins and almonds. Let rise again. Form *stollen* and proceed as directed under "Christmas *Stollen.*"

Almond Stollen

7 lbs. flour	6 cups flour
8 ozs. yeast	4 cakes yeast
1¼ quarts milk	1 cup milk (generous)
4 lbs. butter	1 lb. butter
1 lb. 8 ozs. sugar	1 cup sugar
1 tsp. salt	¼ tsp. salt
6 ozs. almond paste	1½ ozs. almond paste
1 lb. 8 ozs. citron peel	1 cup citron peel
1 lb. 8 ozs. almonds, chopped	1½ cups almonds, chopped
4 lemon rinds, grated	1 lemon rind, grated
2 orange rinds, grated	½ orange rind, grated
1 tsp. nutmeg	¼ tsp. nutmeg
1 tsp. cardamon	¼ tsp. cardamon
vanilla	vanilla

Method

Proceed as directed under "Christmas *Stollen.*"

THE EASTER SEASON

Eggs, rabbits, chicks, ducks, and other Easter articles are very easy to make. Most of these figures, for greater efficiency, are pressed into forms rather than freely molded. The following section will demonstrate the superiority and greater appeal of hand-decorated Easter articles, compared to the standard, machine-made goods.

Chocolate Eggs

The quality of the chocolate will determine success or failure in this undertaking. It never pays to buy cheap chocolate. Cheap chocolate contains more sugar than cocoa butter. This causes the goods to stick to the forms, resulting in unnecessary breakage. Good semi-sweet chocolate is recognized by its reddish-brown color, rich cocoa aroma, and last, but not least, its price.

Egg forms come in different sizes and are usually made of metal with chromium plating inside. This chrome surface must be treated very carefully and should never be scraped with metal objects. Even the faintest scratches will cause the chocolate to stick. Much more practical are forms made of plexi-glass which not only have a greater flexibility but also are easier to keep clean. The forms should never be greased or oiled, as this will cause streaks in the chocolate. To clean forms properly, use cotton. Eggs are made in two parts and are stuck together with melted chocolate. Other hollow articles are made in one operation. The treatment of chocolate has been described under "The Preparation of Chocolate." (*See Index.*) Properly cooled chocolate should be of a consistency which resembles the flow of heavy syrup. If good chocolate has been bought in the first place, this consistency may be reached by melting it and adding a few ounces of cocoa butter. The exact amount of cocoa butter varies with the many different kinds of chocolates.

The cool chocolate is poured into the egg forms and immediately turned upside down onto a wire screen. The liquid chocolate should harden within a few minutes, after which the drops formed on the edges by the outflowing chocolate are cut off with a knife. The forms are left in a cool place. Under the influence of cool temperatures the cocoa butter molecules will contract, separating the chocolate shell from the form. The chocolate egg should come out easily when banged slightly on the table.

Hollow chocolate figures are poured in one operation. The two half forms are secured together with metal pins and treated exactly as described above. After the figures have been taken from the molds, the bottoms are fixed. Spread a thin layer of cooled chocolate on waxed paper and set the figures in it. As soon as the chocolate has hardened, break away the excess chocolate.

The chocolate eggs are filled with pralines and individually decorated. They may be decorated with either marzipan, royal icing or sugar flowers. Silk ribbons are an attractive addition to any decoration. The eggs may be wrapped in colored aluminum foil or cellophane.

Marzipan Eggs and Animals

Combine one part of almond paste and one part of sifted powdered sugar. Knead well to form smooth marzipan dough. Do not mix by machine or in a warm place as this will cause the almond oil to separate. Oily marzipan will not bind up properly.

Eggs are formed, by pressing marzipan into an egg mold, allowing a wall $\frac{1}{4}''$ thick. The inside is then brushed with cool chocolate and left to harden. The half shells should be allowed to dry for two days before joining together.

Animals or other figures are usually pressed into sulphur molds (*see Index*) and left solid rather than hollow. If hollow figures are desired, the excess marzipan must be cut away with a pointed knife. To make certain that the figures slide easily from the molds, dip a wad of cotton into talcum powder and dust molds evenly.

As the surfaces of marzipan eggs are perfectly smooth and neutral, they are usually painted with vegetable colors. Animals, however, should merely be touched up with make-up powder. (*See Index.*) The animal bottoms may be dipped in chocolate and sprinkled with green cocoanut to imitate grass.

Italian Easter Panetoni

(1) Sponge

8 ozs. bread flour	1½ cups bread flour
1½ ozs. yeast	(generous)
8 ozs. milk	3 cakes yeast
	scant 1 cup milk

(2) Beat over warm water in double boiler until thick

2½ ozs. sugar	⅜ cup sugar
4 egg yolks	4 egg yolks
5 eggs	5 eggs
⅓ oz. salt	2 tsp. salt
1 lemon rind, grated	1 lemon rind, grated

(3) Cream well

5 ozs. butter	⅝ cup butter
1½ ozs. sugar	scant ¼ cup sugar
4 egg yolks	4 egg yolks
2 ozs. salad oil	scant ¼ cup salad oil

(4) Mix together

1 lb. bread flour	3¼ cups bread flour
1½ ozs. currants	¼ cup currants
1½ ozs. raisins	¼ cup raisins
1½ ozs. candied orange peel	¼ cup candied orange peel
1½ ozs. mixed fruit	¼ cup mixed fruit

A selection of decorated Easter eggs. Rabbits and chicks made from sugar and little eggs in foreground from marzipan.

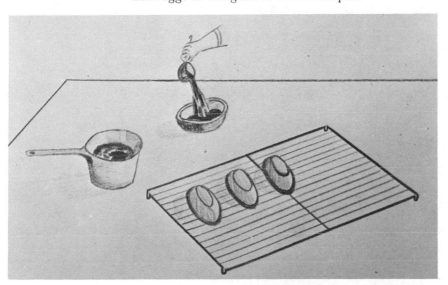

The cold liquid chocolate is poured into the molds and turned upside down onto a wire screen.

Taking the chilled shells from the molds

Chocolate eggs decorated with colored royal icing

Chocolate egg wrapped in aluminum foil

Giant Easter egg made entirely from sugar plastic. Decorations are made from colored royal icing. The egg was used as a centerpiece for an Easter buffet.

A selection of sugar animals and Easter eggs

Rabbits made from marzipan.

Chicks made from marzipan

Nests are made from shortbread iced with chocolate and sprinkled with cocoanut.
Eggs are from colored marzipan.

These eggs are usually made from sponge or butter cake, iced with pale colored
fondant and decorated with royal icings.

Easter *panetoni*

Method

Let sponge rise well. Add *1* and *2*. Stir constantly. Blend in *3*. Mix well. Line a round cake tin with brown paper, making certain the sides are at least 6″ high. After dough has risen slightly, fill tin two thirds of its depth. The dough should be a smooth, rounded piece. Let rise, then cut a cross in the top, and egg wash. Place a piece of butter on top and bake at 300° F. to 325° F. Use a wooden tester to see if cake is baked in the center. The piece of wood should come out clean. This delicious cake is served as an Easter speciality in Italy.

APPENDIXES

Conversion Tables

Leavenings

Ammonium carbonate	1/12 oz. = 1 tsp.
Baking powder, cream of tartar type	$\frac{1}{8}$ oz. = 1 tsp.
Baking powder, phosphate type	$\frac{1}{6}$ oz. = 1 tsp.
Baking soda	$\frac{1}{6}$ oz. = 1 tsp.
Cream of tartar	$\frac{1}{8}$ oz. = 1 tsp.
Monocalcium phosphate	$\frac{1}{8}$ oz. = 1 tsp.
Potassium carbonate	$\frac{1}{8}$ oz. = 1 tsp.
Sodium pyrophosphate	$\frac{1}{8}$ oz. = 1 tsp.
Yeast, compressed	$\frac{1}{2}$ oz. = 1 cake
Yeast, dried	1 pkg. = 1 cake

Flours and Cereals

Bran	2 ozs. = 1 cup
Crumbs, bread	$3\frac{1}{2}$ ozs. = 1 cup
Crumbs, cake	3 ozs. = 1 cup
Farina, uncooked	6 ozs. = 1 cup
Flour, bread unsifted	$4\frac{3}{4}$ ozs. = 1 cup
Flour, bread sifted	$4\frac{1}{4}$ ozs. = 1 cup
Flour, cake unsifted	$4\frac{1}{4}$ ozs. = 1 cup
Flour, cake sifted	$3\frac{7}{8}$ ozs. = 1 cup
Flour, potato	$4\frac{1}{2}$ ozs. = 1 cup
Flour, rice	4 ozs. = 1 cup
Flour, whole wheat	$3\frac{1}{2}$ ozs. = 1 cup
Cornstarch, unsifted	8 ozs. = 1 cup
Cornstarch, sifted	$6\frac{1}{2}$ ozs. = 1 cup
Tapioca, ground	5 ozs. = 1 cup

Eggs

Eggs, whole (1 egg = $1\frac{3}{4}$ ozs. approx.)	5 (8 ozs.) = 1 cup
Eggs, whites (1 white = 1 oz. approx.)	8 (8 ozs.) = 1 cup
Eggs, yolks (1 yolk = $\frac{3}{4}$ oz. approx.)	12 (8 ozs.) = 1 cup
Eggs, dried	1 oz. = $6\frac{1}{2}$ tbsp.

Professional Measures for Eggs

Eggs, whole	20 eggs = 1 quart
Egg yolks	50 yolks = 1 quart
Egg whites	40 whites = 1 quart

Sugar

Sugar, brown	$5\frac{1}{2}$ ozs. = 1 cup
Sugar, corn	$6\frac{1}{2}$ ozs. = 1 cup
Sugar, fruit	$7\frac{3}{4}$ ozs. = 1 cup
Sugar, granulated	7 ozs. = 1 cup
Sugar, powdered	5 ozs. = 1 cup
Sugar, 4x	$4\frac{1}{2}$ ozs. = 1 cup

Liquids

Cream	$8\frac{3}{8}$ ozs. = 1 cup
Fruit juice	$8\frac{1}{2}$ ozs. = 1 cup
Milk, liquid	$8\frac{1}{2}$ ozs. = 1 cup
Milk, evaporated	9 ozs. = 1 cup
Milk, condensed	$10\frac{1}{4}$ ozs. = 1 cup
Vinegar	8 ozs. = 1 cup
Water	8 ozs. = 1 cup

Fats

Butter	$7\frac{3}{4}$ ozs. = 1 cup
Butter, shortening 50/50	$6\frac{3}{4}$ ozs. = 1 cup
Lard	$7\frac{3}{4}$ ozs. = 1 cup
Oil	7 ozs. = 1 cup
Puff paste shortening	7 ozs. = 1 cup

Syrups

Honey	12 ozs. = 1 cup
Malt	$11\frac{3}{4}$ ozs. = 1 cup
Maple syrup	$11\frac{1}{2}$ ozs. = 1 cup
Molasses	11 ozs. = 1 cup
Glucose	12 ozs. = 1 cup

Nuts

Almonds, chopped	$4\frac{1}{8}$ ozs. = 1 cup
Almonds, ground	$2\frac{2}{3}$ ozs. = 1 cup
Brazil nuts, whole	$5\frac{1}{2}$ ozs. = 1 cup
Brazil nuts, ground	$2\frac{1}{4}$ ozs. = 1 cup
California walnuts, whole	$4\frac{1}{2}$ ozs. = 1 cup
Filberts, whole	5 ozs. = 1 cup
Filberts, broken	4 ozs. = 1 cup
Filberts, ground	$2\frac{2}{3}$ ozs. = 1 cup
Peanuts, whole	5 ozs. = 1 cup
Peanuts, ground	4 ozs. = 1 cup
Pecans	4 ozs. = 1 cup

Fruits

Apples, medium	1 piece = 6 ozs.
Apple sauce	8 ozs. = 1 cup

Bananas, peeled	1 banana = $3\frac{1}{2}$ ozs.
Bananas, crushed	14 ozs. = 1 cup
Bananas, dried	$3\frac{3}{8}$ ozs. = 1 cup
Blueberries, fresh	$5\frac{1}{4}$ ozs. = 1 cup
Cherries, candied	6 ozs. = 1 cup
Citron, in syrup, sliced	7 ozs. = 1 cup
Citron, in syrup, cubed	7 ozs. = 1 cup
Citron, dry	$6\frac{1}{2}$ ozs. = 1 cup
Cocoanut, shredded, dry	$3\frac{1}{2}$ ozs. = 1 cup
Cocoanut dessicated, dry	$2\frac{1}{2}$ ozs. = 1 cup
Cocoanut, moist, canned	4 ozs. = 1 can
Cocoanut with milk	10 ozs. = 1 can
Currants	$4\frac{3}{4}$ ozs. = 1 cup
Dates, stoned	5 ozs. = 1 cup
Figs	5 ozs. = 1 cup
Pineapple, crushed	8 ozs. = 1 cup
Prunes, pitted, uncooked	5 ozs. = 1 cup
Prunes, pitted, cooked	7 ozs. = 1 cup
Peel, grated	$\frac{3}{8}$ ozs. = 1 tbsp.
Peel, candied	4 ozs. = 1 cup
Raisins	$4\frac{1}{2}$ ozs. = 1 cup

Miscellaneous

Cheese, cottage	7 ozs. = 1 cup
Cheese, grated	4 ozs. = 1 cup
Cheese, parmesan, grated	$3\frac{1}{2}$ ozs. = 1 cup
Cheese, cream	4 ozs. = 1 pkg.
Chocolate, melted	$8\frac{1}{2}$ ozs. = 1 cup
Chocolate, chipped	$3\frac{3}{4}$ ozs. = 1 cup
Cocoa	1 oz. = $4\frac{1}{2}$ tbsp.
Cocoa	$3\frac{1}{2}$ ozs. = 1 cup
Coffee, ground	3 ozs. = 1 cup
Cornmeal	$5\frac{1}{3}$ ozs. = 1 cup
Gelatine	1 oz. = 3 tbsp.
Gelatine	$5\frac{1}{2}$ ozs. = 1 cup

Gelatine, leaves	10 pieces = $1\frac{1}{2}$ ozs.
Jam	11 ozs. = 1 cup
Jelly	11 ozs. = 1 cup
Marmalade	11 ozs. = 1 cup
Milk, powdered	$4\frac{3}{8}$ ozs. = 1 cup
Milk, powdered	1/10 oz. = 1 tsp.
Oats, rolled	$2\frac{1}{2}$ ozs. = 1 cup
Rice, uncooked	8 ozs. = 1 cup

Flavoring and Spices

Anis seed, ground	1/15 oz. = 1 tsp.
Caraway seed, ground	1/12 oz. = 1 tsp. (generous)
Cardamon seed, ground	1/15 oz. = 1 tsp.
Cinnamon, ground	1/12 oz. = 1 tsp. (generous)
Cloves, ground	1/12 oz. = 1 tsp. (generous)
Extracts	$\frac{1}{8}$ oz. = 1 tsp.
Ginger, ground	1/12 oz. = 1 tsp. (scant)
Mace, ground	1/12 oz. = 1 tsp. (generous)
Nutmeg, ground	1/12 oz. = 1 tsp. (generous)
Poppy seed, whole	5 ozs. = 1 cup
Salt	1/24 oz. = 1 dash
Salt	$\frac{1}{6}$ oz. = 1 tsp.

Weights

To convert grams into ounces divide by 31.
For example: 500 grams divided by 31 = 16 ozs.

CONVERSION TABLE

Centigrade Degrees into Fahrenheit Degrees

C°	F°	C°	F°	C°	F°	C°	F°
0	32.0	44	111.2	88	190.4	132	269.6
1	33.8	45	113.0	89	192.2	133	271.4
2	35.6	46	114.8	90	194.0	134	273.2
3	37.4	47	116.6	91	195.8	135	275.0
4	39.2	48	118.4	92	197.6	136	276.8
5	41.0	49	120.2	93	199.4	137	278.6
6	42.8	50	122.0	94	201.2	138	280.4
7	44.6	51	123.8	95	203.0	139	282.2
8	46.4	52	125.6	96	204.8	140	284.0
9	48.2	53	127.4	97	206.6	141	285.8
10	50.0	54	129.2	98	208.4	142	287.6
11	51.8	55	131.0	99	210.2	143	289.4
12	53.6	56	132.8	100	212.0	144	291.2
13	55.4	57	134.6	101	213.8	145	293.0
14	57.2	58	136.4	102	215.6	146	294.8
15	59.0	59	138.2	103	217.4	147	296.6
16	60.8	60	140.0	104	219.2	148	298.4
17	62.6	61	141.8	105	221.0	149	300.2
18	64.4	62	143.6	106	222.8	150	302.0
19	66.2	63	145.4	107	224.6	151	303.8
20	68.0	64	147.2	108	226.4	152	305.6
21	69.8	65	149.0	109	228.2	153	307.4
22	71.6	66	150.8	110	230.0	154	309.2
23	73.4	67	152.6	111	231.8	155	311.0
24	75.2	68	154.4	112	233.6	156	312.8
25	77.0	69	156.2	113	235.4	157	314.6
26	78.8	70	158.0	114	237.2	158	316.4
27	80.6	71	159.8	115	239.0	159	318.2
28	82.4	72	161.6	116	240.8	160	320.0
29	84.2	73	163.4	117	242.6	161	321.8
30	86.0	74	165.2	118	244.4	162	323.6
31	87.8	75	167.0	119	246.2	163	321.4
32	89.6	76	168.8	120	248.0	164	327.2
33	91.4	77	170.6	121	249.8	165	329.0
34	93.2	78	172.4	122	251.6	166	330.8
35	95.0	79	174.2	123	253.4	167	332.6
36	96.8	80	176.0	124	255.2	168	334.4
37	98.6	81	177.8	125	257.0	169	336.2
38	100.4	82	179.6	126	255.8	170	338.0
39	102.2	83	181.4	127	260.6	171	339.8
40	104.0	84	183.2	128	262.4	172	341.6
41	105.8	85	185.0	129	264.2	173	343.4
42	107.6	86	186.8	130	266.4	174	345.2
43	109.4	87	188.6	131	267.8	175	347.0

Centigrade Degrees into Fahrenheit

C°	F°	C°	F°	C°	F°	C°	F°
176	348.8	183	361.4	189	372.2	195	383.0
177	350.6	184	363.2	190	374.0	196	384.8
178	352.4	185	365.0	191	375.8	197	386.6
179	354.2	186	366.8	192	377.6	198	388.4
180	356.0	187	368.6	193	379.4	199	390.2
181	357.8	188	370.4	194	381.2	200	392.0
182	359.6						

CONVERSION TABLE

Reaumur Degrees into Fahrenheit Degrees

	R°	F°	R°	F°	R°	F°
Numbers 1–25	26	90.5	51	146.7	76	203.0
in Reaumur	27	92.7	52	149.0	77	205.2
are not	28	95.0	53	151.2	78	207.5
used.	29	97.2	54	153.5	79	209.7
	30	99.5	55	155.7	80	212.0
	31	101.7	56	158.0	81	214.2
	32	104.0	57	160.2	82	216.5
	33	106.2	58	162.5	83	218.7
	34	108.5	59	164.7	84	221.0
	35	110.7	60	167.0	85	223.2
	36	113.0	61	169.2	86	225.5
	37	115.2	62	171.5	87	227.7
	38	117.5	63	173.7	88	230.0
	39	119.7	64	176.0	89	232.2
	40	122.0	65	178.2	90	234.5
	41	124.2	66	180.5	91	236.7
	42	126.5	67	182.7	92	239.0
	43	128.7	68	185.0	93	241.2
	44	131.0	69	187.2	94	243.5
	45	133.2	70	189.5	95	245.7
	46	135.5	71	191.7	96	248.0
	47	137.7	72	194.0	97	250.2
	48	140.0	73	196.2	98	252.5
	49	142.2	74	198.5	99	254.7
	50	144.5	75	200.7	100	257.0

R°	F°	R°	F°	R°	F°	R°	F°
101	259.2	126	315.5	151	371.7	176	428.0
102	261.5	127	317.7	152	374.0	177	430.2
103	263.7	128	320.0	153	376.2	178	432.5
104	266.0	129	322.2	154	378.5	179	434.7
105	268.2	130	324.5	155	380.7	180	437.0
106	270.5	131	326.7	156	383.0	181	439.2
107	272.7	132	329.0	157	385.2	182	441.5
108	275.0	133	331.2	158	387.5	183	443.7
109	277.2	134	333.5	159	389.7	184	446.0
110	279.5	135	335.7	160	392.0	185	448.2
111	281.7	136	338.0	161	394.2	186	450.5
112	284.0	137	340.2	162	396.5	187	452.7
113	286.2	138	342.5	163	398.7	188	454.0
114	288.5	139	344.7	164	401.0	189	457.2
115	290.7	140	347.0	165	403.2	190	459.5
116	293.0	141	349.2	166	405.5	191	461.7
117	295.2	142	351.5	167	407.7	192	464.0
118	297.5	143	353.7	168	410.0	193	466.2
119	299.7	144	356.0	169	412.2	194	468.5
120	302.0	145	358.2	170	414.5	195	470.7
121	304.2	146	360.5	171	416.7	196	473.0
122	306.5	147	362.7	172	419.0	197	475.2
123	308.7	148	365.0	173	421.2	198	477.5
124	311.0	149	367.2	174	423.5	199	479.7
125	313.2	150	369.5	175	425.7	200	482.0

To convert Reaumur degrees into Fahrenheit   *Formula:* $R° \times 9/4 + 32 = F°$

Example : to convert $8°R.$ to $F°$; $(8 \times 9/4) + 32 = 50°F.$

Analysis of Materials and Terms

Acid	The chemically distilled, sour substance of fruits.
Agar agar	East Indian sea plant with approximately eight times the jellifying power of gelatine.
Alabaster	A white marble-like mineral of the gypsum family, used for making plaster molds.
Alcohol	A colorless and inflammable liquid, produced by fermentation and distillation.
Aleuron	Vegetable protein substance in wheat. Used for diabetic diets.
Alkali	A soda or potash that neutralizes acids and forms salts.
Allspice	The dried, nearly ripe fruit of *pimenta officinalis*.
Almond extract	A flavoring distilled from bitter almonds.
Almond paste	Containing two parts of almonds and one part of sugar.
Ammonium	The oldest known leavening, mainly used for heavy, spicy cookies and *lebkuchen*.
Ananas	The central European name for pineapple.
Angel food	A cake made with egg whites and sugar as basic materials.
Angelica	A herb of which the stems and leaves are candied and used as a decorating material. Angelica is also used as a flavoring medium in liqueur manufacturing, notably chartreuse.
Anis seed	The dried fruit of *pimpinella anisum*.
Antiseptic	Free of germs.
Apéritif	An alcoholic drink.
Apple gelée	Apple juice mixed with sugar and cooked until thickened.
Arancini	Stringed, candied orange peel.
Aroma	Fragrance, as in plants, wine, and other substances. A pleasant spicy odor.
Arrack	The distilled, spirituous liquor from palms, molasses, or rice, of Oriental origin.
Aspic	A jelly in which meat, fish, fruits, et cetera, are molded.
Azure	Sky blue.
Baba	A dessert of yeast risen dough.
Baiser	A baked, French meringue.
Baked Alaska	An ice cream dish, covered with meringue, browned in a hot oven.
Baking powder	A mixture of cream of tartar and soda, used as a leavening agent.
Baking soda	Bicarbonate of soda.
Ball stage	Sugar cooked from 244° F to 250° F. with water and glucose.
Bear claws	A pastry made of yeast dough.
Beaume	An instrument named after the inventor to measure percentage of sugar in syrup.
Beignets	The French name for doughnuts and other deep fried sweets.
Benzoic acid	A crystallized acid used as an antiseptic preservative.
Blanch	To neutralize a color in fruits, to remove skin of almonds with hot water.
Blancmange	A dessert made of milk, gelatine, sugar, and starch, formed in a mold and served with cream.
Bombe	A selection of various ice-creams, shaped like a bomb and served with a sauce or whipped cream.
Bonbon	A soft candy, sugar or chocolate coated.
Borax	A crystallized salt used in fruit preservation.
Bran	The coarse husk of grain, separate from the flour.
Brandy	An alcoholic liquor distilled from wine, used as flavoring medium for creams, ice-creams, and sauces.

Brioche	A yeast dough, rich in butter and eggs.
Butterscotch	A candy made of brown sugar and butter.
Cafe Glacè	Vanilla ice cream and strong coffee, served as a drink.
Canadian cheese	A pastry made of cooked meringue, filled with marron-flavored butter cream.
Candied blossoms	Used in decorating cakes, et cetera. Most popular are roses, violets, carnations.
Caramel	Sugar, water, and glucose solution boiled between 260° F. and 360° F.
Cardamon	An East Indian herb. The seed is used as a spice.
Cassia	A liqueur made from the bark of the cassia tree. Excellent flavoring medium for moistening cakes.
Casting sugar	Boiled sugar for the purpose of being formed in a mold made of plaster of paris.
Chateau	A wine foam. Served warm as dessert or as sauce with puddings.
Citron	A lemon-like fruit, containing less acid than a lemon. Candied citron rind is used as flavoring and decorating medium.
Clove	The dried blossom of a tropical tree. Used as a spice.
Cobbler	A drink of fruit-flavored wine, served with cracked ice.
Cocoa butter	A fat substance derived from the cocoa beans. The binding medium is chocolate.
Couleur	Burned sugar diluted with water. Used as a coloring medium. Excellent for strengthening coffee colors.
Coup	Ice cream dish served in glasses, decorated with fruits and whipped cream.
Cream of tartar	Crystallized tartar used in baking powder. Used instead of glucose in boiling of sugar to prevent formation of sugar crystals.
Crepes	The French equivalent of pancakes.
Croissant	A delicate French roll, crescent-shaped, made of rich Danish yeast dough.
Croquem-bouché	Small caramellized cream puffs, set together like a pyramid.
Crystallized	Candies, pastries, et cetera, coated with sugar crystals. Accidental crystallization caused by faulty treatment of sugar.
Curaçao	A fine liqueur flavored with dried orange peel.
Demi glacè	French name for half-frozen ice cream.
Dextrin	Carbohydrate occuring in decomposition of starch, used as polisher when dissolved in hot water.
Diabetic	A person who has sugar diabetes. Special diets are required.
Dice	To cut food into small pieces.
Dipping	The process of coating sweet goods either wholly or partially in chocolate, fondant, liqueur syrups, et cetera.
Dobosh torte	Named after the inventor Dobos, a Hungarian confectioner. Usually of six to eight layers, filled with butter cream and glazed with brown caramel.
Dragées	Candies which are coated with sugar through a special process and glazed by machine.
Dressing	The act of spreading icings or creams through an icing bag and tube.
Duchesse	The name of a European delicacy made of filberts, sugar, and egg whites, filled with nougat.
Éclairs	Small oblong cakes, made of cream puff dough, filled with either whipped or custard cream and iced with chocolate.
Egg white albumin	Fresh, dried and crystallized egg whites, easily soluble in water.
Emulsifier	A machine to make artificial whipping cream from a hot milk-fat solution.
Enzyme	An organic substance that aids in certain transformations of materials in the digestion of food.
Essence	Concentrated extract used as a flavoring medium.

Extract	A part taken from a substance by distillation.
Fermentation	The chemical change that takes place in an organic substance caused by certain fungi, such as the activity of yeast on doughs.
Fleurons	Small half-moon shaped objects cut from puff paste.
Florentines	The name for flat pastries made almost entirely of cream, almonds and candied fruits.
Fondant	A cooked sugar icing of fine, creamy consistency.
French pastries	A wide variety of small, individually decorated and iced sweets or desserts.
Fritter	A small cake made of batter and fruits, deep fried.
Fruit cake	Heavy poundcake mixture with dried fruits.
Fruit gelée	Extracted fruit juice, thickened with sugar, which hardens through its natural jellying power.
Fruit purée	Cooked, strained fruit, sweetened or unsweetened. Can be conserved with chemical preservatives and used as flavoring medium for ice creams as well as fat creams.
Fudge	A soft, creamy confection of sugar, butter, and chocolate.
Gelatine	A substance derived from animal tissues, used as binder for creams, jellies, et cetera.
Gin	A liquor distilled from grain and flavored with juniper berries. Used as flavoring medium in ice cream dishes or fruit cocktails.
Ginger	The ground root of a tropical herb used as spice.
Glaze	A transparent liquid finish for foodstuff which dries with a shine.
Glucose	A form of sugar found in fruits or honey. Prevents formation of crystals in cooking sugar. Used as a thickener in liqueur manufacturing.
Glycerin	A natural substance of fats, transparent and odorless. Used as softener in marzipan, or insulator in caramel sugar work.
Graham flour	Named after the American diet specialist Dr. Sylvester Graham (unbolted wheat fiour).
Granulated	Formed of sugar crystals.
Grillage	Or krokant. Made of toasted nuts, bound with brown caramel sugar.
Guava	A tropical fruit used in making jelly and ice cream.
Gugelhopf	An Austrian specialty, baked in a corrugated dome-shaped form. Made of yeast dough or pound cake.
Gum arabic	Obtained from different species of acacia. Soluble in water. Used as glaze.
Honey cake	Sweetened entirely with honey, containing no sugar.
Ice carving	To carve a figure from a solid block of ice, using special chisels. Used for decorative purposes.
Icings	Under the name of icings are all the different kinds combined. We classify as follows: *Sugar Icings*: fondant, powdered sugar, caramel. *Fat Icings:* Butter creams. *Egg White Icings:* royal icing, marshmallow. *Chocolate Icings:* boiled or melted chocolate.
Illuminated ice	Special figures carved from crystal ice, with hole on the bottom, containing an electric light source.
Invert sugar	A combination of dextrose and levulose formed by inverting sucrose. Invert sugar is used in artificial honey manufacturing or added to sugar instead of glucose in candy cookeries. Invert sugar is often added to baked goods because of its ability to brown in golden-yellow tones.
Jams	Contrary to marmalade the whole fruits are cooked and thickened with sugar without straining.
Jelly	A semi-transparent substance obtained by boiling either whole fruits or fruit juices.

Kernel paste	Imitation marzipan. Made of apricot kernels. Often mixed with almond paste for the purpose of economy.
Kirsch or Kirschwasser	A syrup substance distilled from fermented cherry juice. Used as flavoring medium in fat or ice creams.
Kuchen	The general term cake, or cake-like sweets made of egg or yeast risen doughs.
Krokant	Molten sugar with almonds or filberts mixed in. Used for building showpieces or in ground form as flavoring medium.
Kuemmel	A delicious liqueur, flavored with caraway seed and cumin. Used for special sauces.
Leavenings	Substances, such as the following, used to induce a dough to rise :
	Baking powder, cream of tartar type
	Baking powder phosphate S.A.S. type
	Baking soda
	Cream of tartar
	Ammonium carbonate
	Monocalcium phosphate
	Potassium carbonate
	Sodium pyrophosphate
	Yeast
Linzer Torte	Named after the city of Linz, Austria. A butter-rich shortbread filled with jam.
Lebkuchen	A spicy dough, sweetened with either honey or sugar, mixed with glazed fruits. Nurmberg *Lebkuchen* — an international delicacy.
Lime	The powder obtained from limestone. Used to absorb dampness in glass cases containing pulled sugar articles. Also a small, sour citrus fruit.
Liqueur	An alcoholic drink, sweetened and perfumed. Excellent flavoring medium for cocktails, creams, et cetera.
Liqueur confections	Candies with liquid liqueur filling, coated with chocolate.
Luebecker marzipan	Named after the city of Luebeck, Germany. It consists of almond paste with very little sugar pressed into fancy sulphur molds and sold all over the world (Protected Brand Name).
Macaroons	Cooky-like sweets consisting of one part nuts (almonds, walnuts, filberts), two parts of sugar, and egg whites or egg yolks.
Mace	The powdered husk of the nutmeg. Used as a spice.
Make-up powder	Talcum powder or starch colored with food colorings.
Mandoletti	An Italian confection consisting of white nougat, fruits, and egg whites.
Maraschino	A liqueur made from fermented juice of small, bitter cherries. An excellent flavoring medium that resembles bitter almonds. Used in icings, creams, puddings, et cetera.
Margarine	A butter substitute of various vegetable fats. Sometimes attains a butter-like consistency, but never approaches real butter flavor.
Marron	A sweet chestnut from the marron tree of southern Europe.
Marron *glacè*	A sugar-coated chestnut confection.
Marzipan	The basic material is almond paste to which powdered sugar and glucose are added. The most versatile and decorative medium of all.
Melange	A mixture of different types of candies and chocolates.
Meringue	Beaten egg whites and sugar.
Milles Feuilles	The name of puff pastry. Specifically : "thousand leaves cake," pertaining to the dough's leaf-like appearance.
Mint	The distilled oil from the peppermint plant. Used for mint patties, mint liqueur, and mint candies.

Mocha	A fine strongly-brewed coffee which originated in Arabia. Used for mocha creams, icings, and ice creams.
Mocha extract	Same as above, thickened and condensed, with sugar *couleur* added.
Mocha paste	Fine coffee powder, mixed with cocoa butter or other hard fats. Excellent flavoring medium for chocolates and butter creams.
Molasses	The thick, black syrup left over from the sugar refining process.
Molds	A hollow form in which foodstuffs can be poured or pressed for shaping. Besides metal or porcelain molds, plaster of paris is also useful.
Mousse	A frozen dessert of whipped cream and fruits.
Nougat	Melted sugar plus toasted almonds, or hazelnuts, ground to a fine paste and bound with cocoa butter or other hard vegetable shortening. Used for chocolates, ice and butter creams.
Nutmeg	The flavorful kernel of an East Indian tree. The nuts are sold whole or powdered.
Omelette Soufflé	A light egg mixture, baked swiftly and served at once.
Othellos	A light and fluffy egg white-yolks mixture. Dressed onto paper in small mounds.
Panetoni	An Italian Easter specialty made of yeast dough, fruits, and eggs.
Parfait	A half-frozen, flavored ice cream, whipping cream dessert served in glasses.
Parmesan	A half-fat Italian cheese. Its hard texture is excellent for grating.
Pastille	Products made of tragant or gum sugar solution.
Pastillage	Gum paste or sugar plastic.
Pectin	A substance found in various fruits which aids in the formation of jelly. Apples have the highest pectin content.
Petit fours	A selection of various small, sweet goods.
Pignoli	The white kernel-like fruit from a tree of the pine family. Often used instead of almonds.
Pistachios	The dried, green nuts of an Asian tree. Used sliced as a decorative material.
Plasticine	A modelling clay. Plasticine models are used for making plaster or sulphur molds.
Poppy seeds	The dark blue seed of the poppy flower. Excellent for fillings. Must be ground to obtain delicate flavor.
Pound cake	All ingredients are measured in pounds. One pound butter, one pound sugar, one pound flour, one pound eggs.
Pralines	Chocolate-coated candies.
Rice paper	An edible paper-like product made of rice starch.
Rice powder	Or rice starch. Used as a base for making liquid chocolates or fondant pralines. Rice powder may also be added to sugar plastic for extra smoothness.
Rock sugar	Boiled caramel sugar to which royal icing is added. The foamy substance hardens with a rock-like appearance.
Rosette	Round, flat, cooky-like object with corrugated edge.
Rose water	An oily liquid distilled from rose leaves. Fine flavoring medium for fondants.
Roulade	A light sponge cake filled with jelly, butter, or whipped cream, and rolled like a jelly roll.
Rum	An alcoholic beverage. Excellent flavoring medium for syrups, creams, and desserts. Best type is Jamaica rum.
Rye	A grain of the wheat family. Its flour is used for making bread, bread rolls, and *lebkuchen*.
Saccharin	A substance distilled from coal tar, of great sweetness.
Sacher *torte*	A rich cake named after the famous Hotel Sacher in Vienna.
Saffron	A plant, stringy reddish-brown in color. Dissolved in water it turns to deep yellow. Used as food coloring in making bonbons and candies.

Sausage roll	A meat mixture such as hamburger, rolled into puff paste.
Shellac	A chemical glaze used for inedible showpieces.
Sherbet	A cool beverage of fruit juices, ice cream, and alcohol.
Silver dragées	Are basically made of sugar and have decorative value only.
Soufflé	A sweet dish, for which the egg whites are beaten stiffly, mixed with other ingredients and baked.
Soy flour	Derived from the soy bean. Used in baking for diabetics.
Spekulatius	A German-Dutch butter cooky, pressed in a wooden mold and then baked.
Springerle	A Bavarian Christmas cooky, made as *Spekulatius* but dried before baking.
Spritz	The method of pressing a substance through a tube.
Spun Sugar	Sugar which has been cooked to 300° F. is spun over metal rods. A purely decorative product.
Sterilize	To free from bacteria. In fruit preservation to bring to the boiling point.
Stollen	A German Christmas delicacy. Its basic materials are yeast dough, butter, and fruits. The *Dresdener Stollen* are internationally famous (Protected Brand Name).
Strudel	An Austrian specialty made of paper-thin pulled flour dough with various fruit fillings.
Streusel	A crumb-like mixture of flour and fat.
Sulphur	A non-metallic, yellow, brittle element. Used for making molds, whereby the chemical is melted and becomes a liquid substance.
Talcum	A powder derived from the soapstone. Used to prevent hand perspiration in sugar work, or in candy manufacturing.
Torte	The German name for a cake.
Tortelettes	Small round cakes.
Tragant	The gum-like liquid substance of an Asian tree. Easily soluble in cold water brought to a boil. Used as glaze and as binder in sugar plastic as well as ice cream manufacturing.
Truffle	A potato-shaped fungus growing underground, served as a flavorful table specialty. Also used in chocolate manufacturing.
Tutti Frutti	The Italian term for mixed, glazed fruits.
Vanilla	The most versatile aroma in pastry making. The vanilla in its original form is a plant of the orchid family which grows in South America. Its fruits are dried in the sun and change to a deep, shiny black. The dried fruits are packed in tins and sold all over the world. The most flavorful is the *Vanille de Ley* from Mexico.
Vanillin	A chemical product from which vanilla extracts are made.
Violets	The candied violet blossoms. Purely decorative value.
Wax	We distinguish between bee and vegetable (paraffin) wax. Because of its high degree of heat resistance, wax is an excellent insulator.
Water glass	A chemical preservative for eggs.
Wiener	Pertaining to anything Viennese or originating in Vienna.
Wine	An alcoholic beverage distilled from fermented grapes. Only the best kinds should be used in baking.
Yeast	A multi-celled sponge that causes fermentation. Used as a leavening.
Yogurt	A fermented, thick milk drink from Turkey.
Zwieback	A yeast-raised dough which is baked in loaf tins, sliced and toasted.

Useful Hints and Information

1. Sliced bananas won't turn black when dipped into lemon juice.
2. Egg whites whip better when a little salt is added. Grease is its worst enemy. Egg whites which turn smeary after the sugar has been added may be saved by adding a dash of cream of tartar.
3. Vinegar in puff paste will increase flavor and lifting power.
4. Oxidation of metal in bowls can be removed with salt and lemon juice.
5. Cakes will stay moist longer when kept wrapped in damp cloth.
6. Sour whipping cream may be turned to butter when beaten long enough.
7. Stale cakes and pastries make excellent fillings when mixed with rum syrup.
8. Dinner rolls will soften again when placed in hot oven for several minutes.
9. Butter may be desalted by soaking and rinsing in fresh water.
10. Icings will shine better when pastries are brushed with hot jam before application of icing.
11. Stale *croissant* rolls taste excellent when split open, buttered, and toasted in hot oven.
12. Puff paste will get extra lift when baked on wet pans, or if a cup of water is poured into hot oven.
13. Butter cream will turn smooth again when warmed a little and beaten for a few minutes.
14. Cakes will be perfectly even when joined as follows : Cut top and use as bottom, brown side up. Use bottom as top.
15. Apricot jam between layers of cake insures moistness.
16. Sour milk will turn to cottage cheese when kept in warm place.
17. Sterilization of fruit is accomplished by heating it in water to 180° F.
18. Macaroons or cookies which stick to paper will come loose easily when set on wet table top.
19. Icings dry quickly and with high shine when placed for a few minutes in warm oven.
20. Glucose prevents sugar from crystallizing.
21. Glucose won't stick to wet hands.
22. Ice cream with high sugar content will not freeze solid.
23. Binding mediums are corn, rice, wheat, and potato starches, as well as all gelatine and jelly substances.
24. Cakes cut cleanly when knife is dipped into hot water frequently.
25. Whipping cream has better stand when cream, bowl, and beater are cooled on ice.
26. Butter rich dough will not soften when table top has been cooled with pans filled with shaved ice.
27. Heavy goods with long baking time will not turn black on top when kept covered with paper after crust has browned slightly.
28. The richer it is, the faster egg wash will brown.
29. Meringue and other egg white products will be perfectly white when a few drops of blue coloring are added.
30. Gelatine will dissolve easily in cold water and will not burn when cooked in double boiler.

31. Ice *bombes* slide easily from the molds when held under cold water for a few minutes.
32. Icings will stay soft when covered with a wet rag.
33. Chocolate will become flexible when mixed with oil.
34. Cherries will turn white when soaked in a vinegar-water solution.
35. Puddings won't burn when cooked in a water bath.
36. Royal icings will become softer when glycerin is added after beating.
37. Marzipan will not ferment when processed and used under perfectly clean conditions.
38. Tart shells will keep shape better if bean-filled paper cups are placed in tart centers during baking process.
39. Danish pastries will stay soft all day when kept in a warm, moist compartment.
40. Hardened fondant will soften up again when kept under hot, wet rags.
41. To dry canned fruits, place between two layers of absorbent paper.
42. Jelly surfaces cut clean with hot knife.
43. Egg yolks will increase tenderness of pastries and cakes.
44. Pastry and cooky glaze is applied more easily with an atomizer.
45. Fruit pie bottoms won't get soggy when covered with crumbs.
46. Pie crusts become crispy when sprinkled with granulated sugar before baking.
47. Lemon rinds grated and mixed with granulated sugar make excellent flavoring mediums. Keep in non-metal containers.
48. Caramellized pastries stay crisp when kept in warm place.
49. Colors in powder form mixed with alcohol will dry fast. Thickened with sugar syrup they will blend more easily into fat creams.
50. Burned surfaces can be scraped off easily with a fine lemon grater.
51. Chocolate dilutes with cocoa butter only.
52. Yeast doughs rise faster with sugar added to yeast sponge.
53. Vegetable colors on hands come off easily when washed with lemon juice.
54. Vanilla sticks stuck into a can of powdered sugar transmit their fine flavor into every sugar crystal.

Index

198

PERSONAL RECIPES

PERSONAL RECIPES

PERSONAL RECIPES

PERSONAL RECIPES

PERSONAL RECIPES

PERSONAL RECIPES

PERSONAL RECIPES

PERSONAL RECIPES

PERSONAL RECIPES

PERSONAL RECIPES